CCENT Countdown Calen

The lines after the countdown number allow you to add the actual calendar days for re

31

Network Devices,
Components, and
Applications

30

Network
Models
Data Fl

D0286241

29

28

Switchin
Concept
Operatic

24

The IPv4 Address

23

IPv4 Subnetting
and VLSM

22

IPv6 Addressing
Concepts

21

Impleme
IPv6 Add

17

Basic Router
Configuration:
IPv6

16

Static and
Default Route
Configuration

15

Single-Area
OSPFv2

14

Single-A
OSPFv3

10

Basic ACL
Configuration

9

NAT

8

Basic Device
Security

7

Switch S
Configur

3

Troubleshoot
ACL Issues

2

Troubleshoot
Layer 1 Issues

1

CCENT Skills
Review and
Practice

EX

Time

Locatior

AM DAY

31 Days Before Your CCENT Certification Exam

Second Edition

Allan Johnson

Cisco Press ▪ 800 East 96th Street ▪ Indianapolis, Indiana 46240 USA

31 Days Before Your CCENT Certification Exam
Second Edition

A Day-By-Day Review Guide for the ICND1 (100-101) Certification Exam

Allan Johnson

Copyright© 2014 Cisco Systems, Inc.

Published by:
Cisco Press
800 East 96th Street
Indianapolis, IN 46240 USA

Printed in the United States of America

2   16

Library of Congress Control Number: 2013953096

ISBN-13: 978-1-58720-453-1

ISBN-10: 1-58720-453-3

Warning and Disclaimer

This book is designed to provide information about exam topics for the Cisco Certified Entry Networking Technician (CCENT) Exam 100-101 ICND1. Every effort has been made to make this book as complete and as accurate as possible, but no warranty or fitness is implied.

The information is provided on an "as is" basis. The authors, Cisco Press, and Cisco Systems, Inc. shall have neither liability nor responsibility to any person or entity with respect to any loss or damages arising from the information contained in this book or from the use of the discs or programs that may accompany it.

The opinions expressed in this book belong to the author and are not necessarily those of Cisco Systems, Inc.

Special Sales

For information about buying this title in bulk quantities, or for special sales opportunities (which may include electronic versions; custom cover designs; and content particular to your business, training goals, marketing focus, or branding interests), please contact our corporate sales department at corpsales@pearsoned.com or (800) 382-3419.

For government sales inquiries, please contact governmentsales@pearsoned.com.

For questions about sales outside the U.S., please contact international@pearsoned.com.

Feedback Information

At Cisco Press, our goal is to create in-depth technical books of the highest quality and value. Each book is crafted with care and precision, undergoing rigorous development that involves the unique expertise of members from the professional technical community.

Readers' feedback is a natural continuation of this process. If you have any comments regarding how we could improve the quality of this book, or otherwise alter it to better suit your needs, you can contact us through email at feedback@ciscopress.com. Please make sure to include the book title and ISBN in your message.

We greatly appreciate your assistance.

Publisher	Paul Boger
Associate Publisher	Dave Dusthimer
Business Operation Manager, Cisco Press	Jan Cornelssen
Executive Editor	Mary Beth Ray
Managing Editor	Sandra Schroeder
Senior Development Editor	Christopher Cleveland
Senior Project Editor	Tonya Simpson
Copy Editor	John Edwards
Technical Editor	Steve Stiles
Editorial Assistant	Vanessa Evans
Cover Designer	Mark Shirar
Composition	Bronkella Publishing
Senior Indexer	Erika Millen
Proofreader	Megan Wade-Taxter

Trademark Acknowledgments

All terms mentioned in this book that are known to be trademarks or service marks have been appropriately capitalized. Cisco Press or Cisco Systems, Inc. cannot attest to the accuracy of this information. Use of a term in this book should not be regarded as affecting the validity of any trademark or service mark.

Americas Headquarters	Asia Pacific Headquarters	Europe Headquarters
Cisco Systems, Inc.	Cisco Systems (USA) Pte. Ltd.	Cisco Systems International BV
San Jose, CA	Singapore	Amsterdam, The Netherlands

Cisco has more than 200 offices worldwide. Addresses, phone numbers, and fax numbers are listed on the Cisco Website at **www.cisco.com/go/offices.**

CCDE, CCENT, Cisco Eos, Cisco HealthPresence, the Cisco logo, Cisco Lumin, Cisco Nexus, Cisco StadiumVision, Cisco TelePresence, Cisco WebEx, DCE, and Welcome to the Human Network are trademarks; Changing the Way We Work, Live, Play, and Learn and Cisco Store are service marks; and Access Registrar, Aironet, AsyncOS, Bringing the Meeting To You, Catalyst, CCDA, CCDP, CCIE, CCIP, CCNA, CCNP, CCSP, CCVP, Cisco, the Cisco Certified Internetwork Expert logo, Cisco IOS, Cisco Press, Cisco Systems, Cisco Systems Capital, the Cisco Systems logo, Cisco Unity, Collaboration Without Limitation, EtherFast, EtherSwitch, Event Center, Fast Step, Follow Me Browsing, FormShare, GigaDrive, HomeLink, Internet Quotient, IOS, iPhone, iQuick Study, IronPort, the IronPort logo, LightStream, Linksys, MediaTone, MeetingPlace, MeetingPlace Chime Sound, MGX, Networkers, Networking Academy, Network Registrar, PCNow, PIX, PowerPanels, ProConnect, ScriptShare, SenderBase, SMARTnet, Spectrum Expert, StackWise, The Fastest Way to Increase Your Internet Quotient, TransPath, WebEx, and the WebEx logo are registered trademarks of Cisco Systems, Inc. and/or its affiliates in the United States and certain other countries.

All other trademarks mentioned in this document or website are the property of their respective owners. The use of the word partner does not imply a partnership relationship between Cisco and any other company. (0812R)

About the Author

Allan Johnson entered the academic world in 1999 after ten years as a business owner/ operator to dedicate his efforts to his passion for teaching. He holds both an MBA and an M.Ed. in occupational training and development. He taught CCNA courses at the high school level for seven years and has taught both CCNA and CCNP courses at Del Mar College in Corpus Christi, Texas. In 2003, Allan began to commit much of his time and energy to the CCNA Instructional Support Team, providing services to Networking Academy instructors worldwide and creating training materials. He now works full time for Cisco Networking Academy as a learning systems developer.

About the Technical Reviewer

Steve Stiles is a Cisco Networking Academy Instructor for Rhodes State College and a Cisco Certified Instructor Trainer, having earned CCNA Security and CCNP level certifications. He was the recipient of the 2012 Outstanding Teacher of the Year award by the Ohio Association of Two Year Colleges and co-recipient of the Outstanding Faculty of the Year award at Rhodes State College.

Dedication

For my wife, Becky. Without the sacrifices you made during the project, this work would not have come to fruition. Thank you for providing me the comfort and resting place only you can give.

Acknowledgments

When I began to think of whom I would like to have as a technical editor for this work, Steve Stiles immediately came to mind. With his instructor and industry background, as well as his excellent work building activities for the new Cisco Networking Academy curriculum, he was an obvious choice. Thankfully, when Mary Beth Ray contacted him, he was willing and able to do the arduous review work necessary to make sure that you get a book that is both technically accurate and unambiguous.

This book is a concise summary of the work of Cisco Press CCNA authors. Wendell Odom's *Cisco CCENT/CCNA ICND1 100-101 Official Cert Guide* and Anthony Sequeira's *Interconnecting Cisco Network Devices, Part 1 (ICND1) Foundation Learning Guide* were two of my main sources. The different approaches that these two authors—both CCIEs—take toward the CCNA material gives the reader the breadth and the depth needed to master the CCNA exam topics.

The Cisco Networking Academy authors for the online curriculum and series of Companion Guides take the reader deeper, past the CCNA exam topics, with the ultimate goal of not only preparing the student for CCNA certification, but also for more advanced college-level technology courses and degrees. Thank you especially to Amy Gerrie and her team of authors—Rick Graziani, Wayne Lewis, and Bob Vachon—for their excellent treatment of the material; it is reflected throughout this book.

Mary Beth Ray, executive editor, amazes me with her ability to juggle multiple projects at once, steering each from beginning to end. I can always count on her to make the tough decisions. Thank you, Mary Beth, for bringing this project to me.

This is my fifth project with Christopher Cleveland as development editor. His dedication to perfection pays dividends in countless, unseen ways. Thank you again, Chris, for providing me with much needed guidance and support. This book could not be a reality without your persistence.

Contents at a Glance

Contents

Icons Used in This Book

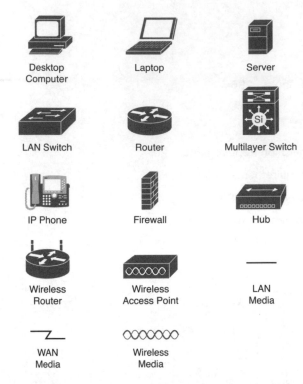

Desktop Computer

Laptop

Server

LAN Switch

Router

Multilayer Switch

IP Phone

Firewall

Hub

Wireless Router

Wireless Access Point

LAN Media

WAN Media

Wireless Media

Command Syntax Conventions

The conventions used to present command syntax in this book are the same conventions used in the IOS Command Reference. The Command Reference describes these conventions as follows:

- **Boldface** indicates commands and keywords that are entered literally as shown. In actual configuration examples and output (not general command syntax), boldface indicates commands that are manually input by the user (such as a **show** command).

- *Italic* indicates arguments for which you supply actual values.

- Vertical bars (|) separate alternative, mutually exclusive elements.

- Square brackets ([ ]) indicate an optional element.

- Braces ({ }) indicate a required choice.

- Braces within brackets ([{ }]) indicate a required choice within an optional element.

Introduction

You are almost there! If you're reading this Introduction, you've probably already spent a considerable amount of time and energy pursuing your CCENT certification. Regardless of how you got to this point in your travels through your CCENT studies, *31 Days Before Your CCENT Certification Exam* most likely represents the last leg of your journey on your way to the destination: to become a Cisco Certified Entry Networking Technician. However, if you are like I am, you might be reading this book at the beginning of your studies. If such is the case, this book provides you with an excellent overview of the material that you must now spend a great deal of time studying and practicing. However, I must warn you: Unless you are extremely well-versed in networking technologies and have considerable experience configuring and troubleshooting Cisco routers and switches, this book will not serve you well as the sole resource for CCENT exam preparation. Therefore, let me spend some time discussing my recommendations for study resources.

Study Resources

Cisco Press offers an abundance of CCNA-related books to serve as your primary source for learning how to install, configure, operate, and troubleshoot small- to medium-size routed and switched networks.

Primary Resources

First on the list must be Wendell Odom's *Cisco CCENT/CCNA ICND1 100-101 Official Cert Guide* (ISBN: 9781587143854). If you do not buy any other books, buy this one. Wendell's method of teaching, combined with his technical expertise and down-to-earth style, is unsurpassed in our industry. As you read through his books, you sense that he is sitting right there next to you walking you through the material. The practice exams and study materials on the DVD in the back of the book are worth the price of the book. There is no better resource on the market for a CCNA candidate.

Next on the list must be Anthony Sequeira's *Interconnecting Cisco Network Devices, Part 1 (ICND1) Foundation Learning Guide* (ISBN: 9781587143762). This book is indispensable to those students who take the first of two Cisco-recommended training class for CCNA preparation: Interconnecting Cisco Network Devices 1 (ICND1). These courses, available through Cisco Training Partners in a variety of formats, are usually of a very short duration (one to six weeks) and are geared toward the industry professional already working in the field of networking. Anthony's book serves the reader well as a concise, but thorough, treatment of the CCENT exam topics. His method and approach often differ and complement Wendell's approach. I recommend that you also refer to this book.

If you are a Cisco Networking Academy student, you are blessed with access to the online version of the CCNA Routing and Switching curriculum and the wildly popular Packet Tracer network simulator. Although there are currently two paths for the CCNA curriculum, I used the Introduction to Networking (ITN) and Routing and Switching Essential (RSE) courses in my daily review of the exam topics. ITN introduces basic concepts of computer networks, including deep dives into the seven layers of the OSI model, IP addressing, and the fundamentals of Ethernet. Successfully completing the course means that you should be able to build small LANs and implement basic addressing and configurations on routers and switches. RSE expands on ITN, taking the student further into basic router and switch configuration. Successfully completing the course means that you should be able to configure and troubleshoot routers and switches using a variety of technologies including RIPv2, single-area OSPF, VLANs, and inter-VLAN routing for both IPv4 and IPv6 networks. To learn more about CCNA Routing and Switching courses and to find an Academy near you, visit www.netacad.com.

However, if you are not an Academy student but would like to benefit from the extensive authoring done for these courses, you can buy any or all the CCNA Routing and Switching Companion Guides (CG) and Lab Manuals (LM) of the Academy's popular online curriculum. Although you will not have access to the Packet Tracer network simulator software, you will have access to the tireless work of an outstanding team of Cisco Academy Instructors dedicated to providing students with comprehensive and engaging CCNA preparation course material. The titles and ISBNs for the CCNA Routing and Switching CGs and LMs are as follows:

- Introduction to Networks Companion Guide (ISBN: 9781587133169)

- Introduction to Networks Lab Manual (ISBN: 9781587133121)

- Routing and Switching Essentials Companion Guide (ISBN: 9781587133183)

- Routing and Switching Essentials Lab Manual (ISBN: 9781587133206)

You can find these books at www.ciscopress.com by clicking the **Cisco Networking Academy** link.

Supplemental Resources

In addition to the book you hold in your hands, there are four more supplemental resources I recommend to augment your final 31 days of review and preparation.

First, a plug for my own book, the *CCENT Practice and Study Guide, Exercises, Activities and Scenarios to Prepare for the ICND1/CCENT (100-101) Certification Exam* (ISBN: 9781587133459). The subtitle is a concise summary of what you will get. Although an appropriate resource for anyone, this book is specifically geared toward the Cisco Networking Academy instructors and students who want a resource to supplement the online curriculum. Mirroring the chapter layout of the first two online courses, the CCENT PSG offers exercises that help you learn the concepts and configurations that are crucial to your success as a CCENT candidate.

Second, Wendell Odom and Sean Wilkins have created over 250 structured labs that are available in the Cisco CCENT ICND1 100-101 Network Simulator (ISBN: 9780789750433). These simulations map precisely to chapters in his book, but are also a great practice resource for anyone. The four types of labs in this product present you with progressively more difficult real-world challenges. Skill builder labs help you practice short, focused configuration tasks. Subnetting exercises help you improve the speed and accuracy of your subnetting calculations. Complex Configuration Scenario labs present realistic multilayered, multitechnology configuration tasks. Finally, challenging Troubleshooting Scenario labs provide you with an opportunity to test your problem identification and resolution skills. If you need that extra edge or are struggling with a particular configuration or troubleshooting concept, you'll find these simulations very helpful.

Third, Eric Rivard is the author of *Cisco CCENT ICND1 100-101 Flash Cards and Exam Practice Pack* (ISBN: 9781587203992). The text portion of the book includes over 450 flash cards that quickly review exam topics in bite-sized pieces. Also included is over 100 pages in the Quick Reference Guide, which is designed for late-stage exam preparation. And on the included CD, you will find a test engine with over 150 CCENT practice exam questions.

> **NOTE:** If you are certain that you will be also pursuing your CCNA certification, the more economical purchase might be to buy the *Cisco CCNA Routing and Switching 200-120 Flash Cards and Exam Practice Pack* (ISBN: 9781587204005). The first half of this book is a repeat of the CCENT version.

Fourth, there is Scott Empson's very popular *CCNA Routing and Switching Portable Command Guide, Third Edition* (ISBN: 9781587204302). This guide is way more than just a listing of commands and what they do. Yes, it summarizes all the CCNA certification-level IOS commands, keywords, command arguments, and associated prompts. But it also provides you with tips and examples of how to apply the commands to real-world scenarios. Configuration examples throughout the book provide you with a better understanding of how these commands are used in simple network designs.

The Cisco Learning Network

Finally, if you have not done so already, you should now register with The Cisco Learning Network at https://learningnetwork.cisco.com. Sponsored by Cisco, The Cisco Learning Network is a free social learning network where IT professionals can engage in the common pursuit of enhancing and advancing their IT careers. Here you will find many resources to help you prepare for your CCNA exam as well as a community of like-minded people ready to answer your questions, help you with your struggles, and share in your triumphs.

So which resources should you buy? That question is largely up to how deep your pockets are or how much you like books. If you're like I am, you must have it all! I admit it. My bookcase is a testament to my Cisco "geekness." But if you are on a budget, choose one of the primary study resources and one of the supplemental resources, such as Wendell Odom's certification book and my practice study guide. Whatever you choose, you will be in good hands. Any or all of these authors will serve you well.

Goals and Methods

The main goal of this book is to provide you with a clear and succinct review of the CCENT objectives. Each day's exam topics are grouped into a common conceptual framework and use the following format:

- A title for the day that concisely states the overall topic

- A list of one or more CCENT 100-101 ICND1 Exam Topics to be reviewed

- A Key Topics section to introduce the review material and quickly orient you to the day's focus

- An extensive review section consisting of short paragraphs, lists, tables, examples, and graphics

- A Study Resources section to provide you with a quick reference for locating more in-depth treatment of the day's topics

The book counts down starting with Day 31 and continues through exam day to provide post-test information. You will also find a calendar and checklist that you can tear out and use during your exam preparation inside the book.

Use the calendar to enter each actual date beside the countdown day and the exact day, time, and location of your CCENT exam. The calendar provides a visual for the time that you can dedicate to each CCENT exam topic.

The checklist highlights important tasks and deadlines leading up to your exam. Use it to help you map out your studies.

Who Should Read This Book

The audience for this book is anyone finishing his or her preparation for taking the CCENT 100-101 ICND1 exam. A secondary audience is anyone needing a refresher review of CCENT exam topics—possibly before attempting to recertify or sit for another certification to which the CCNA is a prerequisite.

Getting to Know the CCENT 100-101 ICND1 Exam

For the current certifications, announced in spring 2013, Cisco created the ICND1 (100-101) and ICND2 (200-101) exams, along with the CCNA (200-120) exam. To become CCENT certified, you only need to pass the ICND1 exam. To become CCNA Routing and Switching certified, you must pass both the ICND1 and ICND2 exams, or just the CCNA exam. The CCNA exam simply covers all the topics of the ICND1 and ICND2 exams, giving you two options for gaining your CCNA Routing and Switching certification. The two-exam path gives people with less experience a chance to study for a smaller set of topics at one time. The one-exam option provides a more cost-effective certification path for those who want to prepare for all the topics at once. This book focuses exclusively on the CCENT path, using the entire list of topics published for the CCENT 100-101 ICND1 exam.

Currently for the CCENT exam, you are allowed 90 minutes to answer 50–60 questions. Use the following steps to access a tutorial at home that demonstrates the exam environment before you go to take the exam:

Step 1.   Visit www.vue.com/cisco.

Step 2.   Look for a link to the certification tutorial. Currently, it can be found on the right side of the web page under the heading "Related Links."

Step 3.   Click the certification tutorial link.

When you get to the testing center and check in, the proctor verifies your identity, gives you some general instructions and then takes you into a quiet room containing a PC. When you're at the PC, you have a few things to do before the timer starts on your exam. For instance, you can take the tutorial to get accustomed to the PC and the testing engine. Every time I sit for an exam, I go through the tutorial even though I know how the test engine works. It helps me settle my nerves and get focused. Anyone who has user-level skills in getting around a PC should have no problems with the testing environment.

When you start the exam, you are asked a series of questions. Each question is presented one at a time and must be answered before moving on to the next question. The exam engine does not let you go back and change your answer. The exam questions can be in one of the following formats:

- Multiple choice
- Fill-in-the-blank
- Drag-and-drop
- Testlet
- Simlet
- Simulation

The multiple-choice format simply requires that you point and click a circle or check box next to the correct answer or answers. Cisco traditionally tells you how many answers you need to choose, and the testing software prevents you from choosing too many or too few.

Fill-in-the-blank questions typically only require you to type numbers. However, if words are requested, the case does not matter unless the answer is a command that is case sensitive (such as passwords and device names when configuring authentication).

Drag-and-drop questions require you to click and hold, move a button or icon to another area, and release the mouse button to place the object somewhere else—typically in a list. For some questions, to get the question correct, you might need to put a list of five things in the proper order.

Testlets contain one general scenario and several multiple-choice questions about the scenario. These are ideal if you are confident in your knowledge of the scenario's content because you can leverage your strength over multiple questions.

A simlet is similar to a testlet in that you are given a scenario with several multiple-choice questions. However, a simlet uses a network simulator to allow you access to a simulation of the command line of Cisco IOS Software. You can then use **show** commands to examine a network's current behavior and answer the question.

A simulation also uses a network simulator, but you are given a task to accomplish such as implementing a network solution or troubleshooting an existing network implementation. You do this by configuring one or more routers and switches. The exam then grades the question based on the configuration you changed or added. A newer form of the simulation question is the GUI-based simulation, where a graphical interface like that found on a Linksys router or the Cisco Security Device Manager are simulated.

What Topics Are Covered on the CCENT Exam?

The topics of the CCENT 100-101 ICND1 exam focus on the following seven key categories:

- Operation of IP Data Networks
- LAN Switching Technologies
- IP Addressing for IPv4 and IPv6
- IP Routing Technologies
- IP Services
- Network Device Security
- Troubleshooting

Although Cisco outlines general exam topics, it is possible that not all topics will appear on the CCENT exam and that topics that are not specifically listed might appear on the exam. The exam topics provided by Cisco and included in this book are a general framework for exam preparation. Be sure to check the Cisco website for the latest exam topics.

Registering for the CCENT 100-101 Exam

If you are starting your *31 Days to Your CCENT Certification Exam* today, register for the exam right now. In my testing experience, there is no better motivator than a scheduled test date staring me in the face. I'm willing to bet that it's the same for you. Don't worry about unforeseen circumstances. You can cancel your exam registration for a full refund up to 24 hours before taking the exam. So if you're ready, you should gather the following information in Table I-1 and register right now!

Table I-1   Personal Information for CCENT 100-101 ICND1 Exam Registration

Item	Notes
Legal Name	
Social Security or Passport Number	
Cisco Certification ID or Test ID[1]	
Cisco Academy Username[2]	
Cisco Academy ID Number[2]	
Company Name	
Valid Email Address	
Voucher Number[2]	
Method of Payment	

[1]Applies to exam candidates who have previously taken a Cisco certification exam

[2]Applies to Cisco Networking Academy students only

To register for an exam, visit Pearson VUE online at www.vue.com/cisco. The process and available test times will vary based on the local testing center you choose.

Remember, there is no better motivation for study than an actual test date. *Sign up today.*

Network Devices, Components, and Applications

CCENT 100-101 ICND1 Exam Topics

- Recognize the purpose and functions of various network devices such as routers, switches, bridges, and hubs.

- Select the components required to meet a given network specification.

- Identify the appropriate media, cables, ports, and connectors to connect Cisco network devices to other network devices and hosts in a LAN.

- Identify common applications and their impact on the network.

Key Points

At its most fundamental level, a network can be divided into four elements:

- The devices
- The media
- The rules
- The messages

For today's exam topics, we will focus on the devices used in today's networks, the media used to interconnect those devices, and the different types of network topologies.

Devices

In today's networks, switches are almost exclusively used to connect end devices to a single LAN. On occasion, you might see a hub connecting end devices. But hubs are really legacy devices. The following describes the difference between a hub and a switch:

- Hubs were typically chosen as an intermediary device within a very small LAN, where bandwidth usage was not an issue or there were cost limitations. In today's networks, hubs have been replaced by switches.

- Switches replaced hubs as the local area network (LAN) intermediary device because a switch can segment collision domains and provide enhanced security.

Switches

When choosing a switch, the main factors to consider are the following:

- **Cost:** Determined by the number and type of ports, network management capabilities, embedded security technologies, and optional advanced switching technologies.

- **Interface characteristics:** Sufficient number of ports for now as well as for future expansion, uplink speeds, mixture of UTP and fiber, and modularity.

- **Hierarchical network layer:** Switches at the access layer have different requirements than switches at the distribution or core layers.

Access Layer Switches

Access layer switches facilitate the connection of end devices to the network. Features of access layer switches include the following:

- Port security

- VLANs

- Fast Ethernet/Gigabit Ethernet

- Power over Ethernet (PoE)

- Link aggregation

- Quality of service (QoS)

Distribution Layer Switches

Distribution layer switches receive the data from the access layer switches and forward it to the core layer switches. Features of distribution layer switches include the following:

- Layer 3 support

- High forwarding rate

- Gigabit Ethernet/10 Gigabit Ethernet

- Redundant components

- Security policies/access control lists

- Link aggregation

- Quality of service (QoS)

Core Layer Switches

Core layer switches make up the backbone and are responsible for handling the majority of data on a switched LAN. Features of core layer switches include the following:

- Layer 3 support

- Very high forwarding rate

- Gigabit Ethernet/10 Gigabit Ethernet

- Redundant components

- Link aggregation

- Quality of service (QoS)

Routers

Routers are the primary devices used to interconnect networks—LANs, WANs, and WLANs. When choosing a router, the main factors to consider are the following:

- **Expandability:** Provides flexibility to add new modules as needs change.

- **Media:** Determines the type of interfaces the router needs to support the various network connections.

- **Operating system features:** Determines the version of IOS loaded on the router. Different IOS versions support different feature sets. Features to consider include security, QoS, Voice over IP (VoIP), routing complexity, and other services.

Figure 31-1 shows a Cisco 1941 router, which provides the following connections:

- **Console ports:** Two console ports for the initial configuration using a regular RJ-45 port and a new USB Type-B (mini-B USB) connector

- **AUX port:** An RJ-45 port for remote management access

- **LAN interfaces:** Two Gigabit Ethernet interfaces for LAN access

- **Enhanced high-speed WAN interface card (eHWIC) slots:** Two slots that support different types of interface modules, including serial, digital subscriber line (DSL), switch port, and wireless

Also shown in Figure 31-1 are two 4GB compact flash slots to provide increased storage space.

Figure 31-1   Backplane of the Cisco 1941 Router

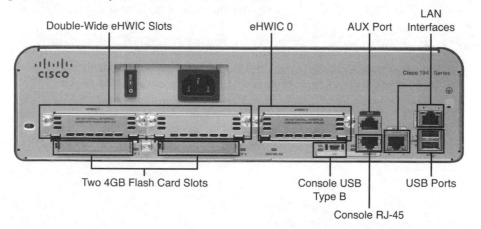

Physical Layer

Before any network communications can occur, a wired or wireless physical connection must be established. The type of physical connection depends on the network setup. In larger networks, switches and wireless access points (WAP) are often two separate dedicated devices. In a very small business (three or four employees) or home network, integrated service routers (ISR) are usually implemented. These ISRs offer a switching component with multiple ports and a WAP, which allows wireless devices to connect as well. Figure 31-2 shows the Linksys E2500, a typical small network ISR.

Figure 31-2   Example of an ISR: Linksys E2500

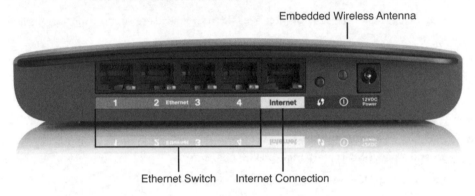

Network Media Forms and Standards

There are three basic forms of network media:

- **Copper cable:** The signals are patterns of electrical pulses.

- **Fiber-optic cable:** The signals are patterns of light.

- **Wireless:** The signals are patterns of microwave transmissions.

Messages are encoded and then placed on the media. Encoding is the process of converting data into patterns of electrical, light, or electromagnetic energy so that it can be carried on the media.

Table 31-1 summarizes the three most common networking media in use today.

Table 31-1   Networking Media

Media	Physical Components	Frame Encoding Technique	Signaling Methods
Copper cable	UTP	Manchester encoding	Changes in the electromagnetic field.
	Coaxial	Non-Return to Zero (NRZ) techniques	
	Connectors		Intensity of the electromagnetic field.
	NICs	4B/5B codes are used with Multi-Level Transition Level 3 (MLT-3) signaling	
	Ports		Phase of the electromagnetic wave.
	Interfaces	8B/10B	
		PAM5	
Fiber-optic cable	Single-mode fiber	Pulses of light	A pulse equals 1.
	Multimode fiber	Wavelength multiplexing using different colors	No pulse is 0.
	Connectors		
	NICs		
	Interfaces		
	Lasers and LEDs		
	Photoreceptors		
Wireless	Access points	DSSS (direct-sequence spread-spectrum)	Radio waves.
	NICs		
	Radio	OFDM (orthogonal frequency division multiplexing)	
	Antennas		

Each media type has its advantages and disadvantages. When choosing the media, consider each of the following:

- **Cable length:** Does the cable need to span across a room or from building to building?

- **Cost:** Does the budget allow for using a more expensive media type?

- **Bandwidth:** Does the technology used with the media provide adequate bandwidth?

- **Ease of installation:** Does the implementation team have the ability to install the cable, or is a vendor required?

- **Susceptible to EMI/RFI:** Is the local environment going to interfere with the signal?

Table 31-2 summarizes media standards for LAN cabling.

Table 31-2   Media Standard, Cable Length, and Bandwidth

Ethernet Type	Bandwidth	Cable Type	Maximum Distance
10BASE-T	10Mbps	Cat3/Cat5 UTP	100 m
100BASE-TX	100Mbps	Cat5 UTP	100 m
100BASE-TX	200Mbps	Cat5 UTP	100 m
100BASE-FX	100Mbps	Multimode fiber	400 m
100BASE-FX	200Mbps	Multimode fiber	2 km
1000BASE-T	1Gbps	Cat5e UTP	100 m
1000BASE-TX	1Gbps	Cat6 UTP	100 m
1000BASE-SX	1Gbps	Multimode fiber	550 m
1000BASE-LX	1Gbps	Single-mode fiber	2 km
10GBASE-T	10Gbps	Cat6a/Cat7 UTP	100 m
10GBASE-SX4	10Gbps	Multimode fiber	550 m
10GBASE-LX4	10Gbps	Single-mode fiber	2 km

LAN Device Connection Guidelines

End devices are those pieces of equipment that are either the original source or the final destination of a message. Intermediary devices connect end devices to the network to assist in getting a message from the source end device to the destination end device.

Connecting devices in a LAN is usually done with unshielded twisted-pair (UTP) cabling. Although many newer devices have an automatic crossover feature that allows you to connect either a straight-through or crossover cable, you should still know the following basic rules:

Use straight-through cables for the following connections:

- Switch to router Ethernet port
- Computer to switch
- Computer to hub

Use crossover cable for the following connections:

- Switch to switch
- Switch to hub
- Hub to hub
- Router to router (Ethernet ports)
- Computer to computer
- Computer to router Ethernet port

LANs and WANs

A local area network (LAN) is a network of computers and other components located relatively close together in a limited area. LANs can vary widely in size from one computer connected to a router in a home office to hundreds of computers in a corporate office; however, in general, a LAN spans a limited geographical area. The fundamental components of a LAN include the following:

- Computers

- Interconnections (NICs and the media)

- Networking devices (hubs, switches, and routers)

- Protocols (Ethernet, IP, ARP, DHCP, DNS, and so on)

A wide area network (WAN) generally connects LANs that are geographically separated. A collection of LANs connected by one or more WANs is called an *internetwork*—thus, we have the Internet. The term *intranet* is often used to refer to a privately owned connection of LANs and WANs.

Depending on the type of service, connecting to the WAN is normally done in one of four ways:

- RJ-11 connection to a dialup or DSL modem

- Cable coaxial connection to a cable modem

- 60-pin serial connection to a CSU/DSU

- RJ-45 T1 controller connection to a CSU/DSU

With the growing number of teleworkers, enterprises have an increasing need for secure, reliable, and cost-effective ways to connect people working in small offices or home offices (SOHO) or other remote locations to resources on corporate sites. Remote connection technologies to support teleworkers include the following:

- Traditional private WAN technologies, including Frame Relay, ATM, and leased lines

- IPsec virtual private networks (VPN)

- Remote secure VPN access through a broadband connection over the public Internet

Components needed for teleworker connectivity include the following:

- **Home office components:** Computer, broadband access (cable or DSL), and a VPN router or VPN client software installed on the computer

- **Corporate components:** VPN-capable routers, VPN concentrators, multifunction security appliances, authentication, and central management devices for resilient aggregation and termination of the VPN connections

Networking Icons

Before you can interpret networking diagrams or topologies, you first must understand the symbols or icons used to represent different networking devices and media. The icons shown in Figure 31-3 are the most common networking symbols for CCNA studies.

Figure 31-3   Networking Icons

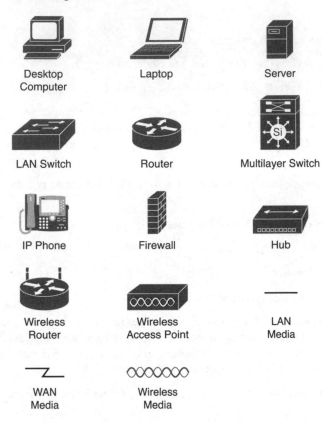

Physical and Logical Topologies

Network diagrams are more often referred to as *topologies*. A topology graphically displays the interconnection methods used between devices.

Physical topologies refer to the physical layout of devices and how they are cabled. There are seven basic physical topologies, as shown in Figure 31-4.

Figure 31-4   Physical Topologies

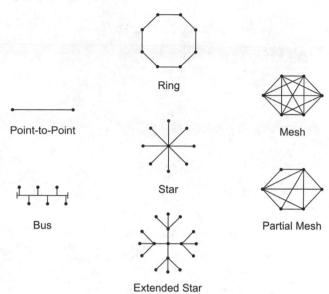

Logical topologies refer to the way that a signal travels from one point on the network to another and are largely determined by the access method—deterministic or nondeterministic. Ethernet is a nondeterministic access method. Logically, Ethernet operates as a bus topology. However, Ethernet networks are almost always physically designed as a star or extended star.

Other access methods use a deterministic access method. Token Ring and Fiber Distributed Data Interface (FDDI) both logically operate as ring, passing data from one station to the next. Although these networks can be designed as a physical ring, like Ethernet, they are often designed as a star or extended star. But logically, they operate like a ring.

Cisco Borderless Network

Figure 31-5 illustrates the Cisco Borderless Network architecture, which uses a tiered approach to virtually collapse the network into a single borderless network. The topology uses several devices that are beyond the scope of a CCNA candidate. However, you can see that a large collection of routers and switches play a major role in the design. Also notice the presence of multilayer switches at the core of the network.

The Cisco Borderless Network is a next-generation network architecture that allows organizations to connect anyone, anywhere, anytime, and on any device—securely, reliably, and seamlessly.

Figure 31-5   Cisco Borderless Network

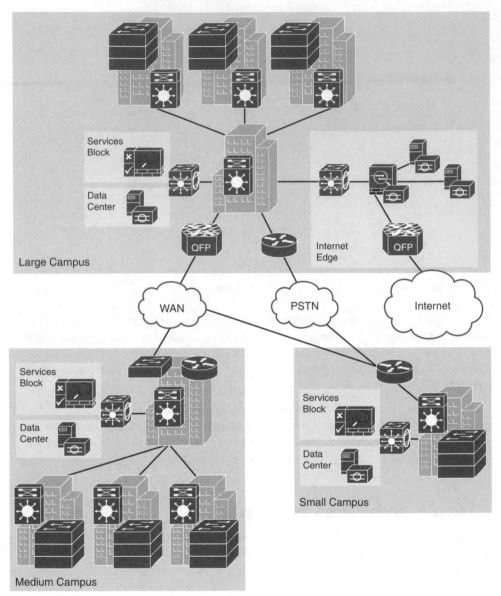

Hierarchy in a Borderless Network

Hierarchical network design involves dividing the network into discrete layers. Each layer provides specific functions that define its role within the overall network. By separating the various functions that exist on a network, the network design becomes modular, which facilitates scalability and performance. The hierarchical design model is broken up into three layers as follows:

- **Access layer:** Provides local and remote user access

- **Distribution layer:** Controls the flow of data between the access and core layers

- **Core layer:** High-speed redundant backbone

Figure 31-6 shows an example of the three-tiered hierarchical campus network design. For smaller networks, the core is often collapsed into the distribution layer for a two-tiered designed. And for very small networks and home networks, all three tiers can be seen in one device, such as the ISR shown earlier in Figure 31-2.

Figure 31-6   The Hierarchical Model

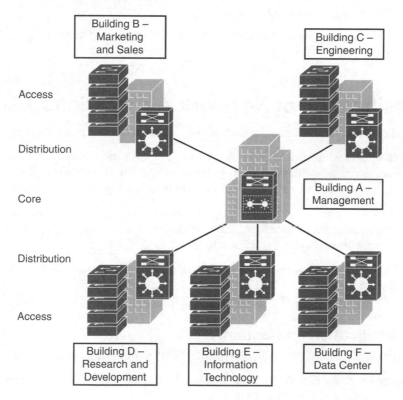

Network Documentation

Documentation for your network should include, at a minimum, the following major categories:

- **Router and switch documentation:** Includes device type, IOS image, host name, location, addresses, and other important information

- **End-system documentation:** Includes device names, OS, addressing details, and network impact (such as bandwidth usage)
- **Network topology diagram:** Includes all devices and shows the connections as well as the interface designations and addressing scheme

More often than not, a network's documentation is less than complete. To complete the documentation, you might have to gather information directly from the devices. Commands that are useful to this process include the following:

- **ping:** Tests direct connectivity between two devices
- **telnet:** Tests remote access as well as Layer 7 functionality
- **show ip interface brief:** Verifies interface statuses
- **show ip route:** Verifies routing operations
- **show cdp neighbor detail:** Gathers useful information about directly connected Cisco devices

Classification of Network Applications

User applications can be classified into three broad categories of network impact:

- **Batch applications,** such as File Transfer Protocol (FTP) and other file transfer utilities that initially require a human to set up, but then run until completion without further human interaction. For these applications, bandwidth is important but not critical.
- **Interactive applications,** such as database queries where a human is requesting and inputting information into an application is more response-sensitive. Delays can be annoying, but bandwidth is still not critical.
- **Real-time applications,** such as Voice over IP (VoIP) and video, demand much more bandwidth. Installation of VoIP systems must be carefully provisioned so that the current network is not adversely affected.

User Application Interaction

There are basically two types of user interactions with a network application:

- **Client-server:** A client device requests information from a server. Requesting a web page from a server is an example of a client-server interaction.
- **Peer-to-peer:** A device acts as both a client and a server within the same communication. Each device in the network running the application can act as a client or a server for the other devices in the network. Text messaging is an example of a peer-to-peer interaction.

Common Network Applications

The following list briefly describes the most common network applications:

- **Hypertext Transfer Protocol (HTTP)** uses GET, POST, and PUT messages to transfer data between a web browser on a client device and a web server. For more secure communications, HTTPS uses authentication and encryption between the client and server.

- **Simple Mail Transfer Protocol (SMTP)** is used by an email client to send email messages to an email server.

- **Post Office Protocol (POP)** is used by an email client to download email messages from an email server.

- **Domain Name System (DNS)** is a distributed system of servers that resolves domain names to IP addresses. To access a web page, client devices must use the IP address. DNS discovers the IP address for a given Uniform Resource Locator (URL) or web address.

- **Dynamic Host Configuration Protocol (DHCP)** provides a method for a device to get IP addressing information from the network when it boots up or renews its IP address.

- **File Transfer Protocol (FTP)** is used by client devices to push and pull data to and from an FTP server.

- **Server Message Block (SMB)** is a file-sharing protocol that is common today in Microsoft networking. After a client device establishes a connection to server, the user can access resources on the server as if the resource is local to the client device.

Growth of Network-Based Applications

Besides all the common applications we discuss in networking studies, programmers and entrepreneurs are continuously developing applications to take advantage of network resources and the Internet. Today, people create, store, and access information as well as communicate with others on the network using a variety of applications. In addition to the traditional email and web browser applications, people are increasingly using newer forms of communication, including instant messaging, blogs, podcasting, peer-to-peer file sharing, wikis, and collaborative tools that allow viewing and working on documents simultaneously. The online gaming industry has grown exponentially over the last decade. All of these applications and online experiences place great demands on the network infrastructure and resources. One way of handling the sheer volume of data is to rank packets based on the quality of service that the source application needs—especially considering the increased use of the network in general and the recent rise of voice and video applications that have a very low tolerance for delay and jitter.

Quality of Service

The priority and guaranteed level of service to the flow of data through the network are increasingly important as new applications place greater demands on the processing power and bandwidth of the networks we use. When we place a call over an IP phone, we want at least as good a service as we receive on a traditional land line. Therefore, networks need to use quality of service (QoS) mechanisms to ensure that limited network resources are prioritized based on traffic content. Without QoS implementation, an email message or web page request crossing a switch or a router will have the same priority as voice or video traffic.

Each type of application can be analyzed in terms of its QoS requirements on the network, so if the network meets those requirements, the application will work well.

Increased Network Usage

Applications have tended to increase the need for more bandwidth while, at the same time, demanding lower delay. Here are some of the types of data applications that have entered the marketplace and their impact on the network:

- **Graphics-capable terminals and printers:** Increase the required bytes for the same interaction as the old text-based terminals and printers

- **File transfers:** Introduce much larger volumes of data, but with no significant response time requirements

- **File servers:** Allow users to store files on a server—which might require a large volume of data transfer, but with a much smaller end-user response time requirement

- **The maturation of database technology:** Makes vast amounts of data available to casual users, vastly increasing the number of users wanting access to data

- **The migration of common applications to web browsers:** Encourages more users to access data

- **The growth of email:** The general acceptance of email as both a personal and business communications service has greatly increased the amount of email traffic.

- **The rapid commercialization of the Internet:** Enables companies to offer data directly to their customers through the data network rather than through phone calls

The Impact of Voice and Video on the Network

Currently, voice and video are in the midst of a migration to traditional IP data networks. Before the late 1990s, voice and video used separate networking facilities. Most companies today are either migrating or plan to migrate to IP phones, which pass voice data over the data network inside IP packets using application protocols generally referred to as Voice over IP (VoIP).

Figure 31-7 show a few details of how VoIP works from a home high-speed Internet connection, with a generic voice adapter (VA) converting the analog signal from a normal telephone to an IP packet.

Figure 31-7   Converting from Sound to Packets with a VA

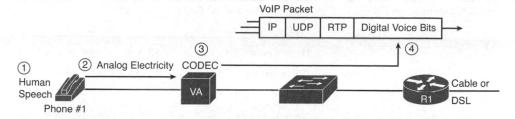

The demand that VoIP places on the data network is not for capacity. A voice call typically consumes less the 30kbps of bandwidth. However, VoIP is sensitive to delay, jitter, and packet loss:

- **Low delay:** VoIP requires a very low delay between the sending phone and the receiving phone—typically less than 200 milliseconds (0.2 seconds). This is a much lower delay than what is required by typical data applications.

- **Low jitter:** Jitter is the variation in delay. VoIP requires very low jitter as well, whereas data applications can tolerate much higher jitter. For example, the jitter for consecutive VoIP packets should not exceed 30 milliseconds (0.03 seconds), or the quality degrades.

- **Loss:** If a VoIP packet is lost in transit because of errors or because a router doesn't have room to store the packet while waiting to send it, the lost VoIP packet is not retransmitted across the network. Lost packets can sound like a break in the sound of the VoIP call.

Video over IP has the same performance issues as voice. However, video requires a lot more bandwidth—anywhere from 300kbps to 10Mbps, depending on the quality demanded.

To support the QoS requirements of voice, video, and other quality- or time-sensitive applications, routers and switches can be configured with a wide variety of QoS tools. These configurations are beyond the scope of the CCNA exam topics.

Study Resources

For today's exam topics, refer to the following resources for more study.

Resource	Location	Topic
Primary Resources		
Network Basics	1.3	LANs, WANs, and the Internet
	1.4	The Expanding Network
	4.1.2	How Application Protocols Interact with End-User Applications
	4.2	Well-Known Application Layer Protocols and Services
	9.3	Physical Layer
	9.4	Network Media

Resource	Location	Topic
Introduction to Networks	1.3	LANs, WANs, and the Internet
	1.4	The Expanding Network
	10.1.2	How Application Protocols Interact with End-User Applications
	10.2	Well-Known Application Layer Protocols and Services
	4.1	Physical Layer Protocols
	4.2	Network Media
Routing Protocols	1.1.1	Functions of a Router
	1.1.2	Connect Devices
Switched Networks	1 (all)	Introduction to Switched Networks
Routing and Switching Essentials	1.1	LAN Design
ICND1 Official Cert Guide	1	TCP/IP Application Layer
	2	An Overview of LANs
		Building Physical Ethernet Networks with UTP
	5	TCP/IP Applications
	6	Historical Progression: Hubs, Bridges, and Switches
		Choosing Ethernet Technology for a Campus LAN
		Autonegotiation
	15	Installing Cisco Routers
ICND1 Foundation Learning Guide	3	All
Supplemental Resources		
CCENT Practice and Study Guide	1	LANs, WANs, and the Internet
		The Expanding Network
	4	Physical Layer Protocols
		Network Media
	10	All
Flash Cards	1	All

Networking Models and Data Flow

CCENT 100-101 ICND1 Exam Topics

- Describe the purpose and basic operation of the protocols in the OSI and TCP/IP models.

- Predict the data flow between two hosts across a network.

Key Points

As a new student to networking, one of the very first topics you probably learned was the layers of the OSI and TCP/IP models. Now that you have completed your studies and are reviewing for your certification exam, you more than likely can see the benefit of using these models. Each helps our understanding of networks in its own way. Much of today's review is a quick summary of the TCP/IP layers and their operations as data is sent from source to destination. Many of the key points will be fleshed out more fully in upcoming days. However, this is the only day we will discuss the operation of the transport layer. So we will spend quite a bit of time on the Transmission Control Protocol (TCP) and the User Datagram Protocol (UDP).

The OSI and TCP/IP Models

To understand how communication occurs across the network, we use layered models as a framework for representing and explaining networking concepts and technologies. Network models provide a variety of benefits:

- Reduce complexity

- Standardize interfaces

- Assist understanding

- Promote rapid product development

- Support interoperability

- Facilitate modular engineering

Initially, networks were built on proprietary standards and hardware. Layered models, such as the TCP/IP and OSI models, support interoperability between competing vendor product lines.

The OSI model development began in the 1970s with the goal of providing a standards-based suite of protocols that would allow communication among all computer systems. Although the U.S. government required the use of OSI products in the 1980s and 1990s, the

Defense Advanced Research Projects Agency (DARPA) under the Department of Defense—and with the help of researchers at various universities—had designed the competing TCP/IP model. For various reasons, including the popularity of TCP/IP, by 1983, the ARPANET had chosen TCP/IP as its principal protocol suit. By 1994, all U.S. government agencies were required to switch over from OSI protocols to TCP/IP.

Today, we use the OSI model principally as a tool for explaining networking concepts. However, the protocols of the TCP/IP suite are the rules by which networks now operate. Because both models are important, you should be well versed in each model's layers as well as how the models map to each other. Figure 30-1 summarizes the two models.

Figure 30-1   OSI and TCP/IP Models

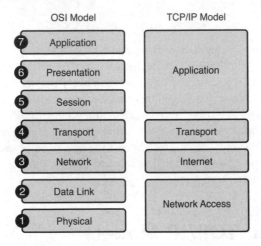

It can be confusing using two models; however, these simple guidelines might help:

- When discussing layers of a model, we are usually referring to the OSI model.

- When discussing protocols, we are usually referring to the TCP/IP model.

So let's quickly review the OSI layers and the TCP/IP protocols.

OSI Layers

Table 30-1 summarizes the layers of the OSI model and provides a brief functional description.

Table 30-1   OSI Model Layers and Functions

Layer	Functional Description
Application (7)	Refers to interfaces between network and application software. Also includes authentication services.
Presentation (6)	Defines the format and organization of data. Includes encryption.
Session (5)	Establishes and maintains end-to-end bidirectional flows between endpoints. Includes managing transaction flows.

Layer	Functional Description
Transport (4)	Provides a variety of services between two host computers, including connection establishment and termination, flow control, error recovery, and segmentation of large data blocks into smaller parts for transmission.
Network (3)	Refers to logical addressing, routing, and path determination.
Data link (2)	Formats data into frames appropriate for transmission onto some physical medium. Defines rules for when the medium can be used. Defines means by which to recognize transmission errors.
Physical (1)	Defines the electrical, optical, cabling, connectors, and procedural details required for transmitting bits, represented as some form of energy passing over a physical medium.

The following mnemonic phrase, where the first letter represents the layer ("A" stands for "Application"), can be helpful in memorizing the name and order of the layers from top to bottom:

All People Seem To Need Data Processing

TCP/IP Layers and Protocols

The TCP/IP model defines four categories of functions that must occur for communications to be successful. Most protocol models describe a vendor-specific protocol stack. However, because the TCP/IP model is an open standard, one company does not control the definition of the model.

Table 30-2 summarizes the TCP/IP layers, their functions, and the most common protocols.

Table 30-2   TCP/IP Layer Functions

TCP/IP Layer	Function	Example Protocols
Application	Represents data to the user and controls dialogue	DNS, Telnet, SMTP, POP3, IMAP, DHCP, HTTP, FTP, SNMP
Transport	Supports communication between diverse devices across diverse networks	TCP, UDP
Internet	Determines the best path through the network	IP, ARP, ICMP
Network access	Controls the hardware devices and media that make up the network	Ethernet, Frame Relay

In the coming days, we will review these protocols in more detail. For now, a brief description of the main TCP/IP protocols follows:

- **Domain Name System (DNS):** Provides the IP address of a website or domain name so that a host can connect to it

- **Telnet:** Allows administrators to log in to a host from a remote location

- **Simple Mail Transfer Protocol (SMTP), Post Office Protocol (POP3), and Internet Message Access Protocol (IMAP):** Used to send email messages between clients and servers

- **Dynamic Host Configuration Protocol (DHCP):** Assigns IP addressing to requesting clients

- **Hypertext Transfer Protocol (HTTP):** Used to transfer information between web clients and web servers

- **File Transfer Protocol (FTP):** Allows the download and upload of files between an FTP client and FTP server

- **Simple Network Management Protocol (SNMP):** Used by network management systems to monitor devices attached to the network

- **Transmission Control Protocol (TCP):** Allows virtual connections between hosts on the network to provide reliable delivery of data

- **User Datagram Protocol (UDP):** Allows faster, unreliable delivery of data that is either lightweight or time-sensitive

- **Internet Protocol (IP):** Provides a unique global address to computers for communicating over the network

- **Address Resolution Protocol (ARP):** Finds a host's hardware address when only the IP address is known

- **Internet Control Message Protocol (ICMP):** Used to send error and control messages, including reachability to another host and availability of services

- **Ethernet:** The most popular LAN standard for framing and preparing data for transmission onto the media

- **Frame Relay:** Also a framing standard; one of the most cost-effective WAN technologies used to connect LANs

Protocol Data Units and Encapsulation

As application data is passed down the protocol stack on its way to be transmitted across the network media, various protocols add information to it at each level. This is commonly known as the *encapsulation process*. The data structure at any given layer is called a *protocol data unit (PDU)*. Table 30-3 lists the PDUs at each layer of the OSI model.

Table 30-3   PDUs at Each Layer of the OSI Model

OSI Layer	PDU
Application	Data
Presentation	Data
Session	Data
Transport	Segment

OSI Layer	PDU
Network	Packet
Data link	Frame
Physical	Bits

The communication process from any source to any destination can be summarized with the following steps:

1. Creation of data at the application layer of the originating source device

2. Segmentation and encapsulation of data as it passes down the protocol stack in the source device

3. Generation of the data onto the media at the network access layer of the stack

4. Transportation of the data through the internetwork, which consists of media and any intermediary devices

5. Reception of the data at the network access layer of the destination device

6. Decapsulation and reassembly of the data as it passes up the stack in the destination device

7. Passing this data to the destination application at the application layer of the destination device

The TCP/IP Application Layer

The application layer of the TCP/IP model provides an interface between software, like a web browser, and the network itself. The process of requesting and receiving a web page works like this:

1. HTTP request sent, including an instruction to "get" a file—which is often a website's home page.

2. HTTP response sent from the web server with a code in the header—usually either 200 (request succeeded and information is returned in response) or 404 (page not found).

The HTTP request and the HTTP response are encapsulated in headers. The content of headers allows the application layers on each end device to communicate. Regardless of the application layer protocol (HTTP, FTP, DNS, and so on), all use the same general process for communicating between application layers on the end devices.

The TCP/IP Transport Layer

The transport layer, through TCP, provides a mechanism to guarantee delivery of data across the network. TCP supports error recovery to the application layer through the use of basic acknowledgment logic. Adding to the process for requesting a web page, TCP operation works like this:

1. Web client sends an HTTP request for a specific web server down to the transport layer.

2. TCP encapsulates the HTTP request with a TCP header and includes the destination port number for HTTP.

3. Lower layers process and send the request to the web server.

4. Web server receives HTTP requests and sends a TCP acknowledgment back to the requesting web client.

5. Web server sends the HTTP response down to the transport layer.

6. TCP encapsulates the HTTP data with a TCP header.

7. Lower layers process and send the response to the requesting web client.

8. Requesting web client sends acknowledgment back to the web server.

If data is lost at any point during this process, it is TCP's job to recover the data. HTTP at the application layer does not get involved in error recovery.

In addition to TCP, the transport layer provides UDP—a connectionless, unreliable protocol for sending data that does not require nor need error recovery. Table 30-4 lists the main features supported by the transport protocols. The first item is supported by TCP and UDP. The remaining items are supported only by TCP.

Table 30-4   TCP/IP Transport Layer Features

Function	Description
Multiplexing using ports	Function that allows receiving hosts to choose the correct application for which the data is destined, based on the destination port number.
Error recovery (reliability)	Process of numbering and acknowledging data with Sequence and Acknowledgment header fields.
Flow control using windowing	Process that uses a sliding window size that is dynamically agreed upon by the two end devices at various points during the virtual connection. The window size, represented in bytes, is the maximum amount of data the source will send before receiving an acknowledgment from the destination.
Connection establishment and termination	Process used to initialize port numbers, Sequence and Acknowledgment fields.
Ordered data transfer and data segmentation	Continuous stream of bytes from an upper-layer process that is "segmented" for transmission and delivered to upper-layer processes at the receiving device, with the bytes in the same order.

TCP Header

TCP provides error recovery, but to do so, it consumes more bandwidth and uses more processing cycles than UDP. TCP and UDP rely on IP for end-to-end delivery. TCP is concerned with providing services to the applications of the sending and receiving computers. To provide all these services, TCP uses a variety of fields in its header. Figure 30-2 shows the fields of the TCP header.

Figure 30-2   TCP Header

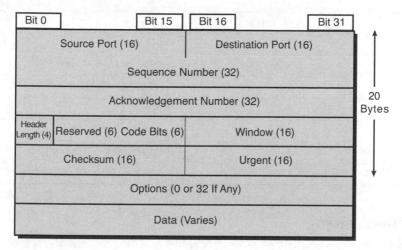

Port Numbers

The first two fields of the TCP header—source and destination ports—are also part of the UDP header shown later in Figure 30-6. Port numbers provide TCP (and UDP) with a way to multiplex multiple applications on the same computer. Web browsers now support multiple tabs or pages. Each time you open a new tab and request another web page, TCP assigns a different source port number and sometimes multiple port numbers. For example, you might have five web pages open. TCP will almost always assign destination port 80 for all five sessions. However, the source port for each will be different. This is how TCP (and UDP) multiplexes the conversation so that the web browser knows in which tab to display the data.

Source ports are usually dynamically assigned by TCP and UDP from the range starting 1024 up to a maximum of 65535. Port numbers below 1024 are reserved for well-known applications. Table 30-5 lists several popular applications and their well-known port numbers.

Table 30-5   Popular Applications and Their Well-Known Port Numbers

Port Number	Protocol	Application
20	TCP	FTP data
21	TCP	FTP control
22	TCP	SSH
23	TCP	Telnet
25	TCP	SMTP
53	UDP, TCP	DNS
67, 68	UDP	DHCP
69	UDP	TFTP
80	TCP	HTTP (WWW)
110	TCP	POP3
161	UDP	SNMP
443	TCP	HTTPS (SSL)
16,384–32,767	UDP	RTP-based voice (VoIP) and video

Error Recovery

Also known as *reliability*, TCP provides error recovery during data transfer sessions between two end devices that have established a connection. The sequence and acknowledgment fields in the TCP header are used to track every byte of data transfer and ensure that missing bytes are retransmitted.

In Figure 30-3, the Acknowledgment field sent by the web client (4000) implies the next byte to be received; this is called *positive acknowledgment*.

Figure 30-3   TCP Acknowledgment Without Errors

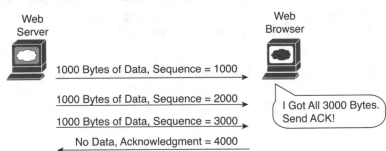

Figure 30-4 depicts the same scenario, except that now we have some errors. The second TCP segment was lost in transmission. Therefore, the web client replies with an ACK field set to 2000. This is called a positive acknowledgment with retransmission (PAR) because the web client is requesting that some of the data be retransmitted. The web server will now resend data starting at segment 2000. In this way, lost data is recovered.

Figure 30-4   TCP Acknowledgment with Errors

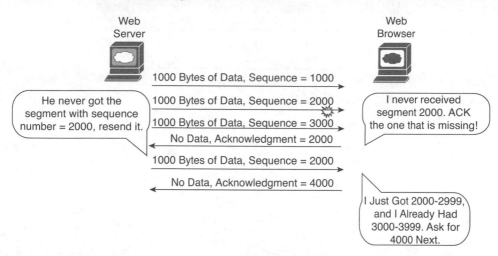

Although not shown, the web server also sets a retransmission timer, awaiting acknowledgment, just in case the acknowledgment is lost or all transmitted segments are lost. If that timer expires, the web server sends all segments again.

Flow Control

Flow control is handled by TCP through a process called *windowing*. The two end devices negotiate the window size when initially establishing the connection; then they dynamically renegotiate window size during the life of the connection, increasing its size until it reaches the maximum window size of 65,535 bytes or until errors occur. Window size is specified in the Window field of the TCP header. After sending the amount of data specified in the window size, the source must receive an acknowledgment before sending the next window size of data.

Connection Establishment and Termination

Connection establishment is the process of initializing sequence and acknowledgment fields and agreeing on port numbers and window size. The three-way connection establishment phase shown in Figure 30-5 must occur before data transfer can proceed.

In the figure, DPORT and SPORT are the destination and source ports. SEQ is the sequence number. In bold are SYN and ACK, which each represent a 1-bit flag in the TCP header used to signal connection establishment. TCP initializes the Sequence Number and Acknowledgment Number fields to any number that fits into the 4-byte fields. The initial Sequence Number is a random 32-bit number generated with each new transmission. The Acknowledgment Number is received back and increments the sender's sequence number by 1.

After data transfer is complete, a four-way termination sequence occurs that uses an additional flag, called the FIN bit, as shown in Figure 30-6.

Figure 30-5   TCP Connection Establishment

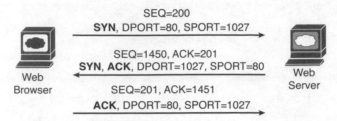

Figure 30-6   TCP Connection Termination

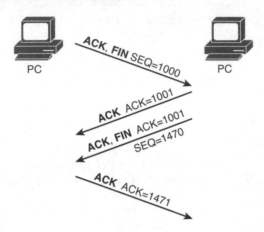

UDP

TCP establishes and terminates connections between endpoints, whereas UDP does not. Therefore, UDP is called a *connectionless protocol*. It provides no reliability, no windowing, and no reordering of the data. However, UDP does provide data transfer and multiplexing using port numbers, and it does so with fewer bytes of overhead and less processing than TCP. Applications that use UDP are ones that can trade the possibility of some data loss for less delay, such as VoIP. Figure 30-7 compares the two headers.

Figure 30-7   TCP and UDP Headers

2	2	4	4	4 bits	6 bits	6 bits	2	2	2	3	1
Source Port	Dest. Port	Sequence Number	Ack. Number	Offset	Reserved	Flags	Window Size	Checksum	Urgent	Options	PAD

TCP Header

2	2	2	2
Source Port	Dest. Port	Length	Checksum

UDP Header

* Unless Specified, Lengths Shown
  Are the Numbers of Bytes

The TCP/IP Internet Layer

The Internet layer of the TCP/IP model and its Internet Protocol (IP) define addresses so that each host computer can have a different IP address. In addition, the Internet layer defines the process of routing so that routers can determine the best path to send packets to the destination. Continuing with the web page example, IP addresses the data as it passes from the transport layer to the Internet layer:

1. Web client sends an HTTP request.

2. TCP encapsulates the HTTP request.

3. IP encapsulates the transports segment into a packet, adding source and destination addresses.

4. Lower layers process and send the request to the web server.

5. Web server receives HTTP requests and sends a TCP acknowledgment back to the requesting web client.

6. Web server sends the HTTP response down to the transport layer.

7. TCP encapsulates the HTTP data.

8. IP encapsulates the transport segment into a packet, adding source and destination addresses.

9. Lower layers process and send the response to the requesting web client.

10. Requesting web client sends acknowledgment back to the web server.

The operation of IP not only includes addressing but also the process of routing the data from source to destination. IP will be further discussed and reviewed in the upcoming days.

The TCP/IP Network Access Layer

IP depends on the network access layer to deliver IP packets across a physical network. Therefore, the network access layer defines the protocols and hardware required to deliver data across some physical network by specifying exactly how to physically connect a networked device to the physical media over which data can be transmitted.

The network access layer includes a large number of protocols to deal with the different types of media that data can cross on its way from source device to destination device. For example, data might need to travel first on an Ethernet link, then cross a Point-to-Point (PPP) link, then a Frame Relay link, then an Asynchronous Transfer Mode (ATM) link, and then finally an Ethernet link to the destination. At each transition from one media type to another, the network access layer provides the protocols, cabling standards, headers, and trailers to send data across the physical network.

Many times, a local link address is needed to transfer data from one hop to the next. For example, in an Ethernet LAN, Media Access Control (MAC) addresses are used between the sending device and its local gateway router. At the gateway router—depending on the needs of the outbound interface—the Ethernet header might be replaced with a Frame Relay header that will include data-link connection identifier (DLCI) addresses. In Frame Relay, DLCI addresses serve the same purpose as MAC addresses in Ethernet—to get the data across the link from one hop to the next so that the data can continue its journey to the destination. Some protocols, such as Point-to-Point Protocol (PPP), do not need a link address because only one other device is on the link that can receive the data.

With the network access layer, we can now finalize our web page example. The following greatly simplifies and summarizes the process of requesting and sending a web page:

1. Web client sends an HTTP request.

2. TCP encapsulates the HTTP request.

3. IP encapsulates the transport segment into a packet, adding source and destination addresses.

4. Network access layer encapsulates packet in a frame, addressing it for the local link.

5. Network access layer sends the frame out as bits on the media.

6. Intermediary devices process the bits at the network access and Internet layers and then forward the data toward the destination.

7. Web server receives the bits on the physical interface and sends them up through the network access and Internet layers.

8. Web server sends a TCP acknowledgment back to the requesting web client.

9. Web server sends the HTTP response down to the transport layer.

10. TCP encapsulates the HTTP data.

11. IP encapsulates the transport segment into a packet, adding source and destination addresses.

12. Network access layer encapsulates packet in a frame, addressing it for the local link.

13. Network access layer sends the frame out as bits on the media.

14. Lower layers process and send the response to the requesting web client.

15. Response travels back to the source over multiple data links.

16. Requesting web client receives response on the physical interface and sends the data up through the network access and Internet layers.

17. Requesting web client sends a TCP acknowledgment back to the web server.

18. Web page is displayed in requesting device's browser.

Data Encapsulation Summary

Each layer of the TCP/IP model adds its own header information. As the data travels down through the layers, it is encapsulated with a new header. At the network access layer, a trailer is also added. This encapsulation process can be described in five steps:

Step 1. Create and encapsulate the application data with any required application layer headers. For example, the HTTP OK message can be returned in an HTTP header, followed by part of the contents of a web page.

Step 2. Encapsulate the data supplied by the application layer inside a transport layer header. For end-user applications, a TCP or UDP header is typically used.

Step 3. Encapsulate the data supplied by the transport layer inside an Internet layer (IP) header. IP is the only protocol available in the TCP/IP network model at the Internet layer.

Step 4. Encapsulate the data supplied by the Internet layer inside a network access layer header and trailer. This is the only layer that uses both a header and a trailer.

Step 5. Transmit the bits. The physical layer encodes a signal onto the medium to transmit the frame.

The numbers in Figure 30-8 correspond to the five steps in the list, graphically showing the same encapsulation process.

Figure 30-8   Five Steps of Data Encapsulation

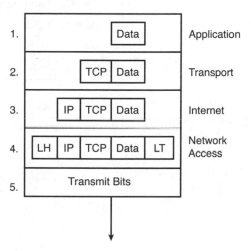

NOTE: The letters LH and LT stand for link header and link trailer, respectively, and refer to the data link layer header and trailer.

Study Resources

For today's exam topics, refer to the following resources for more study.

Resource	Location	Topic
Primary Resources		
Network Basics	3	Protocol Suites
		Reference Models
		Data Encapsulation
	5	All
Introduction to Networks	3	Protocol Suites
		Reference Models
		Data Encapsulation
	7	All
ICND1 Official Cert Guide	1	All
	5	All
ICND1 Foundation Learning Guide	2	All
Supplemental Resources		
CCENT Practice and Study Guide	3	Network Protocols and Standards
		Moving Data in the Network
	7	All
Flash Cards	4	All

Ethernet and Media Access Control

CCENT 100-101 ICND1 Exam Topics

- Determine the technology and media access control method for Ethernet networks.

Key Topics

Ethernet has continued to evolve from the 10BASE2 flavor, capable of speeds up to 10Mbps, to the newest 10GigE (10 Gigabit Ethernet), capable of speeds up to 10Gbps. Since 1985, the IEEE has continued to upgrade the 802.3 standards to provide faster speeds without changing the underlying frame structure. This feature, among others, has made Ethernet the choice for LAN implementations worldwide. Today we review Ethernet technologies and operation at both the data link and physical layers.

Ethernet Overview

802.3 is the IEEE standard for Ethernet, and both terms are commonly used interchangeably. The terms *Ethernet* and *802.3* both refer to a family of standards that together define the physical and data link layers of the definitive LAN technology. Figure 29-1 shows a comparison of Ethernet standards to the OSI model.

Figure 29-1   Ethernet Standards and the OSI Model

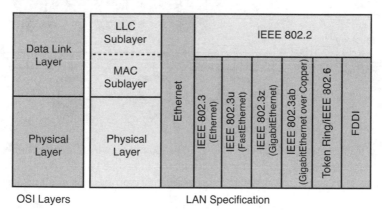

Ethernet separates the functions of the data link layer into two distinct sublayers:

- **Logical Link Control (LLC) sublayer:** Defined in the 802.2 standard
- **Media Access Control (MAC) sublayer:** Defined in the 802.3 standard

The LLC sublayer handles communication between the network layer and the MAC sublayer. In general, LLC provides a way to identify the protocol that is passed from the data link layer to the network layer. In this way, the fields of the MAC sublayer are not populated with protocol type information, as was the case in earlier Ethernet implementations.

The MAC sublayer has two primary responsibilities:

- **Data encapsulation:** Includes frame assembly before transmission, frame parsing upon reception of a frame, data link layer MAC addressing, and error detection.

- **Media Access Control:** Because Ethernet is a shared media and all devices can transmit at any time, media access is controlled by a method called Carrier Sense Multiple Access with Collision Detection (CSMA/CD) when operating in half-duplex mode.

At the physical layer, Ethernet specifies and implements encoding and decoding schemes that enable frame bits to be carried as signals across both unshielded twisted-pair (UTP) copper cables and optical fiber cables. In early implementations, Ethernet used coaxial cabling.

Legacy Ethernet Technologies

Ethernet is best understood by first considering the two early Ethernet specifications—10BASE5 and 10BASE2. With these two specifications, the network engineer installs a series of coaxial cables connecting each device on the Ethernet network, as shown in Figure 29-2.

Figure 29-2   Ethernet Physical and Logical Bus Topology

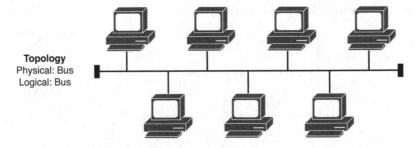

Topology
Physical: Bus
Logical: Bus

The series of cables creates an electrical circuit, called a *bus*, which is shared among all devices on the Ethernet. When a computer wants to send some bits to another computer on the bus, it sends an electrical signal and the electricity propagates to all devices on the Ethernet.

With the change of media to UTP and the introduction of the first hubs, Ethernet physical topologies migrated to a star, as shown in Figure 29-3.

Figure 29-3   Ethernet Physical Star and Logical Bus Topology

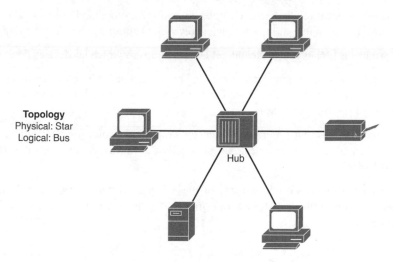

Regardless of the change in the physical topology from a bus to a star, hubs logically operate similarly to a traditional bus topology and require the use of CSMA/CD.

CSMA/CD

Because Ethernet is a shared media where every device has the right to send at any time, it also defines a specification for how to ensure that only one device sends traffic at a time. The CSMA/CD algorithm defines how the Ethernet logical bus is accessed.

CSMA/CD logic helps prevent collisions and also defines how to act when a collision does occur. The CSMA/CD algorithm works like this:

1. A device with a frame to send listens until the Ethernet is not busy.

2. When the Ethernet is not busy, the sender(s) begin(s) sending the frame.

3. The sender(s) listen(s) to make sure that no collision occurred.

4. If a collision occurs, the devices that had been sending a frame each send a jamming signal to ensure that all stations recognize the collision.

5. After the jamming is complete, each sender randomizes a timer and waits that long before trying to resend the collided frame.

6. When each random timer expires, the process starts again from the beginning.

When CSMA/CD is in effect, it also means that a device's network interface card (NIC) is operating in half-duplex mode—either sending or receiving frames. CSMA/CD is disabled when a NIC autodetects that it can operate in—or is manually configured to operate in—full-duplex mode. In full-duplex mode, a NIC can send and receive simultaneously.

Legacy Ethernet Summary

Today, you might occasionally use LAN hubs, but you will more likely use switches instead of hubs. However, keep in mind the following key points about the history of Ethernet:

- The original Ethernet LANs created an electrical bus to which all devices connected.

- 10BASE2 and 10BASE5 repeaters extended the length of LANs by cleaning up the electrical signal and repeating it—a Layer 1 function—but without interpreting the meaning of the electrical signal.

- Hubs are repeaters that provide a centralized connection point for UTP cabling—but they still create a single electrical bus, shared by the various devices, just like 10BASE5 and 10BASE2.

- Because collisions could occur in any of these cases, Ethernet defines the CSMA/CD algorithm, which tells devices how to both avoid collisions and take action when collisions do occur.

Current Ethernet Technologies

Refer to Figure 29-1 and notice the different 802.3 standards. Each new physical layer standard from the IEEE requires many differences at the physical layer. However, each of these physical layer standards uses the same 802.3 header, and each uses the upper LLC sublayer as well. Table 29-1 lists today's most commonly used IEEE Ethernet physical layer standards.

Table 29-1   Today's Most Common Types of Ethernet

Common Name	Speed	Alternative Name	Name of IEEE Standard	Cable Type, Maximum Length
Ethernet	10Mbps	10BASE-T	802.3	Copper, 100 m
Fast Ethernet	100Mbps	100BASE-TX	802.3u	Copper, 100 m
Gigabit Ethernet	1000Mbps	1000BASE-LX	802.3z	Fiber, 550 m
Gigabit Ethernet	1000Mbps	1000BASE-T	802.3ab	Copper, 100 m
10GigE (Gigabit Ethernet)	10Gbps	10GBASE-T	802.3an	Copper, 100 m

UTP Cabling

The three most common Ethernet standards used today—10BASE-T (Ethernet), 100BASE-TX (Fast Ethernet, or FE), and 1000BASE-T (Gigabit Ethernet, or GE)—use UTP cabling. Some key differences exist, particularly with the number of wire pairs needed in each case and in the type (category) of cabling.

The UTP cabling used by popular Ethernet standards includes either two or four pairs of wires. The cable ends typically use an RJ-45 connector. The RJ-45 connector has eight specific physical locations into which the eight wires in the cable can be inserted, called pin positions or, simply, pins.

The Telecommunications Industry Association (TIA) and the Electronics Industry Alliance (EIA) define standards for UTP cabling, color-coding for wires, and standard pinouts on the cables. Figure 29-4 shows two TIA/EIA pinout standards, with the color-coding and pair numbers listed.

Figure 29-4   TIA/EIA Standard Ethernet Cabling Pinouts

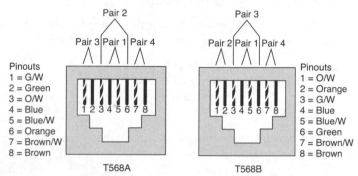

For the exam, you should be well prepared to choose which type of cable (straight-through or crossover) is needed in each part of the network. In short, devices on opposite ends of a cable that use the same pair of pins to transmit need a crossover cable. Devices that use an opposite pair of pins to transmit need a straight-through cable. Table 29-2 lists typical devices and the pin pairs they use, assuming that they use 10BASE-T and 100BASE-TX.

Table 29-2   10BASE-T and 100BASE-TX Pin Pairs Used

Devices That Transmit on 1,2 and Receive on 3,6	Devices That Transmit on 3,6 and Receive on 1,2
PC NICs	Hubs
Routers	Switches
Wireless access points (Ethernet interfaces)	—
Networked printers (printers that connect directly to the LAN)	—

1000BASE-T requires four wire pairs because Gigabit Ethernet transmits and receives on each of the four wire pairs simultaneously.

However, Gigabit Ethernet does have a concept of straight-through and crossover cables, with a minor difference in the crossover cables. The pinouts for a straight-through cable are the same—pin 1 to pin 1, pin 2 to pin 2, and so on. The crossover cable crosses the same two-wire pair as the crossover cable for the other types of Ethernet—the pair at pins 1,2 and 3,6—as well as crossing the two other pairs (the pair at pins 4,5 with the pair at pins 7,8).

Benefits of Using Switches

A collision domain is a set of devices whose frames could collide. All devices on a 10BASE2, 10BASE5, or any network using a hub risk collisions between the frames that they send, so all devices on one of these types of Ethernet networks are in the same collision domain and use CSMA/CD to detect and resolve collisions.

LAN switches significantly reduce, or even eliminate, the number of collisions on a LAN. Unlike hubs, switches do not create a single shared bus. Instead, switches do the following:

- They interpret the bits in the received frame so that they can typically send the frame out the one required port, rather than all other ports.

- If a switch needs to forward multiple frames out the same port, the switch buffers the frames in memory, sending one at a time, thereby avoiding collisions.

In addition, switches with only one device cabled to each port of the switch allow the use of full-duplex operation. Full-duplex means that the NIC can send and receive concurrently, effectively doubling the bandwidth of a 100Mbps link to 200Mbps—100Mbps for sending and 100Mbps for receiving.

These seemingly simple switch features provide significant performance improvements as compared with using hubs. In particular:

- If only one device is cabled to each port of a switch, no collisions can occur.

- Devices connected to one switch port do not share their bandwidth with devices connected to another switch port. Each has its own separate bandwidth, meaning that a switch with 100Mbps ports has 100Mbps of bandwidth per port.

Ethernet Addressing

The IEEE defines the format and assignment of LAN addresses. To ensure a unique MAC address, the first half of the address identifies the manufacturer of the card. This code is called the organizationally unique identifier (OUI). Each manufacturer assigns a MAC address with its own OUI as the first half of the address. The second half of the address is assigned by the manufacturer and is never used on another card or network interface with the same OUI. Figure 29-5 shows the structure of a unicast Ethernet address.

Figure 29-5   Structure of a Unicast Ethernet Address

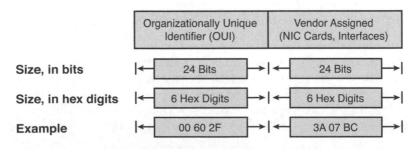

Ethernet also has group addresses, which identify more than one NIC or network interface. The IEEE defines two general categories of group addresses for Ethernet:

- **Broadcast addresses:** The broadcast address implies that all devices on the LAN should process the frame and has a value of FFFF.FFFF.FFFF.

- **Multicast addresses:** Multicast addresses are used to allow a subset of devices on a LAN to communicate. When IP multicasts over an Ethernet, the multicast MAC addresses used by IP follow this format: 0100.5exx.xxxx. The xx.xxxx portion is divided between IPv4 multicast (00:0000–7F.FFFF) and MPLS multicast (80:0000–8F:FFFF). Multiprotocol Label Switching (MPLS) is a CCNP topic.

Ethernet Framing

The physical layer helps you get a string of bits from one device to another. The framing of the bits allows the receiving device to interpret the bits. The term *framing* refers to the definition of the fields assumed to be in the data that is received. Framing defines the meaning of the bits transmitted and received over a network.

The framing used for Ethernet has changed a couple of times over the years. Each iteration of Ethernet is shown in Figure 29-6, with the current version shown at the bottom.

Figure 29-6   Ethernet Frame Formats

DIX

Preamble	Destination	Source	Type	Data and Pad	FCS
8	6	6	2	46 – 1500	4

IEEE 802.3 (Original)

Preamble	SFD	Destination	Source	Length	Data and Pad	FCS
7	1	6	6	2	46 – 1500	4

IEEE 802.3 (Revised 1997)

	Preamble	SFD	Destination	Source	Length/ Type 2	Data and Pad	FCS
Bytes	7	1	6	6		46 – 1500	4

The fields in the last version shown in Figure 29-6 are explained further in Table 29-3.

Table 29-3   IEEE 802.3 Ethernet Field Descriptions

Field	Field Length in Bytes	Description
Preamble	7	Synchronization
Start Frame Delimiter (SFD)	1	Signifies that the next byte begins the Destination MAC field
Destination MAC Address	6	Identifies the intended recipient of this frame
Source MAC Address	6	Identifies the sender of this frame
Length	2	Defines the length of the data field of the frame (either length or type is present, but not both)
Type	2	Defines the type of protocol listed inside the frame (either length or type is present, but not both)
Data and Pad	46–1500	Holds data from a higher layer, typically a Layer 3 PDU (generic), and often an IP packet
Frame Check Sequence (FCS)	4	Provides a method for the receiving NIC to determine whether the frame experienced transmission errors

The Role of the Physical Layer

We have already discussed the most popular cabling used in LANs—UTP. But to fully understand the operation of the network, you should know some additional basic concepts of the physical layer.

The OSI physical layer accepts a complete frame from the data link layer and encodes it as a series of signals that are transmitted onto the local media.

The delivery of frames across the local media requires the following physical layer elements:

- The physical media and associated connectors
- A representation of bits on the media
- Encoding of data and control information
- Transmitter and receiver circuitry on the network devices

There are three basic forms of network media on which data is represented:

- Copper cable
- Fiber
- Wireless (IEEE 802.11)

Bits are represented on the medium by changing one or more of the following characteristics of a signal:

- Amplitude
- Frequency
- Phase

The nature of the actual signals representing the bits on the media will depend on the signaling method in use. Some methods might use one attribute of a signal to represent a single 0 and use another attribute of a signal to represent a single 1. The actual signaling method and its detailed operation are not important to your CCNA exam preparation.

Study Resources

For today's exam topics, refer to the following resources for more study.

Resource	Location	Topic
Primary Resources		
Network Basics	10	All
Introduction to Networks	5	All
ICND1 Official Cert Guide	2	Building Physical Ethernet Networks with UTP
		Sending Data in Ethernet Networks
ICND1 Foundation Learning Guide	3	All
Supplemental Resources		
CCENT Practice and Study Guide	5	All
Flash Cards	3	Relevant Questions
CCNA R&S Portable Command Guide	4	All

Day 28

Switching Concepts and Operation

CCENT 100-101 ICND1 Exam Topics

- Identify basic switching concepts and the operation of Cisco switches.

Key Topics

Today we review the concepts behind switching, including the history of the development of switching, how switching actually works, as well as the variety of switch features. We also review how to access Cisco devices, the basic IOS commands to navigate the command-line interface (CLI), and the details of how configuration files are managed.

Evolution to Switching

Today's LANs almost exclusively use switches to interconnect end devices; however, this was not always the case. Initially, devices were connected to a physical bus—a long run of coaxial backbone cabling. With the introduction of 10BASE-T and UTP cabling, the hub gained popularity as a cheaper, easier way to connect devices. But even 10BASE-T with hubs had the following limitations:

- A frame being sent from one device can collide with a frame sent by another device attached to that LAN segment. Devices were in the same collision domain sharing the bandwidth.

- Broadcasts sent by one device were heard by, and processed by, all other devices on the LAN. Devices were in the same broadcast domain. Similar to hubs, switches forward broadcast frames out all ports except for the incoming port. Switch ports can be configured on various VLANs, which will segment them into broadcast domains.

Ethernet bridges were soon developed to solve some of the inherent problems in a shared LAN. A bridge basically segmented a LAN into two collision domains which

- Reduced the number of collisions that occurred in a LAN segment

- Increased the available bandwidth

When switches arrived on the scene, these devices provided the same benefits of bridges, as well as the following:

- A larger number of interfaces to break up the collision domain into more segments

- Hardware-based switching instead of using software to make the decision

In a LAN where all nodes are connected directly to the switch, the throughput of the network increases dramatically. With each computer connected to a separate port on the switch, each is in a separate collision domain and has its own dedicated segment. The three primary reasons for this increase are as follows:

- Dedicated bandwidth to each port

- Collision-free environment

- Full-duplex operation

Switching Logic

Ethernet switches selectively forward individual frames from a receiving port to the port where the destination node is connected. During this instant, the switch creates a full-bandwidth, logical, point-to-point connection between the two nodes.

Switches create this logical connection based on the source and destination Media Access Control (MAC) addresses in the Ethernet header. Specifically, the primary job of a LAN switch is to receive Ethernet frames and then make a decision: either forward the frame or ignore the frame. To accomplish this, the switch performs three actions:

1. Decides when to forward a frame or when to filter (not forward) a frame, based on the destination MAC address

2. Learns MAC addresses by examining the source MAC address of each frame received by the switch

3. Creates a (Layer 2) loop-free environment with other switches by using Spanning Tree Protocol (STP)

To make the forward or filter decision, the switch uses a dynamically built MAC address table stored in RAM. By comparing the frame's destination MAC address with the fields in the table, the switch decides how to forward and/or filter the frame.

For example, in Figure 28-1, the switch receives a frame from Host A with the destination MAC address OC. The switch looks in its MAC table and finds an entry for the MAC address and forwards the frame out port 6. The switch also filters the frame by not forwarding it out any other port, including the port on which the frame was received.

In addition to forwarding and filtering frames, the switch will also refresh the timestamp for the source MAC address of the frame. In Figure 28-1, the MAC address for Host A, OA, is already in the MAC table. So the switch refreshes the entry. Entries that are not refreshed will eventually be removed (after the default 300 seconds in Cisco IOS).

Continuing the example in Figure 28-1, assume that another device, Host E, is attached to port 10. Host B then sends a frame to the new Host E. The switch does not yet know where Host E is located. So it forwards the frame out all active ports except for the port on which the frame was received. The new Host E will receive the frame. When it replies to Host B, the switch will learn Host E's MAC address and port for the first time and store it in the MAC address table. Subsequent frames destined for Host E will only be sent out port 10.

Figure 28-1   Switch Forwarding Based on MAC Address

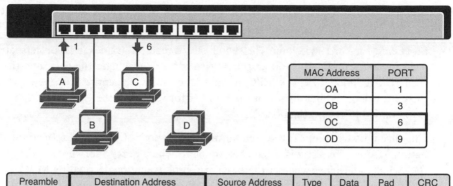

MAC Address	PORT
OA	1
OB	3
OC	6
OD	9

Frame	Preamble	Destination Address	Source Address	Type	Data	Pad	CRC
		OC	OA				

Finally, LAN switches must have a method for creating a loop-free path for frames to take within the LAN. STP provides loop prevention in Ethernet networks where redundant physical links exist.

Collision and Broadcast Domains

A collision domain is the set of LAN interfaces whose frames could collide with each other. All shared media environments, such as those created by using hubs, are collision domains. When one host is attached to a switch port, the switch creates a dedicated connection, thereby eliminating the potential for a collision. Switches reduce collisions and improve bandwidth use on network segments because they provide dedicated bandwidth to each network segment.

Out of the box, however, a switch cannot provide relief from broadcast traffic. A collection of connected switches forms one large broadcast domain. If a frame with the destination address FFFF.FFFF.FFFF crosses a switch port, that switch must then flood the frame out all other active ports. Each attached device must then process the broadcast frame at least up to the network layer. Routers and VLANs are used to segment broadcast domains. Day 26, "VLAN Concepts," reviews the use of VLANs to segment broadcast domains.

Frame Forwarding

Switches operate in several ways to forward frames. They can differ in forwarding methods, port speeds, memory buffering, and the OSI layers used to make the forwarding decision. The sections that follow discuss these concepts in greater detail.

Switch Forwarding Methods

Switches use one of the following forwarding methods for switching data between network ports:

- **Store-and-forward switching:** The switch stores received frames in its buffers, analyzes each frame for information about the destination, and evaluates the data integrity using the cyclic redundancy check (CRC) in the frame trailer. The entire frame is stored and the CRC calculated before any of the frame is forwarded. If the CRC passes, the frame is forwarded to the destination.

- **Cut-through switching:** The switch buffers just enough of the frame to read the destination MAC address so that it can determine to which port to forward the data. After the switch determines whether there is a match between the destination MAC address and an entry in the MAC address table, the frame is forwarded out the appropriate port(s). This happens as the rest of the initial frame is still being received. The switch does not perform any error checking on the frame.

- **Fragment free:** The switch waits for the collision window (64 bytes) to pass before forwarding the frame. This means that each frame will be checked into the data field to make sure that no fragmentation has occurred. Fragment free mode provides better error checking than cut-through, with practically no increase in latency.

Symmetric and Asymmetric Switching

Symmetric switching provides switched connections between ports with the same bandwidth, such as all 100Mbps ports or all 1000Mbps ports. An asymmetric LAN switch provides switched connections between ports of unlike bandwidth, such as a combination of 10Mbps, 100Mbps, and 1000Mbps ports.

Memory Buffering

Switches store frames for a brief time in a memory buffer. There are two methods of memory buffering:

- **Port-based memory:** Frames are stored in queues that are linked to specific incoming ports.

- **Shared memory:** Frames are deposited into a common memory buffer, which all ports on the switch share.

Layer 2 and Layer 3 Switching

A Layer 2 LAN switch performs switching and filtering based only on MAC addresses. A Layer 2 switch is completely transparent to network protocols and user applications. A Layer 3 switch functions similarly to a Layer 2 switch. But instead of using only the Layer 2 MAC address information for forwarding decisions, a Layer 3 switch can also use IP address information. Layer 3 switches are also capable of performing Layer 3 routing functions, reducing the need for dedicated routers on a LAN. Because Layer 3 switches have specialized switching hardware, they can typically route data as quickly as they can switch data.

Accessing and Navigating the Cisco IOS

By now, you are very familiar with connecting to Cisco devices and configuring them using the command-line interface (CLI). Here, we quickly review methods for accessing and navigating the CLI.

Connecting to Cisco Devices

You can access a device directly or from a remote location. Figure 28-2 shows the many ways that you can connect to Cisco devices.

Figure 28-2   Sources for Cisco Device Configuration

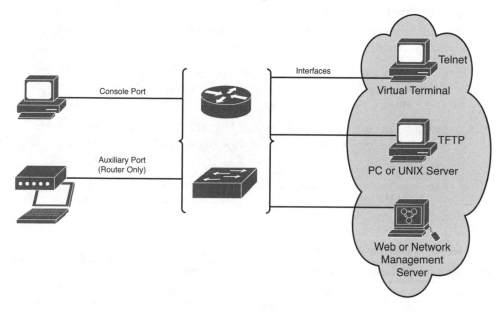

The two ways to configure Cisco devices are as follows:

- **Console terminal:** Use an RJ-45–to–RJ-45 rollover cable and a computer with the terminal communications software (such as HyperTerminal, Tera Term, and so on) to establish a direct connection. Optionally, you can connect a mini-USB cable to the mini-USB console port, if available.

- **Remote terminal:** Use an external modem connected to the auxiliary port—routers only—to remotely configure the device.

After it is configured, you can access the device using three additional methods:

- Establish a terminal (vty) session using Telnet.

- Configure the device through the current connection (console or auxiliary), or download a previously written startup config file from a Trivial File Transfer Protocol (TFTP) server on the network.

- Download a configuration file using a network management software application such as CiscoWorks.

CLI EXEC Sessions

Cisco IOS separates the EXEC session into two basic access levels:

- **User EXEC mode:** Access to only a limited number of basic monitoring and trouble-shooting commands, such as **show** and **ping**.

- **Privileged EXEC mode:** Full access to all device commands, including configuration and management.

Using the Help Facility

Cisco IOS has extensive command-line input help facilities, including context-sensitive help. The following summarizes the two types of help available:

- **Word help:** Enter a character sequence of an incomplete command immediately followed by a question mark (**sh?**) to get a list of available commands that start with the character sequence.

- **Command syntax help:** Enter the **?** command to get command syntax help to see all the available arguments to complete a command (**show ?**). IOS then displays a list of available arguments.

As part of the help facility, IOS displays console error messages when incorrect command syntax is entered. Table 28-1 shows sample error messages, what they mean, and how to get help when they are displayed.

Table 28-1   Console Error Messages

Example Error Message	Meaning	How to Get Help
switch# cl % Ambiguous command: "cl"	You did not enter enough characters for your device to recognize the command.	Reenter the command followed by a question mark (?), without a space between the command and the question mark. The possible keywords that you can enter with the command are displayed.
switch# **clock** % Incomplete command.	You did not enter all the keywords or values required by this command.	Reenter the command followed by a question mark (?), with a space between the command and the question mark.
switch# **clock ste** ^ % Invalid input detected at '^' marker.	You entered the command incorrectly. The caret (^) marks the point of the error.	Enter a question mark (?) to display all the available commands or parameters.

CLI Navigation and Editing Shortcuts

Table 28-2 summarizes the shortcuts for navigating and editing commands in the CLI. Although not specifically tested on the CCNA exam, these shortcuts can save you time when using the simulator during the exam.

Table 28-2   Hot Keys and Shortcuts

Keyboard Command	What Happens
Navigation Key Sequences	
Up arrow or Ctrl-P	This displays the most recently used command. If you press it again, the next most recent command appears, until the history buffer is exhausted. (The P stands for previous.)
Down arrow or Ctrl-N	If you have gone too far back into the history buffer, these keys take you forward to the more recently entered commands. (The N stands for next.)
Left arrow or Ctrl-B	This moves the cursor backward in the currently displayed command without deleting characters. (The B stands for back.)
Right arrow or Ctrl-F	This moves the cursor forward in the currently displayed command without deleting characters. (The F stands for forward.)
Tab	Completes a partial command name entry.
Backspace	This moves the cursor backward in the currently displayed command, deleting characters.
Ctrl-A	This moves the cursor directly to the first character of the currently displayed command.
Ctrl-E	This moves the cursor directly to the end of the currently displayed command.
Ctrl-R	This redisplays the command line with all characters. It's useful when messages clutter the screen.
Ctrl-D	This deletes a single character.
Esc-B	This moves back one word.
Esc-F	This moves forward one word.
At the --More-- Prompt	
Enter key	Displays the next line.
Spacebar	Displays the next screen.
Any other alphanumeric key	Returns to the EXEC prompt.
Break Keys	
Ctrl-C	When in any configuration mode, this ends the configuration mode and returns to privileged EXEC mode. When in setup mode, aborts back to the command prompt.

Keyboard Command	What Happens
Ctrl-Z	When in any configuration mode, this ends the configuration mode and returns to privileged EXEC mode. When in user or privileged EXEC mode, logs you out of the router.
Ctrl-Shift-6	All-purpose break sequence. Use to abort DNS lookups, traceroutes, pings.

Command History

The Cisco IOS, by default, stores the last ten commands you entered in a history buffer. This provides you with a quick way to move backward and forward in the history of commands, choose one, and then edit it before reissuing the command. To view or configure the command history buffer, use the commands shown in Table 28-3. Although the switch prompt is shown here, these commands are also appropriate for a router.

Table 28-3   Command History Buffer Commands

Command Syntax	Description
switch# **show history**	Displays the commands currently stored in the history buffer.
switch# **terminal history**	Enables terminal history. This command can be run from either user or privileged EXEC mode.
switch# **terminal history size 50**	Configures the terminal history size. The terminal history can maintain 0–256 command lines.
switch# **terminal no history size**	Resets the terminal history size to the default value of 20 command lines in IOS 15.
switch# **terminal no history**	Disables terminal history.

IOS Examination Commands

To verify and troubleshoot network operation, you use **show** commands. Figure 28-3 delineates the different **show** commands, as follows:

- If they are applicable to IOS (stored in RAM)
- If they apply to the backup configuration file stored in NVRAM
- If they apply to flash or specific interfaces

Figure 28-3   Typical show Commands and the Information Provided

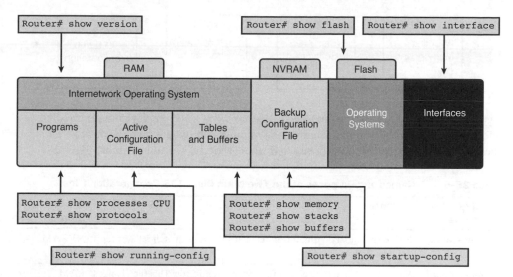

Subconfiguration Modes

To enter global configuration mode, enter the **configure terminal** command. From global configuration mode, IOS provides a multitude of subconfiguration modes. Table 28-4 summarizes the most common subconfiguration modes pertinent to the CCNA exam.

Table 28-4   Cisco Device Subconfiguration Modes

Prompt	Name of Mode	Examples of Commands Used to Reach This Mode
hostname(config)#	Global	configure terminal
hostname(config-line)#	Line	line console 0
		line vty 0 15
hostname(config-if)#	Interface	interface fastethernet 0/0
hostname(config-router)#	Router	router rip
		router eigrp 100

Storing and Erasing Configuration Files

When you configure a Cisco device, it needs to be able to retain the configuration in memory in case the switch or router loses power. Cisco devices have four main types of memory. Figure 28-4 shows these four memory types and the primary function of each.

Figure 28-4   Cisco Device Memory Types

RAM	Flash	ROM	NVRAM
(Working Memory and Running Configuration)	(Cisco IOS Software)	(Bootstrap Program)	(Startup Configuration)

Cisco devices use two configuration files—one file used when the device is powered on and another file for the active, currently used running configuration in RAM. Table 28-5 list the names of these files, their purposes, and where they are stored in memory.

Table 28-5   Names and Purposes of the Two Main Cisco IOS Configuration Files

Configuration Filename	Purpose	Where It Is Stored
Startup-config	Stores the initial configuration used anytime the switch reloads the Cisco IOS.	NVRAM
Running-config	Stores the currently used configuration commands. This file changes dynamically when someone enters commands in configuration mode.	RAM

Configuration files can also be stored on a TFTP server. The configuration files can be copied between RAM, NVRAM, and a TFTP server using the copy commands, as shown in Figure 28-5.

Figure 28-5   Configuration File copy Commands and Storage Locations

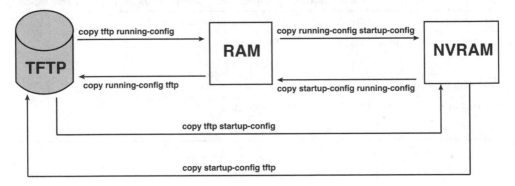

You can use three commands to erase the contents of NVRAM. The **write erase** and **erase startup-config** commands are older, whereas the **erase nvram:** command is the more recent, and recommended, command. All three commands erase the contents of the NVRAM configuration file.

Study Resources

For today's exam topics, refer to the following resources for more study.

Resource	Location	Topic
Primary Resources		
Network Basics	2	IOS Bootcamp
Introduction to Networks	2	IOS Bootcamp
Switched Networks	1	The Switched Environment
Routing and Switching Essentials	1	The Switched Environment
ICND1 Official Cert Guide	6	All
	7	All
ICND1 Foundation Learning Guide	4	All
Supplemental Resources		
CCENT Practice and Study Guide	2	IOS Bootcamp
	12	The Switched Environment
Flash Cards	2	Relevant Questions
CCNA R&S Portable Command Guide	5	All
Network Simulator	10	Switch Forwarding Troubleshooting

Basic Switch Configuration

CCENT 100-101 ICND1 Exam Topics

- Configure and verify initial switch configuration, including remote access management.

- Configure SVI interfaces.

- Verify network status and switch operation using basic utilities such as ping, telnet, and ssh.

Key Topics

Today, we review the commands necessary to perform a basic initial configuration of a switch, including changing the default management VLAN and configuring SSH remote access. We will also review verification techniques such as using **ping**, **traceroute**, and **show** commands.

Basic Switch Configuration Commands

Table 27-1 reviews basic switch configuration commands.

Table 27-1   Basic Switch Configuration Commands

Command Description	Command Syntax
Enter global configuration mode.	Switch# **configure terminal**
Configure a name for the device.	Switch(config)# **hostname S1**
Enter the interface configuration mode for the VLAN 123 interface.	S1(config)# **interface vlan 123**
Configure the interface IP address.	S1(config-if)# **ip address 172.17.99.11 255.255.255.0**
Enable the interface.	S1(config-if)# **no shutdown**
Return to global configuration mode.	S1(config-if)# **exit**
Enter the interface to assign the VLAN.	S1(config)# **interface fastethernet 0/6**
Define the VLAN membership mode for the port.	S1(config-if)# **switchport mode access**
Assign the port to a VLAN.	S1(config-if)# **switchport access vlan 123**
Configure the interface duplex mode to enable AUTO duplex configuration.	S1(config-if)# **duplex auto**
Configure the interface speed and enable AUTO speed configuration.	S1(config-if)# **speed auto**

Command Description	Command Syntax
Enable auto-MDIX on the interface.	`S1(config-if)# mdix auto`
Return to global configuration mode.	`S1(config-if)# exit`
Configure the default gateway on the switch.	`S1(config)# ip default-gateway 172.17.50.1`
Configure the HTTP server for authentication using the **enable** password, which is the default method of HTTP server user authentication.	`S1(config)# ip http authentication enable`
Enable the HTTP server.	`S1(config)# ip http server`
Switch from global configuration mode to line configuration mode for console 0.	`S1(config)# line console 0`
Set **cisco** as the password for the console 0 line on the switch.	`S1(config-line)# password cisco`
Set the console line to require the password to be entered before access is granted.	`S1(config-line)# login`
Return to global configuration mode.	`S1(config-if)# exit`
Switch from global configuration mode to line configuration mode for vty terminals 0–15.	`S1(config)# line vty 0 15`
Set **cisco** as the password for the vty lines on the switch.	`S1(config-line)# password cisco`
Set the vty line to require the password to be entered before access is granted.	`S1(config-line)# login`
Return to global configuration mode.	`S1(config-line)# exit`
Configure **cisco** as the enable password to enter privileged EXEC mode.	`S1(config)# enable password cisco`
Configure **class** as the enable secret password to enter privileged EXEC mode. This password overrides the **enable password**.	`S1(config)# enable secret class`
Encrypt all the system passwords that are stored in clear text.	`S1(config)# service password-encryption`
Configure a login banner. The # character delimits the beginning and end of the banner.	`S1 (config)# banner login #Authorized Personnel Only!#`
Configure a message of the day (MOTD) login banner. The # character delimits the beginning and end of the banner.	`S1(config)# banner motd #Device maintenance will be occurring on Friday!#`
Return to privileged EXEC mode.	`S1(config)# end`
Save the running configuration to the switch startup configuration.	`S1# copy running-config startup -config`

In reference to the commands in Table 27-1, keep in mind the following:

- The default VLAN for all ports is VLAN 1. Because it is a best practice to use a VLAN other than the default VLAN 1 as the management VLAN, the command in the table uses VLAN 123.

- By default, the native VLAN assigned to 802.1Q trunks is also VLAN 1. It is a security best practice to define a dummy VLAN as the native VLAN—a VLAN that is distinct from all other VLANs. We discuss trunking configuration on Day 25, "VLAN and Trunking Configuration."

- Although the **enable password** command is shown in the table for completeness, this command is superseded by the **enable secret** command. If both are entered, IOS ignores the **enable password** command.

- Although the configuration for Telnet is shown, configuring SSH is a best practice. SSH configuration is reviewed in the next section.

- To configure multiple ports with the same command, use the **interface range** command. For example, to configure ports 6–10 as access ports belonging to VLAN 10, you would enter the following:

```
Switch(config)# interface range FastEthernet 0/6 - 10
Switch(config-if-range)# switchport mode access
Switch(config-if-range)# switchport access vlan 10
```

Half-Duplex, Full-Duplex, and Port Speed

Half-duplex communication is unidirectional data flow in which a device can either send or receive on an Ethernet LAN, but not both at the same time. Today's LAN networking devices and end device network interface cards (NIC) operate at full duplex as long as the device is connected to another full-duplex–capable device. Full-duplex communication increases effective bandwidth by allowing both ends of a connection to transmit and receive data simultaneously; this is known as *bidirectional*. This microsegmented LAN is collision free. Gigabit Ethernet and 10Gbps NICs require full-duplex connections to operate. Port speed is simply the bandwidth rating of the port. The most common speeds today are 100Mbps, 1Gbps, and 10Gbps.

Although the default duplex and speed setting for Cisco Catalyst 2960 and 3560 switches is **auto**, the **speed** and **duplex** commands can be manually configured.

NOTE: Setting the duplex mode and speed of switch ports can cause issues if one of the ends is mismatched or set to autonegotiation. Also, all fiber-optic ports, such as 100BASE-FX ports, operate only at one preset speed and are always full duplex.

Automatic Medium-Dependent Interface Crossover (auto-MDIX)

Until recently, switch-to-switch or switch-to-router connections required using different Ethernet cables (crossover or straight-through). Using the automatic medium-dependent interface crossover (auto-MDIX) feature on an interface eliminates this problem. When auto-MDIX is enabled, the interface automatically detects the required cable connection type (straight-through or crossover) and configures the connection appropriately. The auto-MDIX feature is enabled by default on Catalyst 2960 and Catalyst 3560 switches but is not available on the older Catalyst 2950 and Catalyst 3550 switches. The Gigabit Ethernet standard requires auto-MDIX, so any 1000Mbps port will have this capability. When using auto-MDIX on an interface, the interface speed and duplex must be set to **auto** so that the feature operates correctly.

Configuring SSH Access

Secure Shell (SSH) is recommended as the protocol to use for remote device management. Configuring SSH (port 22) is a security best practice because Telnet (port 23) uses insecure plain-text transmission of both the login and the data across the connection. Example 27-1 displays an SSH configuration.

Example 27-1   Configuring SSH Remote Access on a Switch

```
S1# show ip ssh
SSH Disabled - version 1.99
%Please create RSA keys to enable SSH (of at least 768 bits size) to enable SSH v2.
Authentication timeout: 120 secs; Authentication retries: 3
S1# conf t
S1(config)# ip domain-name cisco.com
S1(config)# crypto key generate rsa
The name for the keys will be: S1.cisco.com
Choose the size of the key modulus in the range of 360 to 4096 for your
   General Purpose Keys. Choosing a key modulus greater than 512 may take
   a few minutes.

How many bits in the modulus [512]:1024
% Generating 1024 bit RSA keys, keys will be non-exportable...
[OK] (elapsed time was 4 seconds)

*Mar  1 02:20:18.529: %SSH-5-ENABLED: SSH 1.99 has been enabled
S1(config)# line vty 0 15
S1(config-line)# login local
S1(config-line)# transport input ssh
S1(config-line)# user admin password ccna
```

```
!The following commands are optional SSH configurations.
S1(config)# ip ssh version 2
S1(config)# ip ssh authentication-retries 5
S1(config)# ip ssh time-out 60
S1(config)# end
S1# show ip ssh
SSH Enabled - version 2.0
Authentication timeout: 60 secs; Authentication retries: 5
S1#
```

The following description details the steps shown in Example 27-1:

Step 1. Verify that the switch supports SSH using the **show ip ssh** command. If the command is not recognized, you know that SSH is not supported.

Step 2. Configure a DNS domain name with the **ip domain-name** *domain-name* global configuration command.

Step 3. Configure the switch using the **crypto key generate rsa** command to generate an RSA key pair and automatically enable SSH. When generating RSA keys, you are prompted to enter a modulus length. Cisco recommends a minimum modulus size of 1024 bits, as shown in Example 27-1.

NOTE: To remove the RSA key pair, use the **crypto key zeroize rsa** command. This will disable the SSH service.

Step 4. Change the vty lines to use usernames, with either locally configured usernames or an authentication, authorization, and accounting (AAA) server. In Example 27-1, the **login local** vty subcommand defines the use of local usernames, replacing the **login** vty subcommand.

Step 5. Configure the switch to accept only SSH connections with the **transport input ssh** vty subcommand. (The default is **transport input telnet.**)

Step 6. Add one or more **username** *username* **password** *password* global configuration commands to configure username/password pairs.

Step 7. If desired, you can modify the default SSH configuration to change the SSH version to 2.0, the number of authentication tries, and the timeout, as shown in Example 27-1.

Step 8. Verify your SSH parameters using the **show ip ssh** command.

Verifying Network Connectivity

Using and interpreting the output of various testing tools are often the first steps in isolating the cause of a network connectivity issue. The **ping** command can be used to systematically test connectivity in the following manner:

- Can an end device ping itself?

- Can an end device ping its default gateway?

- Can an end device ping the destination?

By using the **ping** command in this ordered sequence, you can isolate problems faster. If local connectivity is not an issue—in other words, the end device can successfully ping its default gateway—using the traceroute utility can help isolate at what point in the path from source to destination that the traffic stops.

As a first step in the testing sequence, verify the operation of the TCP/IP stack on the local host by pinging the loopback address, 127.0.0.1, as demonstrated in Example 27-2.

Example 27-2   Testing the TCP/IP Stack on a Windows PC

```
C:\> ping 127.0.0.1

Pinging 127.0.0.1 with 32 bytes of data:

Reply from 127.0.0.1: bytes=32 time<1ms TTL=64
Reply from 127.0.0.1: bytes=32 time<1ms TTL=64
Reply from 127.0.0.1: bytes=32 time<1ms TTL=64
Reply from 127.0.0.1: bytes=32 time<1ms TTL=64

Ping statistics for 127.0.0.1:
    Packets: Sent = 4, Received = 4, Lost = 0 (0% loss),
Approximate round trip times in milli-seconds:
    Minimum = 0ms, Maximum = 0ms, Average = 0ms
```

Because this test should succeed regardless of whether the host is connected to the network, a failure indicates a software or hardware problem on the host itself. Either the network interface is not operating properly or possibly support for the TCP/IP stack has been inadvertently removed from the operating system.

Next, verify connectivity to the default gateway. Determine the default gateway address using **ipconfig** and then attempt to ping it, as demonstrated in Example 27-3.

Example 27-3   Testing Connectivity to the Default Gateway on a Windows PC

```
C:\> ipconfig

Windows IP Configuration

Ethernet adapter Local Area Connection:

        Connection-specific DNS Suffix   . : cisco.com
        IP Address. . . . . . . . . . . : 192.168.1.25
        Subnet Mask . . . . . . . . . . : 255.255.255.0
        Default Gateway . . . . . . . . : 192.168.1.1

C:\> ping 192.168.1.1

Pinging 192.168.1.1 with 32 bytes of data:

Reply from 192.168.1.1: bytes=32 time=162ms TTL=255
Reply from 192.168.1.1: bytes=32 time=69ms TTL=255
Reply from 192.168.1.1: bytes=32 time=82ms TTL=255
Reply from 192.168.1.1: bytes=32 time=72ms TTL=255

Ping statistics for 192.168.1.1:
    Packets: Sent = 4, Received = 4, Lost = 0 (0% loss),
Approximate round trip times in milli-seconds:
    Minimum = 69ms, Maximum = 162ms, Average = 96ms
```

Failure here can indicate several problems, each of which will need to be checked in a systematic sequence. One possible order might be the following:

1. Is the cabling from the PC to the switch correct? Are link lights lit?

2. Is the configuration on the PC correct according to the logical map of the network?

3. Are the affected interfaces on the switch the cause of the problem? Is there a duplex, speed, or auto-MDIX mismatch? Are there VLAN misconfigurations?

4. Is the cabling from the switch to the router correct? Are link lights lit?

5. Is the configuration on the router interface correct according to the logical map of the network? Is the interface active?

Finally, verify connectivity to the destination by pinging it. Assume that we are trying to reach a server at 192.168.3.100. Example 27-4 shows a successful ping test to the destination.

Example 27-4   Testing Connectivity to the Destination on a Windows PC

```
PC> ping 192.168.3.100

Pinging 192.168.3.100 with 32 bytes of data:

Reply from 192.168.3.100: bytes=32 time=200ms TTL=126
Reply from 192.168.3.100: bytes=32 time=185ms TTL=126
Reply from 192.168.3.100: bytes=32 time=186ms TTL=126
Reply from 192.168.3.100: bytes=32 time=200ms TTL=126

Ping statistics for 192.168.3.100:
    Packets: Sent = 4, Received = 4, Lost = 0 (0% loss),
Approximate round trip times in milli-seconds:
    Minimum = 185ms, Maximum = 200ms, Average = 192ms
```

Failure here would indicate a failure in the path beyond the default gateway interface because we already successfully tested connectivity to the default gateway. From a Windows PC, the best tool to use to find the break in the path is the **tracert** command, as demonstrated in Example 27-5.

NOTE: Both Mac OS X and Linux use the **traceroute** command.

Example 27-5   Tracing the Route from a Windows PC

```
C:\> tracert 192.168.3.100

Tracing route to 192.168.3.100 over a maximum of 30 hops:

 1    97 ms      75 ms      72 ms      192.168.1.1
 2    104 ms     119 ms     117 ms     192.168.2.2
 3    *          *          *          Request timed out.
 4    *          *          *          Request timed out.
 5    *          *          *          Request timed out.
 6    ^C
C:\>
```

NOTE: The reason for failure at hops 3, 4, and 5 in Example 27-5 could be that these routers are configured to not send ICMP messages back to the source.

The last successful hop on the way to the destination was 192.168.2.2. If you have administrator rights to 192.168.2.2, you could continue your research by remotely accessing the command line on 192.168.2.2 and investigating why traffic will not go any further. Also, other devices between 192.168.2.2 and 192.168.3.100 could be the source of the problem.

The point is, you want to use your ping and tracert tests as well as your network documentation to proceed in a logical sequence from source to destination.

Regardless of how simple or complex your network is, using ping and tracert from the source to the destination is a simple yet powerful way to systematically verify end-to-end connectivity as well as to locate breaks in a path from one source to one destination.

Study Resources

For today's exam topics, refer to the following resources for more study.

Resource	Location	Topic
Primary Resources		
Network Basics	2	Getting Basic
Introduction to Networks	2	Getting Basic
Switched Networks	2	Basic Switch Configuration
		Secure Remote Access
Routing and Switching Essentials	2	Basic Switch Configuration
		Secure Remote Access
ICND1 Official Cert Guide	8	All (except Port Security, which is covered in Day 9)
	18	Testing Connectivity with ping, traceroute, and telnet
ICND1 Foundation Learning Guide	5	All
Supplemental Resources		
CCENT Practice and Study Guide	2	Basic Device Configuration
	13	All
Network Simulator	8	All labs except for those that cover switch security
	18	PC IP Commands II-III
		Traceroute I
		Using and Suspending Telnet Connections
		Switch IP Connectivity
CCNA R&S Portable Command Guide	11	All

VLAN Concepts

CCENT 100-101 ICND1 Exam Topics

- Describe how VLANs create logically separate networks and the need for routing between them.

- Explain network segmentation and basic traffic management concepts.

Key Points

Most large networks today implement virtual local area networks (VLAN). Without VLANs, a switch considers every port to be in the same broadcast domain. With VLANs, switch ports can be grouped into different VLANs, in effect segmenting the broadcast domain. Today, we review VLAN concepts, consider traffic types, discuss VLAN types, and review the concept of trunking including Dynamic Trunking Protocol (DTP).

VLAN Concepts

Although a switch "out of the box" is configured to have only one VLAN, normally a switch will be configured to have two or more VLANs. Doing so creates multiple broadcast domains by putting some interfaces into one VLAN and other interfaces into other VLANs.

Reasons for using VLANs include the following:

- Grouping users by department instead of by physical location

- Segmenting devices into smaller LANs to reduce processing overhead for all devices on the LAN

- Reducing the workload of STP by limiting a VLAN to a single access switch

- Enforcing better security by isolating sensitive data to separate VLANs

- Separating IP voice traffic from data traffic

- Assisting troubleshooting by reducing the size of the failure domain (the number of devices that can cause or be effected by a failure)

Benefits of using VLANs include the following:

- **Security:** Sensitive data can be isolated to one VLAN, separating it from the rest of the network.

- **Cost reduction:** Cost savings result from less need for expensive network upgrades and more efficient use of existing bandwidth and uplinks.

- **Higher performance:** Dividing flat Layer 2 networks into multiple logical broadcast domains reduces unnecessary traffic on the network and boosts performance.

- **Broadcast storm mitigation:** VLAN segmentation prevents a broadcast storm from propagating throughout the entire network.

- **Ease of management and troubleshooting:** A hierarchical addressing scheme groups network addresses contiguously. Because a hierarchical IP addressing scheme makes problem components easier to locate, network management and troubleshooting are more efficient.

Traffic Types

A key factor for VLAN deployment is understanding the traffic patterns and the various traffic types in the organization. Table 26-1 lists the common types of network traffic that you should evaluate before placing devices and configuring VLANs.

Table 26-1   Traffic Types

Traffic Type	Description
Network management	Many types of network management traffic can be present on the network. To make network troubleshooting easier, some designers assign a separate VLAN to carry certain types of network management traffic.
IP telephony	There are two types of IP telephony traffic: signaling information between end devices and the data packets of the voice conversation. Designers often configure the data to and from the IP phones on a separate VLAN designated for voice traffic so that they can apply quality-of-service measures to give high priority to voice traffic.
IP multicast	Multicast traffic can produce a large amount of data streaming across the network. Switches must be configured to keep this traffic from flooding to devices that have not requested it, and routers must be configured to ensure that multicast traffic is forwarded to the network areas where it is requested.
Normal data	Normal data traffic is typical application traffic that is related to file and print services, email, Internet browsing, database access, and other shared network applications.
Scavenger class	Scavenger class includes all traffic with protocols or patterns that exceed their normal data flows. Applications assigned to this class have little or no contribution to the organizational objectives of the enterprise and are typically entertainment oriented in nature.

Types of VLANs

Some VLAN types are defined by the type of traffic they support; others are defined by the specific functions they perform. The principal VLAN types and their descriptions follow:

- **Data VLAN:** Configured to carry only user-generated traffic, ensuring that voice and management traffic is separated from data traffic.

- **Default VLAN:** All the ports on a switch are members of the default VLAN when the switch is reset to factory defaults. The default VLAN for Cisco switches is VLAN 1. VLAN 1 has all the features of any VLAN, except that you cannot rename it and you cannot delete it. It is a security best practice to restrict VLAN 1 to serve as a conduit only for Layer 2 control traffic (for example, CDP), supporting no other traffic.

- **Black hole VLAN:** A security best practice is to define a black hole VLAN to be a dummy VLAN distinct from all other VLANs defined in the switched LAN. All unused switch ports are assigned to the black hole VLAN so that any unauthorized device connecting to an unused switch port will be prevented from communicating beyond the switch to which it is connected.

- **Native VLAN:** This VLAN type serves as a common identifier on opposing ends of a trunk link. A security best practice is to define a native VLAN to be a dummy VLAN distinct from all other VLANs defined in the switched LAN. The native VLAN is not used for any traffic in the switched network unless legacy bridging devices happen to be present in the network or a multiaccess interconnection exists between switches joined by a hub.

- **Management VLAN:** A VLAN defined by the network administrator as a means to access the management capabilities of a switch. By default, VLAN 1 is the management VLAN. It is a security best practice to define the management VLAN to be a VLAN distinct from all other VLANs defined in the switched LAN. You do so by configuring and activating a new VLAN interface.

- **Voice VLANs:** The voice VLAN feature enables switch ports to carry IP voice traffic from an IP phone. The network administrator configures a voice VLAN and assigns it to access ports. Then when an IP phone is connected to the switch port, the switch sends CDP messages that instruct the attached IP phone to send voice traffic tagged with the voice VLAN ID.

Voice VLAN Example

Figure 26-1 shows an example of using one port on a switch to connect a user's IP phone and PC. The switch port is configured to carry data traffic on VLAN 20 and voice traffic on VLAN 150. The Cisco IP Phone contains an integrated three-port 10/100 switch to provide the following dedicated connections:

- Port 1 connects to the switch or other VoIP device.

- Port 2 is an internal 10/100 interface that carries the IP Phone traffic.

- Port 3 (access port) connects to a PC or other device.

Figure 26-1 Cisco IP Phone Switching Voice and Data Traffic

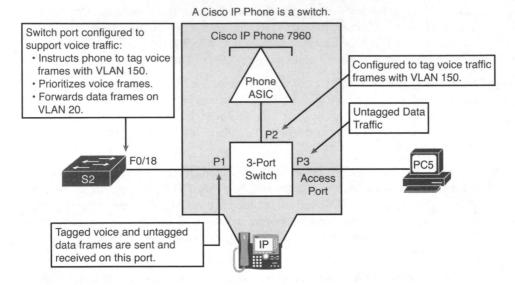

The traffic from the PC5 attached to the IP Phone passes through the IP Phone untagged. The link between S2 and the IP Phone acts as a modified trunk to carry both the tagged voice traffic and the untagged data traffic.

Trunking VLANs

A VLAN trunk is an Ethernet point-to-point link between an Ethernet switch interface and an Ethernet interface on another networking device, such as a router or a switch, carrying the traffic of multiple VLANs over the singular link. A VLAN trunk allows you to extend the VLANs across an entire network. A VLAN trunk does not belong to a specific VLAN; rather, it serves as a conduit for VLANs between switches. Figure 26-2 shows a small switched network with a trunk link between S1 and S2 carrying multiple VLAN traffic.

When a frame is placed on a trunk link, information about the VLAN it belongs to must be added to the frame. This is accomplished by using IEEE 802.1Q frame tagging. When a switch receives a frame on a port configured in access mode and destined for a remote device through a trunk link, the switch takes apart the frame and inserts a VLAN tag, recalculates the frame check sequence (FCS), and sends the tagged frame out the trunk port. Figure 26-3 shows the 802.1Q tag inserted in an Ethernet frame.

Figure 26-2   Example of a VLAN Trunk

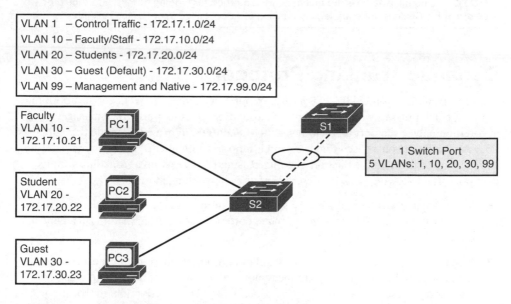

VLAN 1   – Control Traffic - 172.17.1.0/24
VLAN 10 – Faculty/Staff - 172.17.10.0/24
VLAN 20 – Students - 172.17.20.0/24
VLAN 30 – Guest (Default) - 172.17.30.0/24
VLAN 99 – Management and Native - 172.17.99.0/24

Faculty
VLAN 10 -
172.17.10.21

Student
VLAN 20 -
172.17.20.22

Guest
VLAN 30 -
172.17.30.23

1 Switch Port
5 VLANs: 1, 10, 20, 30, 99

Figure 26-3   Fields of the 802.1Q Tag Inside an Ethernet Frame

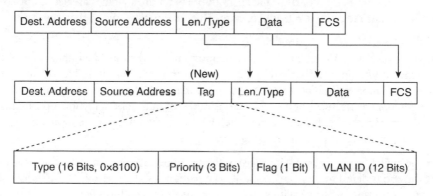

The VLAN tag field consists of a 16-bit Type field called the EtherType field and a Tag control information field. The EtherType field is set to the hexadecimal value of 0x8100. This value is called the tag protocol ID (TPID) value. With the EtherType field set to the TPID value, the switch receiving the frame knows to look for information in the Tag control information field. The Tag control information field contains the following:

- **3 bits of user priority:** Used to provide expedited transmission of Layer 2 frames, such as voice traffic.

- **1 bit of Canonical Format Identifier (CFI):** Enables Token Ring frames to be carried across Ethernet links easily.

- **12 bits of VLAN ID (VID):** VLAN identification numbers.

NOTE: Although 802.1Q is the recommended method for tagging frames, you should be aware of the Cisco proprietary legacy trunking protocol called Inter-Switch Link (ISL).

Dynamic Trunking Protocol

Dynamic Trunking Protocol (DTP) is a Cisco-proprietary protocol that negotiates both the status of trunk ports as well as the trunk encapsulation of trunk ports. DTP manages trunk negotiation only if the port on the other switch is configured in a trunk mode that supports DTP. A switch port on a Cisco Catalyst switch supports a number of trunking modes. The trunking mode defines how the port negotiates using DTP to set up a trunk link with its peer port. The following is a brief description of each trunking mode:

- If the switch is configured with the **switchport mode trunk** command, the switch port periodically sends DTP messages to the remote port, advertising that it is in an unconditional trunking state.

- If the switch is configured with the **switchport mode trunk dynamic auto** command, the local switch port advertises to the remote switch port that it is able to trunk but does not request to go to the trunking state. After a DTP negotiation, the local port ends up in the trunking state only if the remote port trunk mode has been configured so that the status is **on** or **desirable**. If both ports on the switches are set to **auto**, they do not negotiate to be in a trunking state. They negotiate to be in the access mode state.

- If the switch is configured with the **switchport mode dynamic desirable** command, the local switch port advertises to the remote switch port that it is able to trunk and asks the remote switch port to go to the trunking state. If the local port detects that the remote has been configured as **on, desirable**, or **auto** mode, the local port ends up in the trunking state. If the remote switch port is in the **nonegotiate** mode, the local switch port remains as a nontrunking port.

- If the switch is configured with the **switchport nonegotiate** command, the local port is then considered to be in an unconditional trunking state. Use this feature when you need to configure a trunk with a switch from another switch vendor.

Table 26-2 summarizes the results of DTP negotiations based on the different DTP configuration commands on a local and remote port.

Table 26-2   Trunk Negotiation Results Between a Local and a Remote Port

	Dynamic Auto	Dynamic Desirable	Trunk	Access
Dynamic Auto	Access	Trunk	Trunk	Access
Dynamic Desirable	Trunk	Trunk	Trunk	Access
Trunk	Trunk	Trunk	Trunk	Not Recommended
Access	Access	Access	Not Recommended	Access

Study Resources

For today's exam topics, refer to the following resources for more study.

Resource	Location	Topic
Primary Resources		
Switched Networks	3	VLAN Segmentation
		Introduction to DTP
Routing and Switching Essentials	3	VLAN Segmentation
		Introduction to DTP
ICND1 Official Cert Guide	9	Virtual LAN Concepts
ICND1 Foundation Learning Guide	6	Implementing VLANs and Trunks
Supplemental Resources		
CCENT Practice and Study Guide	14	VLAN Segmentation
Flash Cards	9	Questions 1–9

VLAN and Trunking Configuration

CCENT 100-101 ICND1 Exam Topics

- Configure and verify VLANs.

- Configure and verify trunking on Cisco switches.

Key Points

The following sections present a sample topology and the commands to configure and verify VLANs and trunking. The review for today is brief so that you can spend your time practicing your configuration, verification, and troubleshooting skills either on real equipment or on the simulator of your choice.

Sample Topology

For today's exam topics, we will use the topology shown in Figure 25-1 to review the commands for configuring, verifying, and troubleshooting VLAN and trunking. I strongly recommend that you build and configure this topology—either using real equipment or a network simulator—as part of your review for the CCNA exam.

Figure 25-1   Day 25 Sample Topology

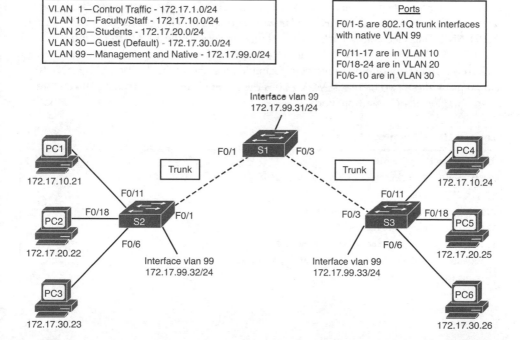

VLAN Configuration and Verification Commands

The default configuration of a Cisco switch is to put all interfaces in VLAN 1, which can be verified with the **show vlan brief** command, as demonstrated for S2 in Example 25-1.

Example 25-1   Default VLAN Configuration

```
S2# show vlan brief

VLAN Name                             Status    Ports
---- -------------------------------- --------- -------------------------------
1    default                          active    Fa0/1, Fa0/2, Fa0/3, Fa0/4
                                                Fa0/5, Fa0/6, Fa0/7, Fa0/8
                                                Fa0/9, Fa0/10, Fa0/11, Fa0/12
                                                Fa0/13, Fa0/14, Fa0/15, Fa0/16
                                                Fa0/17, Fa0/18, Fa0/19, Fa0/20
                                                Fa0/21, Fa0/22, Fa0/23, Fa0/24
                                                Gig1/1, Gig1/2
1002 fddi-default                     active
1003 token-ring-default               active
1004 fddinet-default                  active
1005 trnet-default                    active
```

A VLAN can be created in one of two ways: either in global configuration mode or directly under the interface. The advantage to configuring in global configuration mode is that you can then assign a name with the **name** *vlan-name* command. The advantage to configuring the VLAN in interface configuration mode is that you assign the VLAN to the interface and create the VLAN with just one command. However, to name the VLAN, you still have to go back to the global configuration method. Example 25-2 shows the creation of VLANs 10 and 20 using these two methods. VLAN 20 is then named, and the remaining VLANs are created in global configuration mode.

Example 25-2   Creating VLANs

```
S2# config t
Enter configuration commands, one per line.  End with CNTL/Z.
S2(config)# vlan 10
S2(config-vlan)# name Faculty/Staff
S2(config-vlan)# interface fa 0/18
S2(config-if)# switchport access vlan 20
% Access VLAN does not exist. Creating vlan 20
S2(config-if)# vlan 20
```

```
S2(config-vlan)# name Students
S2(config-vlan)# vlan 30
S2(config-vlan)# name Guest(Default)
S2(config-vlan)# vlan 99
S2(config-vlan)# name Management&Native
S2(config-vlan)# end
%SYS-5-CONFIG_I: Configured from console by console
S2#
```

Notice in Example 25-3 that all the VLANs are created, but only VLAN 20 is assigned to an interface.

Example 25-3   Verifying VLAN Creation

```
S2# show vlan brief

VLAN Name                             Status    Ports
---- -------------------------------- --------- -------------------------------
1    default                          active    Fa0/1, Fa0/2, Fa0/3, Fa0/4
                                                Fa0/5, Fa0/6, Fa0/7, Fa0/8
                                                Fa0/9, Fa0/10, Fa0/11, Fa0/12
                                                Fa0/13, Fa0/14, Fa0/15, Fa0/16
                                                Fa0/17, Fa0/19, Fa0/20, Fa0/21
                                                Fa0/22, Fa0/23, Fa0/24, Gig1/1
                                                Gig1/2
10   Faculty/Staff                    active
20   Students                         active    Fa0/18
30   Guest(Default)                   active
99   Management&Native                active
1002 fddi-default                     active
1003 token-ring-default               active
1004 fddinet-default                  active
1005 trnet-default                    active
S2#
```

To assign the remaining interfaces to the VLANs specified in Figure 25-1, you can configure one interface at a time, or you can use the **range** command to configure all the interfaces that belong to a VLAN with one command, as shown in Example 25-4.

Example 25-4   Assigning VLANs to Interfaces

```
S2# config t
Enter configuration commands, one per line.  End with CNTL/Z.
S2(config)# interface range fa 0/11 - 17
S2(config-if-range)# switchport access vlan 10
S2(config-if-range)# interface range fa 0/18 - 24
S2(config-if-range)# switchport access vlan 20
S2(config-if-range)# interface range fa 0/6 - 10
S2(config-if-range)# switchport access vlan 30
S2(config-if-range)# end
%SYS-5-CONFIG_I: Configured from console by console
S2#
```

The **show vlan brief** command in Example 25-5 verifies that all interfaces specified in Figure 25-1 have been assigned to the appropriate VLAN. Notice that unassigned interfaces still belong to the default VLAN 1.

Example 25-5   Verifying VLAN Assignments to Interfaces

```
S2# show vlan brief

VLAN Name                             Status    Ports
---- -------------------------------- --------- -------------------------------
1    default                          active    Fa0/1, Fa0/2, Fa0/3, Fa0/4
                                                Fa0/5, Gig1/1, Gig1/2
10   Faculty/Staff                    active    Fa0/11, Fa0/12, Fa0/13, Fa0/14
                                                Fa0/15, Fa0/16, Fa0/17
20   Students                         active    Fa0/18, Fa0/19, Fa0/20, Fa0/21
                                                Fa0/22, Fa0/23, Fa0/24
30   Guest(Default)                   active    Fa0/6, Fa0/7, Fa0/8, Fa0/9
                                                Fa0/10
99   Management&Native                active
1002 fddi-default                     active
1003 token-ring-default               active
1004 fddinet-default                  active
1005 trnet-default                    active
S2#
```

You can also verify a specific interface's VLAN assignment with the **show interfaces** *type number* **switchport** command, as shown for FastEthernet 0/11 in Example 25-6.

Example 25-6   Verifying an Interface's VLAN Assignment

```
S2# show interfaces fastethernet 0/11 switchport
Name: Fa0/11
Switchport: Enabled
Administrative Mode: dynamic auto
Operational Mode: static access
Administrative Trunking Encapsulation: dot1q
Operational Trunking Encapsulation: native
Negotiation of Trunking: On
Access Mode VLAN: 10 (Faculty/Staff)
Trunking Native Mode VLAN: 1 (default)
Voice VLAN: none
Administrative private-vlan host-association: none
Administrative private-vlan mapping: none
Administrative private-vlan trunk native VLAN: none
Administrative private-vlan trunk encapsulation: dot1q
Administrative private-vlan trunk normal VLANs: none
Administrative private-vlan trunk private VLANs: none
Operational private-vlan: none
Trunking VLANs Enabled: ALL
Pruning VLANs Enabled: 2-1001
Capture Mode Disabled
Capture VLANs Allowed: ALL
Protected: false
Appliance trust: none
S2#
```

For the sample topology shown in Figure 25-1, you would configure the VLANs on S1 and S3 as well, but only S3 needs VLANs assigned to interfaces.

Configuring and Verifying Trunking

Following security best practices, we are configuring a different VLAN for the management and default VLAN. In a production network, you would want to use a different one for each: one for the management VLAN and one for the native VLAN. However, for expediency, we are using VLAN 99 for both.

To begin, we must first define a new management interface for VLAN 99, as shown in Example 25-7.

Example 25-7   Defining a New Management Interface

```
S1# config t
Enter configuration commands, one per line.  End with CNTL/Z.
S1(config)# interface vlan 99
%LINK-5-CHANGED: Interface Vlan99, changed state to up
S1(config-if)# ip address 172.17.99.31 255.255.255.0
S1(config-if)# end
%SYS-5-CONFIG_I: Configured from console by console
S1#
```

Repeat the configuration on S2 and S3. The IP address is used for testing connectivity to the switch as well as the IP address the network administrator uses for remote access (Telnet, SSH, SDM, HTTP, and so on).

Depending on the switch model and IOS version, DTP might have already established trunking between two switches that are directly connected. For example, the default trunk configuration for 2950 switches is **dynamic desirable**. Therefore, a 2950 will initiate trunk negotiations. For our purposes, we will assume the switches are all 2960s. The 2960 default trunk configuration is **dynamic auto,** in which the interface will not initiate trunk negotiations.

In Example 25-8, the first five interfaces on S1 are configured for trunking. Also, notice that the native VLAN is changed to VLAN 99.

Example 25-8   Trunk Configuration and Native VLAN Assignment

```
S1# config t
Enter configuration commands, one per line.  End with CNTL/Z.
S1(config)# interface range fa0/1 - 5
S1(config-if-range)# switchport mode trunk
S1(config-if-range)# switchport trunk native vlan 99
S1(config-if-range)# end
%SYS-5-CONFIG_I: Configured from console by console
S1#
%CDP-4-NATIVE_VLAN_MISMATCH: Native VLAN mismatch discovered on FastEthernet0/1
   (99), with S2 FastEthernet0/1 (1).
%CDP-4-NATIVE_VLAN_MISMATCH: Native VLAN mismatch discovered on FastEthernet0/3
   (99), with S3 FastEthernet0/3 (1).
```

If you wait for the next round of CDP messages, you should get the error message shown in Example 25-8. Although the trunk is working between S1 and S2 and between S1 and S3, the switches do not agree on the native VLAN. Repeat the trunking commands on S2 and S3 to correct the native VLAN mismatch.

> **NOTE:** The encapsulation type—dot1q or isl—might need to be configured depending on the switch model. If so, the syntax for configuring the encapsulation type is as follows:
>
> ```
> Switch(config-if)# switchport trunk encapsulation { dot1q | isl | negotiate }
> ```

The 2960 Series supports only 802.1Q, so this command is not available.

To verify that trunking is operational, use the commands shown in Example 25-9.

Example 25-9   Verifying Trunk Configuration

```
S1# show interfaces trunk
Port         Mode         Encapsulation  Status        Native vlan
Fa0/1        on           802.1q         trunking      99
Fa0/3        on           802.1q         trunking      99


Port         Vlans allowed on trunk
Fa0/1        1-1005
Fa0/3        1-1005


Port         Vlans allowed and active in management domain
Fa0/1        1,10,20,30,99,1002,1003,1004,1005
Fa0/3        1,10,20,30,99,1002,1003,1004,1005


Port         Vlans in spanning tree forwarding state and not pruned
Fa0/1        1,10,20,30,99,1002,1003,1004,1005
Fa0/3        1,10,20,30,99,1002,1003,1004,1005
S1# show interface fa 0/1 switchport
Name: Fa0/1
Switchport: Enabled
Administrative Mode: trunk
Operational Mode: trunk
Administrative Trunking Encapsulation: dot1q
Operational Trunking Encapsulation: dot1q
Negotiation of Trunking: On
Access Mode VLAN: 1 (default)
Trunking Native Mode VLAN: 99 (Management&Native)
Voice VLAN: none
Administrative private-vlan host-association: none
Administrative private-vlan mapping: none
Administrative private-vlan trunk native VLAN: none
Administrative private-vlan trunk encapsulation: dot1q
Administrative private-vlan trunk normal VLANs: none
Administrative private-vlan trunk private VLANs: none
Operational private-vlan: none
Trunking VLANs Enabled: ALL
```

```
Pruning VLANs Enabled: 2-1001
Capture Mode Disabled
Capture VLANs Allowed: ALL
Protected: false
Appliance trust: none
S1#
```

Remember, hosts on the same VLAN must be configured with an IP address and subnet mask on the same subnet. So, the ultimate test of your configuration is to verify that end devices on the same VLAN can now ping each other. If not, use the verification commands to systematically track down the problem with your configuration. Troubleshooting VLAN and trunking implementations is discussed in detail on Day 5, "Troubleshoot VLAN Issues," and Day 4, "Troubleshoot Trunking Issues."

Study Resources

For today's exam topics, refer to the following resources for more study.

Resource	Location	Topic
Primary Resources		
Switched Networks	3	VLAN Implementations
Routing and Switching Essentials	3	VLAN Implementations
ICND1 Official Cert Guide	9	VLAN and VLAN Trunking Configuration and Verification
ICND1 Foundation Learning Guide	6	Implementing VLANs and Trunks
Supplemental Resources		
CCENT Practice and Study Guide	14	VLAN Implementations
Flash Cards	9	Questions 10–30
Network Simulator		Trunking Configuration I–IV
		VLAN Configuration I–IV
		VLANs I–III
		Configuring VLANs
		VLAN Trunking I
CCNA R&S Portable Command Guide	12, 13	All

The IPv4 Address

CCENT 100-101 ICND1 Exam Topics

- Describe the operation and necessity of using private and public IP addresses for IPv4 addressing.

Key Topics

Today, we focus on reviewing the structure of an IPv4 address, the classes, as well as private and public IPv4 addresses. Tomorrow, we will review IPv4 subnetting.

IPv4 Addressing

Although IPv6 is rapidly permeating the networks of the world, most networks still have a large IPv4 implementation. Especially on private networks, migration away from IPv4 will take years to complete. So IPv4 and your skill in its use are still in demand.

Header Format

To facilitate the routing of packets over a network, the TCP/IP protocol suite uses a 32-bit logical address known as an IP address. This address must be unique for each device in the internetwork.

Figure 24-1 shows the layout of the IPv4 header.

Figure 24-1   IPv4 Header Format

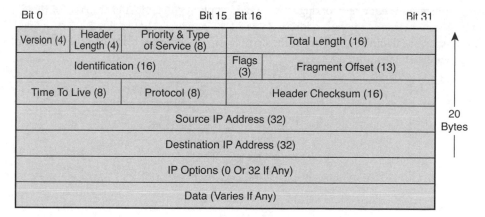

Note that each IP packet carries this header, which includes a source IP address and destination IP address.

An IP address consists of two parts:

- The high-order, or leftmost, bits specify the network address component (network ID) of the address.

- The low-order, or rightmost, bits specify the host address component (host ID) of the address.

Classes of Addresses

From the beginning, IPv4 was designed with class structure: Classes A, B, C, D, and E. Class D is used for multicasting addresses and Class E is reserved for experimentation. Classes A, B, and C are assigned to network hosts. To provide a hierarchical structure, these classes are divided into network and host portions, as shown in Figure 24-2. The high-order bits specify the network ID, and the low-order bits specify the host ID.

Figure 24-2   Network/Host Boundary for Each Class of IPv4 Address

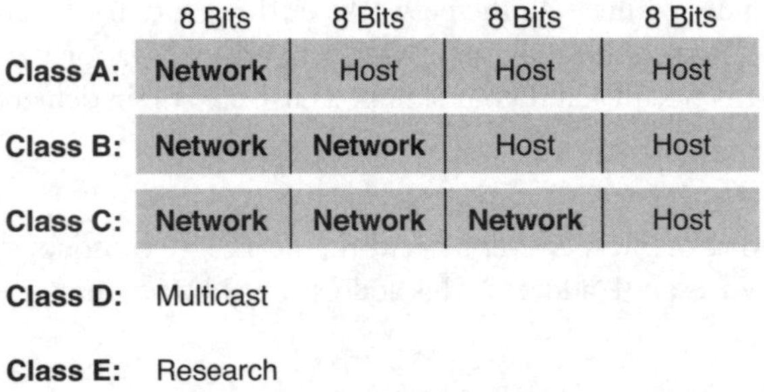

	8 Bits	8 Bits	8 Bits	8 Bits
Class A:	Network	Host	Host	Host
Class B:	Network	Network	Host	Host
Class C:	Network	Network	Network	Host
Class D:	Multicast			
Class E:	Research			

In a classful addressing scheme, devices that operate at Layer 3 can determine the address class of an IP address from the format of the first few bits in the first octet. Initially, this was important so that a networking device could apply the default subnet mask for the address and determine the host address. Table 24-1 summarizes how addresses are divided into classes, the default subnet mask, the number of networks per class, and the number of hosts per classful network address.

Table 24-1   IP Address Classes

Address Class	First Octet Range (Decimal)	First Octet Bits (Highlighted Bits Do Not Change)	Network (N) and Host (H) Portions of Addresses	Default Subnet Mask (Decimal and Binary)	Number of Possible Networks and Hosts per Network
A	1–127	00000000–01111111	N.H.H.H	255.0.0.0 11111111.00000000. 00000000.00000000	2^7 or 128 networks $2^{24}-2$ or 16,777,214 hosts per network
B	128–191	10000000–10111111	N.N.H.H	255.255.0.0 11111111.11111111. 00000000.00000000	2^{14} or 16,384 networks $2^{16}-2$ or 65,534 hosts per network
C	192–223	11000000–11011111	N.N.N.H	255.255.255.0 11111111.11111111. 11111111.00000000	2^{21} or 2,097,152 networks 2^8-2 or 254 hosts per network
D	224–239	11100000–11101111	Not used for host addressing		
E	240–255	11110000–11111111	Not used for host addressing		

In the last column, the "minus 2" for hosts per network is to account for the reserved network and broadcast addresses for each network. These two addresses cannot be assigned to hosts.

NOTE: We are not reviewing the process of converting between binary and decimal. At this point in your studies, you should be very comfortable moving between the two numbering systems. If not, take some time to practice this necessary skill. You can search the Internet for binary conversion tricks, tips, and games to help you practice.

Purpose of the Subnet Mask

Subnet masks are always a series of 1 bits followed by a series of 0 bits. The boundary where the series changes from 1s to 0s is the boundary between the network and host. This is how a device that operates at Layer 3 determines the network address for a packet—by finding the bit boundary where the series of 1 bits ends and the series of 0 bits begins. The bit boundary for default subnet masks breaks on the octet boundary. Determining the network address for an IP address that uses a default mask is easy.

For example, a router receives a packet destined for 192.168.1.51. By "ANDing" the IP address and the subnet mask, the router determines the network address for the packet. By the ANDing rules, a 1 AND a 1 equals 1. All other possibilities equal 0. Table 24-2 shows the results of the ANDing operation. Notice that the host bits in the last octet are ignored.

Table 24-2   ANDing an IP Address and Subnet Mask to Find the Network Address

Destination Address	192.168.1.51	11000000.10101000.00000001.00110011
Subnet Mask	255.255.255.0	11111111.11111111.11111111.00000000
Network Address	192.168.1.0	11000000.10101000.00000001.00000000

The bit boundary can now occur in just about any place in the 32 bits. Table 24-3 summarizes the values for the last nonzero octet in a subnet mask.

Table 24-3   Subnet Mask Binary Values

Mask (Decimal)	Mask (Binary)	Network Bits	Host Bits
0	00000000	0	8
128	10000000	1	7
192	11000000	2	6
224	11100000	3	5
240	11110000	4	4
248	11111000	5	3
252	11111100	6	2
254	11111110	7	1
255	11111111	8	0

Private and Public IP Addressing

RFC 1918, "Address Allocation for Private Internets," eased the demand for IP addresses by reserving the following addresses for use in private internetworks:

- Class A: 10.0.0.0/8 (10.0.0.0–10.255.255.255)

- Class B: 172.16.0.0/12 (172.16.0.0–172.31.255.255)

- Class C: 192.168.0.0/16 (192.168.0.0–192.168.255.255)

If you are addressing a nonpublic intranet, these private addresses are normally used instead of globally unique public addresses. This provides flexibility in your addressing design. Any organization can take full advantage of an entire Class A address (10.0.0.0/8). Forwarding traffic to the public Internet requires translation to a public address using Network Address Translation (NAT). But by overloading an Internet-routable address with many private addresses, a company needs only a handful of public addresses. Day 9 reviews NAT operation and configuration in greater detail.

Study Resources

For today's exam topics, refer to the following resources for more study.

Resource	Location	Topic
Primary Resources		
Network Basics	6	IPv4 Packet
	7	IPv4 Network Addresses
Introduction to Networks	6	IPv4 Packet
	8	IPv4 Network Addresses
ICND1 Official Cert Guide	4	IPv4 Addressing
ICND1 Foundation Learning Guide	7	Understanding TCP/IP's Internet Layer
Supplemental Resources		
CCENT Practice and Study Guide	8	IPv4 Network Addresses
Flash Cards	4	Questions 1–12; 18–20
Network Simulator	14	IP Address Rejection I–XI

IPv4 Subnetting and VLSM

CCENT 100-101 ICND1 Exam Topics

- Identify the appropriate IPv4 addressing scheme using VLSM and summarization to satisfy addressing requirements in a LAN/WAN environment.

Key Topics

By now, you should be able to subnet very quickly. For example, you should be able to quickly answer a question such as If you are given a /16 network, what subnet mask would you use that would maximize the total number of subnets while still providing enough addresses for the largest subnet with 500 hosts? The answer would be 255.255.254.0, or /23. This would give you 128 subnets with 510 usable hosts per subnet. You should be able to calculate this information in very short order.

The CCENT exam promises to contain lots of subnetting and subnetting-related questions. Today we focus on this necessary skill as well as designing addressing schemes using variable-length subnet masking (VLSM) and summarization to optimize your network routing traffic.

Subnetting in Four Steps

Everyone has a preferred method of subnetting. Each teacher will use a slightly different strategy to help students master this crucial skill. Each of the suggested "Study Resources" has a slightly different way of approaching this subject.

The method I prefer can be broken down into four steps:

Step 1.   Determine how many bits to borrow based on the host requirements.

Step 2.   Determine the new subnet mask.

Step 3.   Determine the subnet multiplier.

Step 4.   List the subnets including subnetwork address, host range, and broadcast address.

The best way to demonstrate this method is to use an example. Let's assume that you are given the network address 192.168.1.0 with the default subnet mask 255.255.255.0. The network address and subnet mask can be written as 192.168.1.0/24. The "slash 24" represents the subnet mask in a shorter notation and means that the first 24 bits are network bits.

Let's further assume that you need 30 hosts per network and want to create as many subnets for the given address space as possible. With these network requirements, let's subnet the address space.

Determine How Many Bits to Borrow

To determine the number of bits you can borrow, you first must know how many host bits you have to start with. Because the first 24 bits are network bits in our example, the remaining 8 bits are host bits.

Because our requirement specifies 30 host addresses per subnet, we need to first determine the minimum number of host bits to leave. The remaining bits can be borrowed:

Host Bits = Bits Borrowed + Bits Left

To provide enough address space for 30 hosts, we need to leave 5 bits. Use the following formula:

$2^{BL} - 2$ = number of host addresses

where the exponent BL is bits left in the host portion.

Remember, the "minus 2" is to account for the network and broadcast addresses that cannot be assigned to hosts.

In this example, leaving 5 bits in the host portion will provide the right amount of host addresses:

$2^5 - 2 = 30$

Because we have 3 bits remaining in the original host portion, we borrow all these bits to satisfy the requirement to "create as many subnets as possible." To determine how many subnets we can create, use the following formula:

2^{BB} = number of subnets

where the exponent BB is bits borrowed from the host portion.

In this example, borrowing 3 bits from the host portion will create 8 subnets: $2^3 = 8$.

As shown in Table 23-1, the 3 bits are borrowed from the leftmost bits in the host portion. The highlighted bits in the table show all possible combinations of manipulating the 8 bits borrowed to create the subnets.

Table 23-1   Binary and Decimal Value of the Subnetted Octet

Subnet Number	Last Octet Binary Value	Last Octet Decimal Value
0	00000000	.0
1	00100000	.32
2	01000000	.64
3	01100000	.96
4	10000000	.128
5	10100000	.160
6	11000000	.192
7	11100000	.224

Determine the New Subnet Mask

Notice in Table 23-1 that the network bits now include the 3 borrowed host bits in the last octet. Add these 3 bits to the 24 bits in the original subnet mask and you have a new subnet mask, /27. In decimal format, you turn on the 128, 64, and 32 bits in the last octet for a value of 224. So the new subnet mask is 255.255.255.224.

Determine the Subnet Multiplier

Notice in Table 23-1 that the last octet decimal value increments by 32 with each subnet number. The number 32 is the subnet multiplier. You can quickly find the subnet multiplier using one of two methods:

- **Method 1:** Subtract the last nonzero octet of the subnet mask from 256. In this example, the last nonzero octet is 224. So the subnet multiplier is 256 − 224 = 32.

- **Method 2:** The decimal value of the last bit borrowed is the subnet multiplier. In this example, we borrowed the 128 bit, the 64 bit, and the 32 bit. The 32 bit is the last bit we borrowed and is, therefore, the subnet multiplier.

By using the subnet multiplier, you no longer have to convert binary subnet bits to decimal.

List the Subnets, Host Ranges, and Broadcast Addresses

Listing the subnets, host ranges, and broadcast addresses helps you see the flow of addresses within one address space. Table 23-2 documents our subnet addressing scheme for the 192.168.1.0/24 address space.

Table 23-2   Subnet Addressing Scheme for 192.168.1.0/24: 30 Hosts Per Subnet

Subnet Number	Subnet Address	Host Range	Broadcast Address
0	192.168.1.0	192.168.1.1–192.168.1.30	192.168.1.31
1	192.168.1.32	192.168.1.33–192.168.1.62	192.168.1.63
2	192.168.1.64	192.168.1.65–192.168.1.94	192.168.1.95
3	192.168.1.96	192.168.1.97 192.168.1.126	192.168.1.127
4	192.168.1.128	192.168.1.129–192.168.1.158	192.168.1.159
5	192.168.1.160	192.168.1.161–192.168.1.190	192.168.1.191
6	192.168.1.192	192.168.1.193–192.168.1.222	192.168.1.223
7	192.168.1.224	192.168.1.225–192.168.1.254	192.168.1.255

The following are three examples using the four subnetting steps. For brevity, only the first three subnets are listed in Step 4.

Subnetting Example 1

Subnet the address space 172.16.0.0/16 to provide at least 80 host addresses per subnet while creating as many subnets as possible.

1. There are 16 host bits. Leave 7 bits for host addresses ($2^7 - 2 = 126$ host addresses per subnet). Borrow the first 9 host bits to create as many subnets as possible ($2^9 = 512$ subnets).

2. The original subnet mask is /16, or 255.255.0.0. Turn on the next 9 bits starting in the second octet for a new subnet mask of /25 or 255.255.255.128.

3. The subnet multiplier is 128, which can be found as $256 - 128 = 128$ or because the 128 bit is the last bit borrowed.

4. Table 23-3 lists the first three subnets, host ranges, and broadcast addresses.

Table 23-3   Subnet Addressing Scheme for Example 1

Subnet Number	Subnet Address	Host Range	Broadcast Address
0	172.16.0.0	172.16.0.1–172.16.0.126	172.16.0.127
1	172.16.0.128	172.16.0.129–172.16.0.254	172.16.0.255
2	172.16.1.0	172.16.1.1–172.16.1.126	172.16.1.127

Subnetting Example 2

Subnet the address space 172.16.0.0/16 to provide at least 80 subnet addresses.

1. There are 16 host bits. Borrow the first 7 host bits to create at least 80 subnets ($2^7 - 2 = 126$ subnets). That leaves 9 bits for host addresses, or $2^9 - 2 = 510$ host addresses per subnet.

2. The original subnet mask is /16, or 255.255.0.0. Turn on the next 7 bits starting in the second octet for a new subnet mask of /23, or 255.255.254.0.

3. The subnet multiplier is 2, which can be found as $256 - 254 = 2$ or because the 2 bit is the last bit borrowed.

4. Table 23-4 lists the first three subnets, host ranges, and broadcast addresses.

Table 23-4   Subnet Addressing Scheme for Example 2

Subnet Number	Subnet Address	Host Range	Broadcast Address
0	172.16.0.0	172.16.0.1–172.16.1.254	172.16.1.255
1	172.16.2.0	172.16.2.1–172.16.3.254	172.16.3.255
2	172.16.4.0	172.16.4.1–172.16.5.254	172.16.5.255

Subnetting Example 3

Subnet the address space 172.16.10.0/23 to provide at least 60 host addresses per subnet while creating as many subnets as possible.

1. There are 9 host bits. Leave 6 bits for host addresses ($2^6 - 2 = 62$ host addresses per subnet). Borrow the first 3 host bits to create as many subnets as possible ($2^3 = 8$ subnets).

2. The original subnet mask is /23, or 255.255.254.0. Turn on the next 3 bits starting with the last bit in the second octet for a new subnet mask of /26, or 255.255.255.192.

3. The subnet multiplier is 64, which can be found as 256 − 192 = 64 or because the 64 bit is the last bit borrowed.

4. Table 23-5 lists the first three subnets, host ranges, and broadcast addresses.

Table 23-5   Subnet Addressing Scheme for Example 3

Subnet Number	Subnet Address	Host Range	Broadcast Address
0	172.16.10.0	172.16.10.1–172.16.10.62	172.16.10.63
1	172.16.10.64	172.16.10.65–172.16.10.126	172.16.10.127
2	172.16.10.128	172.16.10.129–172.16.10.190	172.16.10.191

VLSM

You probably noticed that the starting address space in Subnetting Example 3 is not an entire classful address. In fact, it is subnet 5 from Subnetting Example 2. So, in Subnetting Example 3, we "subnetted a subnet." That is what VLSM is in a nutshell—subnetting a subnet.

With VLSM, you can customize your subnets to fit your network. Subnetting works the same way. You just have to do it more than once to complete your addressing scheme. To avoid overlapping address spaces, start with your largest host requirement, create a subnet for it, and then continue with the next-largest host requirement.

Let's use a small example. Given the address space 172.30.4.0/22 and the network requirements shown in Figure 23-1, apply an addressing scheme that conserves the most amount of addresses for future growth.

Figure 23-1   VLSM Example Topology

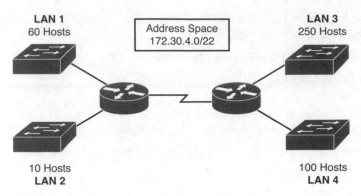

We need five subnets: four LAN subnets and one WAN subnet. Starting with the largest host requirement on LAN 3, begin subnetting the address space.

To satisfy the 250-host requirement, we leave 8 host bits ($2^8 - 2 = 254$ hosts per subnet). Because we have 10 host bits total, we borrow 2 bits to create the first round of subnets ($2^2 = 4$ subnets). The starting subnet mask is /22, or 255.255.252.0. We turn on the next 2 bits in the subnet mask to get /24, or 255.255.255.0. The multiplier is 1. The four subnets are as follows:

- **Subnet 0:** 172.30.4.0/24

- **Subnet 1:** 172.30.5.0/24

- **Subnet 2:** 172.30.6.0/24

- **Subnet 3:** 172.30.7.0/24

Assigning Subnet 0 to LAN 3, we are left with three /24 subnets. Continuing on to the next-largest host requirement on LAN 4, we take Subnet 1, 172.30.5.0/24, and subnet it further.

To satisfy the 100-host requirement, we leave 7 bits ($2^7 - 2 = 128$ hosts per subnet). Because we have 8 host bits total, we can borrow only 1 bit to create the subnets ($2^1 = 2$ subnets). The starting subnet mask is /24, or 255.255.255.0. We turn on the next bit in the subnet mask to get /25, or 255.255.255.128. The multiplier is 128. The two subnets are as follows:

- **Subnet 0:** 172.30.5.0/25

- **Subnet 1:** 172.30.5.128/25

Assigning Subnet 0 to LAN 4, we are left with one /25 subnet and two /24 subnets. Continuing on to the next-largest host requirement on LAN 1, we take Subnet 1, 172.30.5.128/25, and subnet it further.

To satisfy the 60-host requirement, we leave 6 bits ($2^6 - 2 = 62$ hosts per subnet). Because we have 7 host bits total, we borrow 1 bit to create the subnets ($2^1 = 2$ subnets). The starting subnet mask is /25, or 255.255.255.128. We turn on the next bit in the subnet mask to get /26, or 255.255.255.192. The multiplier is 64. The two subnets are as follows:

- **Subnet 0:** 172.30.5.128/26

- **Subnet 1:** 172.30.5.192/26

Assigning Subnet 0 to LAN 1, we are left with one /26 subnet and two /24 subnets. Finishing our LAN subnetting with LAN 2, we take Subnet 1, 172.30.5.192/26, and subnet it further.

To satisfy the 10-host requirement, we leave 4 bits ($2^4 - 2 = 14$ hosts per subnet). Because we have 6 host bits total, we borrow 2 bits to create the subnets ($2^2 = 4$ subnets). The starting subnet mask is /26, or 255.255.255.192. We turn on the next 2 bits in the subnet mask to get /28, or 255.255.255.240. The multiplier is 16. The four subnets are as follows:

- **Subnet 0:** 172.30.5.192/28

- **Subnet 1:** 172.30.5.208/28

- **Subnet 2:** 172.30.5.224/28

- **Subnet 3:** 172.30.5.240/28

Assigning Subnet 0 to LAN 2, we are left with three /28 subnets and two /24 subnets. To finalize our addressing scheme, we need to create a subnet for the WAN link, which needs only 2 host addresses. We take Subnet 1, 172.30.5.208/28, and subnet it further.

To satisfy the 2-host requirement, we leave 2 bits ($2^2 - 2 = 2$ hosts per subnet). Because we have 4 host bits total, we borrow 2 bits to create the subnets ($2^2 = 4$ subnets). The starting subnet mask is /28, or 255.255.255.240. We turn on the next 2 bits in the subnet mask to get /30, or 255.255.255.252. The multiplier is 4. The four subnets are as follows:

- **Subnet 0:** 172.30.5.208/30

- **Subnet 1:** 172.30.5.212/30

- **Subnet 2:** 172.30.5.216/30

- **Subnet 3:** 172.30.5.220/30

We assign Subnet 0 to the WAN link. We are left with three /30 subnets, two /28 subnets, and two /24 subnets.

Summarizing Subnet Addresses

When a network's addressing scheme is designed hierarchically, summarizing addresses to upstream routers makes routing much more efficient. Instead of sending a collection of various subnets, a border router can send one summary route to the next router.

If you are using static routing or configuring a summary route for EIGRP, you might need to calculate the right network prefix and subnet mask.

Referring to Figure 23-2, what summary route would R1 send to the upstream router, BBR (Backbone Router) for the four subnets?

Figure 23-2   Summarizing Subnets: Example 1

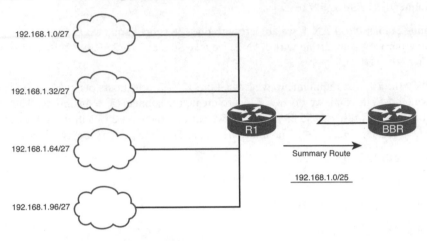

Use the following steps to calculate a summary route:

Step 1.   Write out the networks that you want to summarize in binary, as shown following Step 4.

Step 2.   To find the subnet mask for summarization, start with the leftmost bit.

Step 3.   Work your way to the right, finding all the bits that match consecutively.

Step 4.   When you find a column of bits that do not match, stop. You are at the summary boundary.

```
11000000.10101000.00000001.00000000
11000000.10101000.00000001.00100000
11000000.10101000.00000001.01000000
11000000.10101000.00000001.01100000
```

Step 5.   Count the number of leftmost matching bits, which in this example is 25. This number becomes your subnet mask for the summarized route, /25 or 255.255.255.128.

Step 6.   To find the network address for summarization, copy the matching 25 bits and add all 0 bits to the end to make 32 bits. In this example, the network address is 192.168.1.0.

In production networks, the subnets to be summarized most likely will not have the same subnet mask. For example, the subnets in Figure 23-3 are using three different subnet masks. What summary route would R1 send to BBR for the four subnets?

Figure 23-3   Summarizing Subnets: Example 2

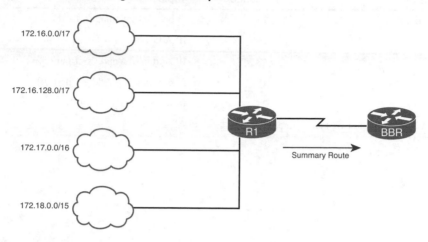

Use the same steps to calculate the summary:

```
10101100.00010000.00000000.00000000
10101100.00010000.10000000.00000000
10101100.00010001.00000000.00000000
10101100.00010010.00000000.00000000
```

Summary Route: 172.16.0.0/14

Study Resources

For today's exam topics, refer to the following resources for more study.

Resource	Location	Topic
Primary Resources		
Network Basics	8	Subnetting an IPv4 Network
		Addressing Schemes
Introduction to Networks	9	Subnetting an IPv4 Network
		Addressing Schemes
ICND1 Official Cert Guide	11, 12, 13, 15	All
ICND1 Foundation Learning Guide	8	All
Supplemental Resources		
CCENT Practice and Study Guide	9	Subnetting an IPv4 Network
		Addressing Schemes
Flash Cards	4	16, 17; 21–30

Resource	Location	Topic
Network Simulator	14	Subnet ID Calculation I–XI
	16	IP Addressing I–III
	18	IP Addressing and Configuration I–II
	19	Subnetting and Addressing I–III
	21	Route Summary Drill I–X
CCNA R&S Portable Command Guide	1, 2, 3	All

IPv6 Addressing Concepts

CCENT 100-101 ICND1 Exam Topics

- Describe IPv6 addresses.

Key Topics

In the early 1990s, the Internet Engineering Task Force (IETF) grew concerned about the exhaustion of the IPv4 network addresses and began to look for a replacement for this protocol. This activity led to the development of what is now known as IPv6. Today's review focuses on an overview of the IPv6 protocol and IPv6 address types.

> **NOTE:** If you have not yet purchased a copy of Rick Graziani's *IPv6 Fundamentals* to add to your library of study tools, now is the time to do so. His book is my definitive source for everything IPv6.

Overview and Benefits of IPv6

The capability to scale networks for future demands requires a limitless supply of IP addresses and improved mobility that private addressing and NAT alone cannot meet. IPv6 satisfies the increasingly complex requirements of hierarchical addressing that IPv4 does not provide. Several of the main benefits and features of IPv6 include

- **Extended address space:** A 128-bit address space represents about 340 trillion trillion trillion addresses. That's enough to assign an address to every atom on the earth and still have enough addresses for another 100 earths.

- **Stateless Address Autoconfiguration:** IPv6 provides host devices with a method for generating their own routable IPv6 addresses. IPv6 also supports stateful configuration using DHCPv6.

- **Eliminates the need for NAT/PAT:** NAT/PAT was conceived as a part of the solution to IPv4 address depletion. With IPv6, address depletion is no longer an issue. NAT64, however, does play an important role in providing backward compatibility with IPv4.

- **Simpler header:** A simpler header offers several advantages over IPv4:
  - Better routing efficiency for performance and forwarding-rate scalability
  - No broadcasts and thus no potential threat of broadcast storms
  - No requirement for processing checksums
  - Simpler and more efficient extension header mechanisms

- **Mobility and security:** Mobility and security help ensure compliance with mobile IP and IPsec standards functionality. Mobility enables people with mobile network devices—many with wireless connectivity—to move around in networks:

  - IPv4 does not automatically enable mobile devices to move without breaks in established network connections.

  - In IPv6, mobility is built in, which means that any IPv6 node can use mobility when necessary.

  - IPsec is enabled on every IPv6 node and is available for use, making the IPv6 Internet more secure.

- **Transition strategies:** You can incorporate existing IPv4 capabilities with the added features of IPv6 in several ways:

  - You can implement a dual-stack method, with both IPv4 and IPv6 configured on the interface of a network device.

  - You can use tunneling, which will become more prominent as the adoption of IPv6 grows.

The IPv6 Protocol

You know the 32-bit IPv4 address as a series of four 8-bit fields, separated by dots. However, larger 128-bit IPv6 addresses need a different representation because of their size. Table 22-1 compares the binary and alphanumeric representations of IPv4 and IPv6 addresses.

Table 22-1   IPv4 and IPv6 Address Comparison

	IPv4 (4 Octets)	IPv6 (16 Octets)
Binary representation	11000000.10101000.00001010.01100101	10100101.00100100.01110010.11010011. 00101100.10000000.11011101.00000010. 00000000.00101001.11101100.01111010. 00000000.00101011.11101010.01110011
Alphanumeric representation	192.168.10.101	A524:72D3:2C80:DD02: 0029:EC7A:002B:EA73
Total IP addresses	4,294,467,295 or 2^{32}	$3.4 * 10^{38}$ or 2^{128}

Figure 22-1 compares the IPv4 header with the main IPv6 header. Notice that the IPv6 header is represented in 64-bit words instead of the 32-bit words used by IPv4.

Figure 22-1   IPv6 Header Format

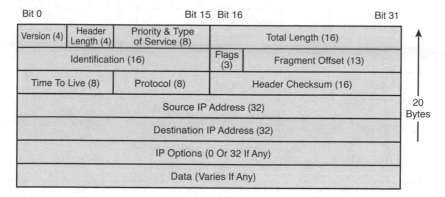

IPv6 Header

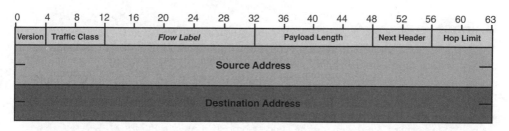

NOTE: Refer to RFC 2460 and "Study Resources" for the full specification of IPv6.

IPv6 Address Types

IPv4 has three address types: unicast, multicast, and broadcast. IPv6 does not use broadcasts. Instead, IPv6 uses unicast, multicast, and anycast. Figure 22-2 illustrates these three types of IPv6 addresses.

Figure 22-2   IPv6 Address Types

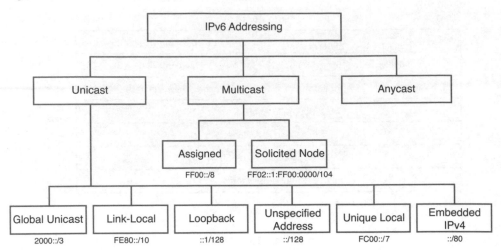

Unicast

The first classification of IPv6 address types shown in Figure 22-2 is the unicast address. A unicast address uniquely identifies an interface on an IPv6 device. A packet sent to a unicast address is received by the interface that is assigned to that address. Similar to IPv4, source IPv6 addresses must be a unicast address. Because unicast addressing—as opposed to multicast and anycast addressing—is, by far, the major focus of a CCENT or CCNA candidate, we will spend some time reviewing the Unicast branch shown in Figure 22-2.

Global Unicast Address

IPv6 has an address format that enables aggregation upward eventually to the ISP. An IPv6 global unicast address is globally unique. Similar to a public IPv4 address, it can be routed in the Internet without any modification. An IPv6 global unicast address consists of a 48-bit global routing prefix, a 16-bit subnet ID, and a 64-bit interface ID. Use Rick Graziani's method of breaking down the IPv6 address with the 3-1-4 Rule (also known as the *pi rule* for 3.14), as shown in Figure 22-3.

Figure 22-3   Graziani's 3-1-4 Rule for Remembering the Global Unicast Address Structure

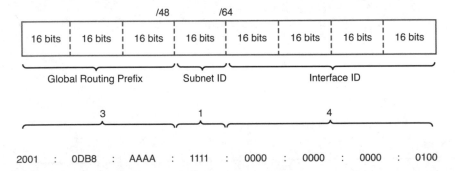

Each number refers to the number of hextets, or 16-bit segments, of that portion of the address:

- **3:** Three hextets for the Global Routing Prefix

- **1:** One hextet for the Subnet ID

- **4:** Four hextets for the Interface ID

The current global unicast address that is assigned by the Internet Assigned Numbers Authority (IANA) uses the range of addresses that start with binary value 001 (2000::/3), which is one-eighth of the total IPv6 address space and is the largest block of assigned addresses. Figure 22-4 shows how the IPv6 address space is divided into an eight-piece pie based on the value of the first 3 bits.

Figure 22-4   Allocation of IPv6 Address Space

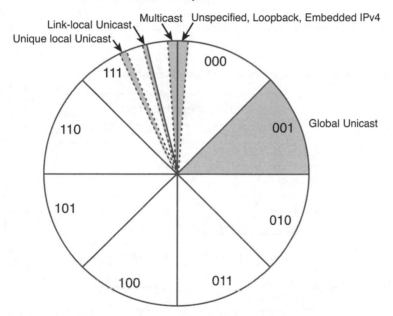

Using the 2000::/3 pie piece, the IANA assigns /23 or shorter address blocks to the five Regional Internet Registries (RIR). From there, ISPs are assigned /32 or shorter address blocks. ISPs then assign sites—their customers—a /48 or shorter address block. Figure 22-5 shows the breakdown of global routing prefixes.

In IPv6, an interface can be configured with multiple global unicast addresses, which can be on the same or different subnets. In addition, an interface does not have to be configured with a global unicast address, but it must at least have a link-local address.

A global unicast address can be further classified into the various configuration options available, as shown in Figure 22-6.

Figure 22-5   Classification of Global Routing Prefix Sizes

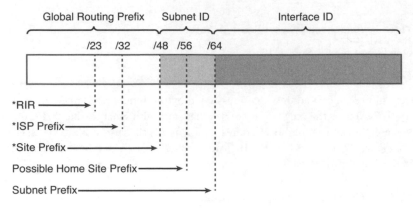

*This is a minimum allocation. The prefix-length may be less if it can be justified.

Figure 22-6   Global Unicast Address Configuration Options

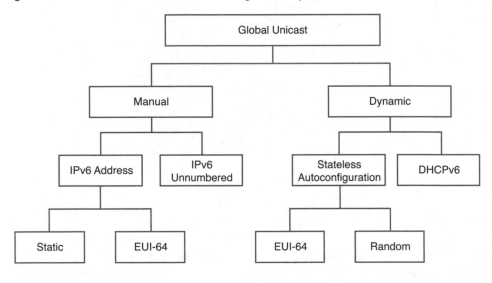

EUI-64 and Stateless Address Autoconfiguration are reviewed in more detail later in this day. The rest of the configuration options shown in Figure 22-6 will be reviewed in more detail in the upcoming days. But for now, we can summarize them as shown in Table 22-2.

Table 22-2   Summary of Global Unicast Configuration Options

Global Unicast Configuration Option		Description
Manual	Static	Similar to IPv4, the IPv6 address and prefix are statically configured on the interface.
	EUI-64	The prefix is configured manually, and the EUI-64 process uses the MAC address to generate the 64-bit interface ID.
	IPv6 Unnumbered	Similar to IPv4, an interface can be configured to use the IPv6 address of another interface on the same device.
Dynamic	Stateless Address Autoconfiguration	SLAAC determines the prefix and prefix length from Neighbor Discovery Router Advertisement messages and then creates the interface ID using the EUI-64 method.
	DHCPv6	Similar to IPv4, a device can receive some or all of its addressing from a DHCPv6 server.

Link-Local Address

As shown earlier in Figure 22-2, link-local addresses are a type of unicast address. Link-local addresses are confined to a single link. They only need to be unique to that link because packets with a link-local source or destination address are not routable off the link.

Link-local addresses are configured in one of three ways:

- Dynamically, using EUI-64

- Random-generated interface ID

- Statically, entering the link-local address manually

Link-local addresses provide a unique benefit in IPv6. A device can create its own link-local address completely on its own. Link-local unicast addresses are in the range of FE80::/10 to FEBF::/10, as shown in Table 22-3.

Table 22-3   Range of Link-Local Unicast Addresses

Link-Local Unicast Address	Range of First Hextet	Range of First Hextet in Binary
FE80::/10	FE80	1111 1110 10 00 0000
	FEBF	1111 1110 10 11 1111

Figure 22-7 shows the format of a link-local unicast address.

Figure 22-7   Link-Local Unicast Address

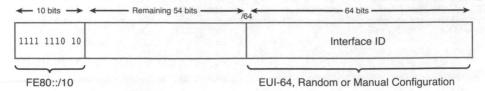

Loopack Address

The loopback address for IPv6 is an all-0s address except for the last bit, which is set to a 1. Like IPv4, the IPv6 loopback address is used by an end device to send an IPv6 packet to itself to test the TCP/IP stack. The loopback address cannot be assigned to an interface and is not routable outside the device.

Unspecified Address

The unspecified unicast address is the all-0s address, represented as ::. It cannot be assigned to an interface but is reserved for communications when the sending device does not have a valid IPv6 address yet. For example, a device will use :: as the source address when using the Duplicate Address Detection (DAD) process. The DAD process ensures a unique link-local address. Before a device can begin using its newly created link-local address, it sends out an all-nodes multicast to all devices on the link with its new address as the destination. If the device receives a response, it knows that link-local address is in use and will, therefore, need to create another link-local address.

Unique Local Address

Unique local addresses (ULA) are defined by RFC 4193, Unique Local IPv6 Unicast Addresses. Figure 22-8 shows the format for ULAs.

Figure 22-8   Unique Local Address

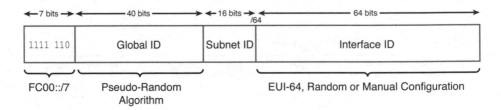

These are private addresses. However, unlike IPv4, IPv6 ULAs are globally unique. This is possible because of the relatively large amount of address space in the Global ID portion shown in Figure 22-8: 40 bits, or more than 1 trillion unique global IDs. As long as a site uses the Pseudo-Random Global ID Algorithm, it will have a very high probability of generating a unique global ID.

Unique local addresses have the following characteristics:

- Possess a globally unique prefix or at least have a very high probability of being unique.

- Allow sites to be combined or privately interconnected without address conflicts or requiring addressing renumbering.

- Are independent of any Internet service provider and can be used within a site without having any Internet connectivity.

- If accidentally leaked outside of a site either by routing or Domain Name System (DNS), there won't be a conflict with any other addresses.

- Can be used just like a global unicast address.

IPv4 Embedded Address

IPv4 and IPv6 packets are not compatible. Features such as NAT-PT (now deprecated) and NAT64 are required to translate between the two address families. IPv4-mapped IPv6 addresses are used by transition mechanisms on hosts and routers to create IPv4 tunnels that deliver IPv6 packets over IPv4 networks.

NOTE: NAT64 is beyond the scope of the CCENT and CCNA exam topics.

To create an IPv4-mapped IPv6 address, the IPv4 address is embedded within the low-order 32 bits of IPv6. Basically, IPv6 just puts an IPv4 address at the end, adds 16 all-1 bits, and pads the rest of the address. The address does not have to be globally unique. Figure 22-9 illustrates this IPv4-mapped IPv6 address structure.

Figure 22-9   IPv4-Mapped IPv6 Address

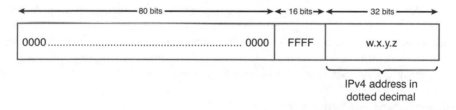

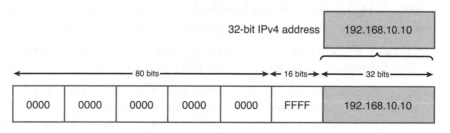

IPv6 compressed format ::FFFF.192.168.10.10

NOTE: Not shown is the IPv4-compatible IPv6 address, which uses all-0s in the 16 bits before the IPv4 address. The IPv4-compatible IPv6 address was rarely used and is now deprecated. Current IPv6 transition mechanisms no longer use this address type.

Multicast

The second major classification of IPv6 address types shown in Figure 22-2 is multicast. Multicast is a technique used for a device to send a single packet to multiple destinations simultaneously. An IPv6 multicast address defines a group of devices known as a multicast group and is equivalent to IPv4 224.0.0.0/4. IPv6 multicast addresses have the prefix FF00::/8.

There are two types of IPv6 multicast addresses:

* Assigned multicast

* Solicited node multicast

Assigned Multicast

Assigned multicast addresses are used in context with specific protocols.

Two common IPv6 assigned multicast groups include

* **FF02::1 All-nodes multicast group:** This is a multicast group that all IPv6-enabled devices join. Similar to a broadcast in IPv4, all IPv6 interfaces on the link process packets sent to this address. For example, a router sending an ICMPv6 Router Advertisement (RA) would use the all-nodes FF02::1 address. IPv6-enabled devices can then use the RA information to learn the link's address information such as prefix, prefix length, and the default gateway.

* **FF02::2 All-routers multicast group:** This is a multicast group that all IPv6 routers join. A router becomes a member of this group when it is enabled as an IPv6 router with the **ipv6 unicast-routing** global configuration command. A packet sent to this group is received and processed by all IPv6 routers on the link or network. For example, IPv6-enabled devices send ICMPv6 Router Solicitation (RS) messages to the all-routers multicast address requesting an RA message.

Solicited-Node Multicast

In addition to every unicast address assigned to an interface, a device will also have a special multicast address known as a solicited-node multicast address, as shown in Figure 22-2. These multicast addresses are automatically created using a special mapping of the device's unicast address with the solicited-node multicast prefix FF02:0:0:0:0:1:FF00::/104.

As shown in Figure 22-10, solicited-node multicast addresses are used for two essential IPv6 mechanisms, both part of Neighbor Discovery Protocol (NDP):

* **Address resolution:** Equivalent to ARP in IPv4, an IPv6 device sends an NS message to a solicited-node multicast address to learn the link layer address of a device on the same link. The device recognizes the IPv6 address of the destination on that link but needs to know its data-link address.

- **Duplicate Address Detection (DAD):** As reviewed earlier, DAD allows a device to verify that its unicast address is unique on the link. An NS message is sent to the device's own solicited-node multicast address to determine whether anyone else has this same address.

Figure 22-10   Uses of Solicited-Node Multicasts

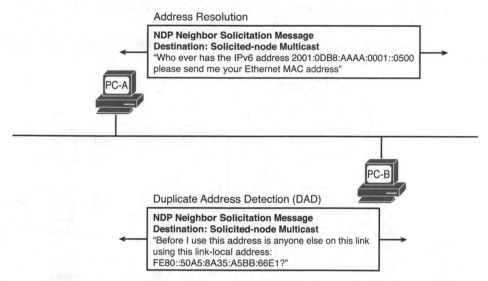

As shown in Figure 22-11, the solicited-node multicast address consists of two parts:

- **FF02:0:0:0:0:FF00::/104 multicast prefix:** This is the first 104 bits of the all solicited-node multicast address.

- **Least significant 24 bits:** These bits are copied from the far-right 24 bits of the global unicast or link-local unicast address of the device.

Figure 22-11   Solicited-Node Multicast Address Structure

Unicast/Anycast Address

	104 bits			24 bits
Global Routing Prefix	Subnet ID	Interface ID		

Solicited-Node Multicast Address

Copy

FF02	0000	0000	0000	0000	0001	FF	

104 bits	24 bits

FF02:0:0:0:0:1:FF00::/104

Anycast

The last major classification of IPv6 address types shown in Figure 22-2 is the anycast address. IPv6 anycast addressing is still somewhat experimental and beyond the scope of the CCENT or CCNA candidate. So, we will only briefly review this address type.

An IPv6 anycast address is an address that can be assigned to more than one device or interface. A packet sent to an anycast address is routed to the "nearest" device that is configured with the anycast address, as shown in Figure 22-12.

Figure 22-12   Example of Anycast Addressing

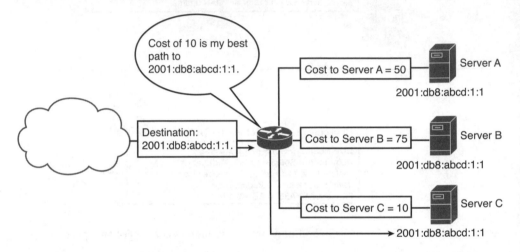

Study Resources

For today's exam topics, refer to the following resources for more study.

Resource	Location	Topic
Primary Resources		
Network Basics	7	IPv4 Issues
		Types of IPv6 Addresses
		IPv6 Unicast Addresses
		IPv6 Multicast Addresses
Introduction to Networks	8	IPv4 Issues
		Types of IPv6 Addresses
		IPv6 Unicast Addresses
		IPv6 Multicast Addresses
IPv6 Fundamentals	2	IPv6 Header
	4	All

Resource	Location	Topic
ICND1 Official Cert Guide	25	Introduction to IPv6
	26	The IPv6 Global Routing Prefix
		Address Ranges for Global Unicast Addresses
		Unique Local Unicast Addresses
ICND1 Foundation Learning Guide	20	Overview of IPv6
Supplemental Resources		
CCENT Practice and Study Guide	8	IPv6 Network Address
	9	Design Considerations for IPv6
Flash Cards	12	Questions 1–12

Implementing IPv6 Addressing

CCENT 100-101 ICND1 Exam Topics

- Identify the appropriate IPv6 addressing scheme to satisfy addressing requirements in a LAN/WAN environment.
- Describe the technological requirements for running IPv6 in conjunction with IPv4.

Key Topics

Today, we review the various ways to implement IPv6 addressing, including subnetting, autoconfiguration of hosts, and running IPv6 and IPv4 in a dual-stack configuration. In later days, we will review more IPv6 implementations, including static routing, OSPFv3, and DHCPv6.

Representing the IPv6 Address

The IPv6 address can look rather intimidating to someone who is used to IPv4 addressing. However, the IPv6 address can be easier to read and is much simpler to subnet than IPv4.

Conventions for Writing IPv6 Addresses

IPv6 conventions use 32 hexadecimal numbers, organized into eight hextets of four hex digits separated by a colon, to represent a 128-bit IPv6 address. For example:

    2340:1111:AAAA:0001:1234:5678:9ABC

To make things a little easier, two rules allow you to shorten what must be typed for an IPv6 address:

- **Rule 1:** Omit the leading 0s in any given hextet.
- **Rule 2:** Omit the all-0s hextets. Represent one or more consecutive hextets of all hex 0s with a double colon (::), but only for one such occurrence in a given address.

NOTE: The term *hextet* refers to four consecutive hexadecimal digits. Eight hextets are in each IPv6 address.

For example, consider the following address. The highlighted hex digits represent the portion of the address that could be abbreviated.

    FE00:0000:0000:0001:0000:0000:0000:0056

This address has two locations in which one or more hextets have four hex 0s, so two main options exist for abbreviating this address, using the :: abbreviation in one or the other location. The following two options show the two briefest valid abbreviations:

- FE00::1:0:0:0:56

- FE00:0:0:1::56

In the first example, the second and third hextets preceding 0001 were replaced with ::. In the second example, the fifth, sixth, and seventh hextets were replaced with ::. In particular, note that the :: abbreviation, meaning "one or more hextets of all 0s," cannot be used twice because that would be ambiguous. So, the abbreviation FE00::1::56 would not be valid.

Conventions for Writing IPv6 Prefixes

IPv6 prefixes represent a range or block of consecutive IPv6 addresses. The number that represents the range of addresses, called a *prefix*, is usually seen in IP routing tables, just like you see IP subnet numbers in IPv4 routing tables.

As with IPv4, when writing or typing a prefix in IPv6, the bits past the end of the prefix length are all binary 0s. The following IPv6 address is an example of an address assigned to a host:

2000:1234:5678:9ABC:1234:5678:9ABC:1111/64

The prefix in which this address resides would be as follows:

2000:1234:5678:9ABC:0000:0000:0000:0000/64

When abbreviated, this would be

2000:1234:5678:9ABC::/64

If the prefix length does not fall on a hextet boundary (is not a multiple of 16), the prefix value should list all the values in the last hextet. For example, assume that the prefix length in the previous example is /56. So, by convention, the rest of the fourth hextet should be written, after being set to binary 0s, as follows:

2000:1234:5678:9A00::/56

The following list summarizes some key points about how to write IPv6 prefixes:

- The prefix has the same value as the IP addresses in the group for the first number of bits, as defined by the prefix length.

- Any bits after the prefix length number of bits are binary 0s.

- The prefix can be abbreviated with the same rules as IPv6 addresses.

- If the prefix length is not on a hextet boundary, write down the value for the entire hextet.

Table 21-1 shows several sample prefixes, their formats, and a brief explanation.

Table 21-1   Example IPv6 Prefixes and Their Meanings

Prefix	Explanation	Incorrect Alternative
2000::/3	All addresses whose first 3 bits are equal to the first 3 bits of hex number 2000 (bits are 001)	2000/3 (omits ::) 2::/3 (omits the rest of the first hextet)
2340:1140::/26	All addresses whose first 26 bits match the listed hex number	2340:114::/26 (omits the last digit in the second hextet)
2340:1111::/32	All addresses whose first 32 bits match the listed hex number	2340:1111/32 (omits ::)

IPv6 Subnetting

In many ways, subnetting IPv6 addresses is much simpler than subnetting IPv4 addresses. A typical site will be assigned an IPv6 address space with a /48 prefix length. Because the least significant bits are used for the interface ID, that leaves 16 bits for the subnet ID and a /64 subnet prefix length, as shown in Figure 21-1.

Figure 21-1   /64 Subnet Prefix

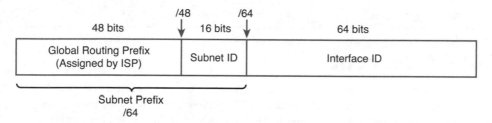

For our subnetting examples, we will use 2001:0DB8:000A::/48, or simply 2001:DB8:A::/48, which includes subnets 2001:DB8:A::/64 through 2001:DB8:A:FFFF::/64. That's 2^{16} or 65,536 subnets, each with 2^{64} or 18 quintillion interface addresses.

Subnetting the Subnet ID

So, to subnet in a small- to medium-size business, simply increment the least significant bits of the subnet ID (as shown in Example 21-1), assign /64 subnets to your networks, and be done with it.

Example 21-1   Subnetting the Subnet ID

```
2001:DB8:A:0001::/64
2001:DB8:A:0002::/64
2001:DB8:A:0003::/64
2001:DB8:A:0004::/64
2001:DB8:A:0005::/64
```

Of course, if you are administering a larger implementation, you can use the four hexadecimal digits of the subnet ID to design a quick and simple four-level hierarchy. There is plenty of room for most large enterprise networks to design a logical address scheme that aggregates addresses for an optimal routing configuration. And if not, applying for and receiving another /48 address is not difficult.

Subnetting into the Interface ID

If you extend your subnetting into the interface ID portion of the address, it is a best practice to subnet on the nibble boundary. A nibble is 4 bits or one hexadecimal digit. For example, let's borrow the first 4 bits from the interface ID portion of the network address 2001:DB8:A:1::/64. That means that the network 2001:DB8:A:1::/64 would now have 2^4 or 16 subnets from 2001:DB8:A:1:0000::/68 to 2001:DB8:A:1:F000::/68. Listing the subnets is easy, as shown in Example 21-2.

Example 21-2   Subnetting into the Interface ID

```
2001:DB8:A:1:0000::/68
2001:DB8:A:1:1000::/68
2001:DB8:A:1:2000::/68
2001:DB8:A:1:3000::/68
      thru
2001:DB8:A:1:F000::/68
```

EUI-64 Concept

Static IPv6 addressing will be reviewed on Day 17, "Basic Router Configuration: IPv6," including how to configure the router to use EUI-64 addressing (EUI stands for Extended Unique Identifier). Today, we are reviewing the concept behind the EUI-64 configuration.

Recall from Figure 21-1 that the second half of the IPv6 address is called the interface ID. The value of the interface ID portion of a global unicast address can be set to any value, as long as no other host in the same subnet attempts to use the same value. However, the size of the interface ID was chosen to allow easy autoconfiguration of IP addresses by plugging the MAC address of a network card into the interface ID field in an IPv6 address.

MAC addresses are 6 bytes (48 bits) in length. So to complete the 64-bit interface ID, IPv6 fills in 2 more bytes by separating the MAC address into two 3-byte halves. It then inserts hex FFFE in between the halves and sets the seventh bit in the first byte to binary 1 to form the interface ID field. Figure 21-2 shows this format, called the EUI-64 format.

For example, the following two lines list a host's MAC address and corresponding EUI-64 format interface ID, assuming the use of an address configuration option that uses the EUI-64 format:

- MAC Address: 0034:5678:9ABC
- EUI-64 Interface ID: 0234:56FF:FE78:9ABC

Figure 21-2   IPv6 Address Format with Interface ID and EUI-64

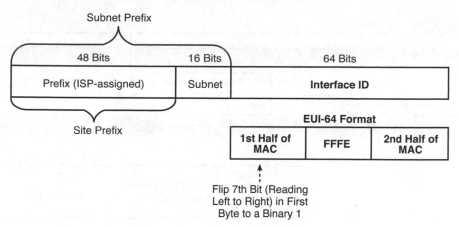

NOTE: To change the seventh bit (reading left to right) in the example, convert hex 00 to binary 00000000, change the seventh bit to 1 (00000010), and then convert back to hex, for hex 02 as the first two digits.

Stateless Address Autoconfiguration

IPv6 supports two methods of dynamic configuration of IPv6 addresses:

- **Stateless Address Autoconfiguration (SLAAC):** A host dynamically learns the /64 prefix through the IPv6 Neighbor Discovery Protocol (NDP) and then calculates the rest of its address by using an EUI-64 method.

- **DHCPv6:** Works the same conceptually as DHCP in IPv4. We will review DHCPv6 on Day 12, "DHCP Configuration."

By using the EUI-64 process and the Neighbor Discovery Protocol (NDP), SLAAC allows a device to determine its entire global unicast address without any manual configuration or a DHCPv6 server. Figure 21-3 illustrates the SLAAC process between a host and a router configured with the **ipv6 unicast-routing** command, which means that it will send and receive NDP messages.

Figure 21-3 Neighbor Discovery and the SLAAC Process

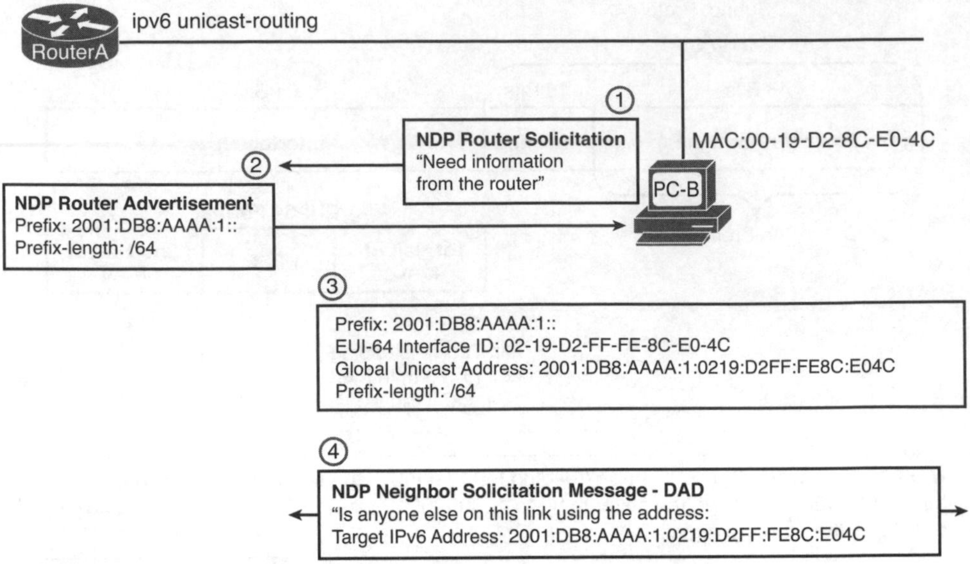

RouterA ipv6 unicast-routing

① NDP Router Solicitation
"Need information from the router"

MAC:00-19-D2-8C-E0-4C

PC-B

② NDP Router Advertisement
Prefix: 2001:DB8:AAAA:1::
Prefix-length: /64

③ Prefix: 2001:DB8:AAAA:1::
EUI-64 Interface ID: 02-19-D2-FF-FE-8C-E0-4C
Global Unicast Address: 2001:DB8:AAAA:1:0219:D2FF:FE8C:E04C
Prefix-length: /64

④ NDP Neighbor Solicitation Message - DAD
"Is anyone else on this link using the address:
Target IPv6 Address: 2001:DB8:AAAA:1:0219:D2FF:FE8C:E04C

Migration to IPv6

Two major transition strategies are currently used to migrate to IPv6:

- **Dual-stacking:** An integration method in which a node has implementation and connectivity to both an IPv4 and IPv6 network. This is the recommended option and involves running IPv4 and IPv6 at the same time.

- **Tunneling:** Tunneling is a method for transporting IPv6 packets over IPv4-only networks by encapsulating the IPv6 packet inside IPv4. Several tunneling techniques are available.

Because of the simplicity of running dual-stack, it will most likely be the preferred strategy as IPv4-only networks begin to disappear. But it will probably still be decades before we see enterprise networks running exclusively IPv6. Figure 21-4 illustrates one way that Wendell Odom thinks about the transition to IPv6, "but who knows how long it will take?"

Remember this advice: "Dual-stack where you can; tunnel where you must." These two methods are the most common techniques to transition from IPv4 to IPv6. Dual-stacking is easy enough. Just configure all your devices to use both IPv4 and IPv6 addressing. Tunneling, however, is more complex and beyond the scope of the CCENT or CCNA exam topics.

Figure 21-4   Transition to IPv6 Using Dual-Stack

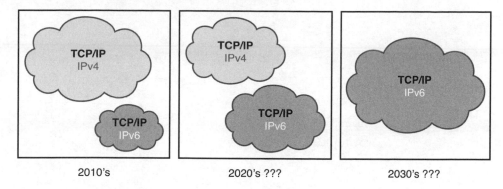

| 2010's | 2020's ??? | 2030's ??? |

Study Resources

For today's exam topics, refer to the following resources for more study.

Resource	Location	Topic
Primary Resources		
Network Basics	7	IPv6 Unicast Addresses
		IPv6 Addressing
Introduction to Networks	8	IPv6 Unicast Addresses
		IPv6 Addressing
IPv6 Fundamentals	3	All
ICND1 Official Cert Guide	25	IPv6 Addressing Formats and Conventions
	26	IPv6 Subnetting Using Global Unicast Addresses
ICND1 Foundation Learning Guide	20	Other IPv6 Features
Supplemental Resources		
CCENT Practice and Study Guide	8	IPv6 Network Address
Flash Cards	12	Questions 13–26
Network Simulator	26	IPv6 Subnet ID Calculations I–X
	27	IPv6 EUI-64 Calculation Drills I–X

Basic Routing Concepts

CCENT 100-101 ICND1 Exam Topics

- Describe basic routing concepts.
- Differentiate methods of routing and routing protocols.

Key Topics

Today we review basic routing concepts, including exactly how a packet is processed by intermediary devices (routers) on its way from source to destination. We then review the basic routing methods, including connected, static, and dynamic routes. Tomorrow's review will dive deeper into dynamic routing.

Packet Forwarding

Packet forwarding by routers is accomplished through path determination and switching functions. The path determination function is the process of how the router determines which path to use when forwarding a packet. To determine the best path, the router searches its routing table for a network address that matches the packet's destination IP address.

One of three path determinations results from this search:

- **Directly connected network:** If the destination IP address of the packet belongs to a device on a network that is directly connected to one of the router's interfaces, that packet is forwarded directly to that device. This means that the destination IP address of the packet is a host address on the same network as this router's interface.

- **Remote network:** If the destination IP address of the packet belongs to a remote network, the packet is forwarded to another router. Remote networks can be reached only by forwarding packets to another router.

- **No route determined:** If the destination IP address of the packet does not belong to either a connected or remote network and the router does not have a default route, the packet is discarded. The router sends an Internet Control Message Protocol (ICMP) Unreachable message to the source IP address of the packet.

In the first two results, the router completes the process by switching the packet out the correct interface. It does this by reencapsulating the IP packet into the appropriate Layer 2 data-link frame format for the exit interface. The type of Layer 2 encapsulation is determined by the type of interface. For example, if the exit interface is Fast Ethernet, the packet is encapsulated in an Ethernet frame. If the exit interface is a serial interface configured for PPP, the IP packet is encapsulated in a PPP frame.

Path Determination and Switching Function Example

Most of the study resources have detailed examples with excellent graphics that explain the path determination and switching functions performed by routers as a packet travels from source to destination.

Although we do not have an abundance of room here to repeat those graphics, we can textually review an example using one graphic, shown in Figure 20-1.

Figure 20-1   Packet Forwarding Sample Topology

For brevity, only the last two octets of the MAC address are shown in the figure:

1. PC1 has a packet to be sent to PC2.

    Using the AND operation on the destination's IP address and PC1's subnet mask, PC1 has determined that the IP source and IP destination addresses are on different networks. Therefore, PC1 checks its Address Resolution Protocol (ARP) table for the IP address of the default gateway and its associated MAC address. It then encapsulates the packet in an Ethernet header and forwards it to R1.

2. Router R1 receives the Ethernet frame.

    Router R1 examines the destination MAC address, which matches the MAC address of the receiving interface, FastEthernet 0/0. R1 will therefore copy the frame into its buffer.

    R1 decapsulates the Ethernet frame and reads the destination IP address. Because it does not match any of R1's directly connected networks, the router consults its routing table to route this packet.

    R1 searches the routing table for a network address and subnet mask that would include this packet's destination IP address as a host address on that network. The entry with the longest match (longest prefix) is selected. R1 then encapsulates the packet in the appropriate frame format for the exit interface and switches the frame to the interface (FastEthernet 0/1 in our example). The interface then forwards it to the next hop.

3. Packet arrives at Router R2.

    R2 performs the same functions as R1, except this time, the exit interface is a serial interface—not Ethernet. Therefore, R2 encapsulates the packet in the appropriate frame format used by the serial interface and sends it to R3. For our example, assume that the interface is using High-Level Data Link Control (HDLC), which uses the data-link address 0x8F. Remember, there are no MAC addresses on serial interfaces.

4. Packet arrives at R3.

    R3 decapsulates the data-link HDLC frame. The search of the routing table results in a network that is one of R3's directly connected networks. Because the exit interface is a directly connected Ethernet network, R3 needs to resolve the destination IP address of the packet with a destination MAC address.

    R3 searches for the packet's destination IP address of 192.168.4.10 in its ARP cache. If the entry is not in the ARP cache, R3 sends an ARP request out its FastEthernet 0/0 interface.

    PC2 sends back an ARP reply with its MAC address. R3 updates its ARP cache with an entry for 192.168.4.10 and the MAC address returned in the ARP reply.

    The IP packet is encapsulated into a new data-link Ethernet frame and sent out R3's FastEthernet 0/0 interface.

5. Ethernet frame with encapsulated IP packet arrives at PC2.

    PC2 examines the destination MAC address, which matches the MAC address of the receiving interface—that is, its own Ethernet NIC. PC2 will therefore copy the rest of the frame. PC2 sees that the Ethernet Type field is 0x800, which means that the Ethernet frame contains an IP packet in the data portion of the frame. PC2 decapsulates the Ethernet frame and passes the IP packet to its operating system's IP process.

Routing Methods

A router can learn routes from three basic sources:

- **Directly connected routes:** Automatically entered in the routing table when an interface is activated with an IP address

- **Static routes:** Manually configured by the network administrator and are entered in the routing table if the exit interface for the static route is active

- **Dynamic routes:** Learned by the routers through sharing routes with other routers that use the same routing protocol

In many cases, the complexity of the network topology, the number of networks, and the need for the network to automatically adjust to changes require the use of a dynamic routing protocol. Dynamic routing certainly has several advantages over static routing; however, static routing is still used in networks today. In fact, networks typically use a combination of both static and dynamic routing.

Table 20-1 compares dynamic and static routing features. From this comparison, you can list the advantages of each routing method. The advantages of one method are the disadvantages of the other.

Table 20-1   Dynamic Versus Static Routing

Feature	Dynamic Routing	Static Routing
Configuration complexity	Generally independent of the network size.	Increases with network size.
Required administrator knowledge	Advanced knowledge required.	No extra knowledge required.
Topology changes	Automatically adapts to topology changes.	Administrator intervention required.
Scaling	Suitable for simple and complex topologies.	Suitable for simple topologies.
Security	Less secure.	More secure.
Resource usage	Uses CPU, memory, and link bandwidth.	No extra resources needed.
Predictability	Route depends on the current topology.	Route to destination is always the same.

Classifying Dynamic Routing Protocols

Figure 20-2 shows a timeline of IP routing protocols along with a chart that will help you memorize the various ways to classify routing protocols.

Figure 20-2   Routing Protocols' Evolution and Classification

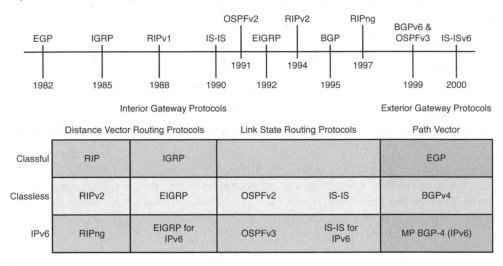

Configuration of single-area Open Shortest Path First version 2 (OSPFv2) and single-area OSPFv3 are included in the CCENT exam topics. Configuration of Enhanced Interior Gateway Routing Protocol (EIGRP) for IPv4, EIGRP for IPv6, multiarea OSPFv2, and multiarea OPSFv3 are part of the CCNA exam topics.

Routing protocols can be classified into different groups according to their characteristics:

- IGP or EGP
- Distance vector or link-state
- Classful or classless

IGP and EGP

An autonomous system (AS) is a collection of routers under a common administration that presents a common, clearly defined routing policy to the Internet. Typical examples are a large company's internal network and an ISP's network. Most company networks are not autonomous systems, only a network within their own ISP's autonomous system. Because the Internet is based on the autonomous system concept, two types of routing protocols are required:

- **Interior gateway protocols (IGP):** Used for intra-AS routing—that is, routing inside an AS
- **Exterior gateway protocols (EGP):** Used for inter-AS routing—that is, routing between autonomous systems

Distance Vector Routing Protocols

Distance vector means that routes are advertised as vectors of distance and direction. Distance is defined in terms of a metric such as hop count, and direction is the next-hop router or exit interface. Distance vector protocols typically use the Bellman-Ford algorithm for the best-path route determination.

Some distance vector protocols periodically send complete routing tables to all connected neighbors. In large networks, these routing updates can become enormous, causing significant traffic on the links.

Although the Bellman-Ford algorithm eventually accumulates enough knowledge to maintain a database of reachable networks, the algorithm does not allow a router to know the exact topology of an internetwork. The router knows only the routing information received from its neighbors.

Distance vector protocols use routers as signposts along the path to the final destination. The only information a router knows about a remote network is the distance or metric to reach that network and which path or interface to use to get there. Distance vector routing protocols do not have an actual map of the network topology.

Distance vector protocols work best in situations where

- The network is simple and flat and does not require a hierarchical design.
- The administrators do not have enough knowledge to configure and troubleshoot link-state protocols.

- Specific types of networks, such as hub-and-spoke networks, are being implemented.

- Worst-case convergence times in a network are not a concern.

Link-State Routing Protocols

In contrast to distance vector routing protocol operation, a router configured with a link-state routing protocol can create a "complete view," or topology, of the network by gathering information from all the other routers. Think of a link-state routing protocol as having a complete map of the network topology. The signposts along the way from source to destination are not necessary because all link-state routers are using an identical "map" of the network. A link-state router uses the link-state information to create a topology map and to select the best path to all destination networks in the topology.

With some distance vector routing protocols, routers send periodic updates of their routing information to their neighbors. Link-state routing protocols do not use periodic updates. After the network has converged, a link-state update is sent only when there is a change in the topology.

Link-state protocols work best in situations where

- The network design is hierarchical, usually occurring in large networks.

- The administrators have a good knowledge of the implemented link-state routing protocol.

- Fast convergence of the network is crucial.

Classful Routing Protocols

Classful routing protocols do not send subnet mask information in routing updates. The first routing protocols, such as Routing Information Protocol (RIP), were classful. This was at a time when network addresses were allocated based on classes: Class A, B, or C. A routing protocol did not need to include the subnet mask in the routing update because the network mask could be determined based on the first octet of the network address.

Classful routing protocols can still be used in some of today's networks, but because they do not include the subnet mask, they cannot be used in all situations. Classful routing protocols cannot be used when a network is subnetted using more than one subnet mask. In other words, classful routing protocols do not support variable-length subnet masking (VLSM).

Other limitations exist to classful routing protocols, including their inability to support discontiguous networks and supernets. Classful routing protocols include Routing Information Protocol version 1 (RIPv1) and Interior Gateway Routing Protocol (IGRP). Neither RIP nor IGRP are included in CCENT or CCNA exam topics.

Classless Routing Protocols

Classless routing protocols include the subnet mask with the network address in routing updates. Today's networks are no longer allocated based on classes, and the subnet mask cannot be determined by the value of the first octet. Classless routing protocols are required in most networks today because of their support for VLSM and discontiguous networks and supernets. Classless routing protocols are Routing Information Protocol version 2 (RIPv2), Enhanced IGRP (EIGRP), Open Shortest Path First (OSPF), Intermediate System–to–Intermediate System (IS-IS), and Border Gateway Protocol (BGP).

Study Resources

For today's exam topics, refer to the following resources for more study.

Resource	Location	Topic
Primary Resources		
Network Basics	6	Routing
Introduction to Networks	6	Routing
Routing Concepts	1	Routing Decisions
		Router Operation
Routing and Switching Essentials	4	Routing Decisions
		Router Operation
ICND1 Official Cert Guide	4	Overview of Network Layer Functions
		IPv4 Routing
ICND1 Foundation Learning Guide	10, 11, 14	All
Supplemental Resources		
CCENT Practice and Study Guide	6	Routing
	15	Routing Decisions
		Router Operation
Flash Cards	5	Questions 1–13
Network Simulator	18	Examining the IP Routing Table
		Routing Analysis I
		IP Route Selection I–X
		Path Analysis I
	28	IPv6 Route Selection I–X

Dynamic Routing Protocols

CCENT 100-101 ICND1 Exam Topics

- Differentiate methods of routing and routing protocols.

Key Topics

Today our review focuses on dynamic routing protocols. Because dynamic routing is such a large CCENT topic area, we spend some time discussing metrics and administrative distance as well as the basic features of distance vector and link-state routing protocols.

Dynamic Routing Metrics

There are cases when a routing protocol learns of more than one route to the same destination from the same routing source. To select the best path, the routing protocol must be able to evaluate and differentiate among the available paths. A *metric* is used for this purpose. Two different routing protocols might choose different paths to the same destination because of using different metrics. Metrics used in IP routing protocols include the following:

- **RIP—Hop count:** Best path is chosen by the route with the lowest hop count.

- **IGRP and EIGRP—Bandwidth, delay, reliability, and load:** Best path is chosen by the route with the smallest composite metric value calculated from these multiple parameters. By default, only bandwidth and delay are used.

- **IS-IS and OSPF—Cost:** Best path is chosen by the route with the lowest cost. The Cisco implementation of OSPF uses bandwidth to determine the cost.

The metric associated with a certain route can be best viewed using the **show ip route** command. The metric value is the second value in the brackets for a routing table entry. In Example 19-1, R2 has a route to the 192.168.8.0/24 network that is two hops away.

Example 19-1   Routing Table for R2

```
R2# show ip route

<output omitted>

Gateway of last resort is not set

R 192.168.1.0/24 [120/1] via 192.168.2.1, 00:00:24, Serial0/0/0
```

```
C 192.168.2.0/24 is directly connected, Serial0/0/0
C 192.168.3.0/24 is directly connected, FastEthernet0/0
C 192.168.4.0/24 is directly connected, Serial0/0/1
R 192.168.5.0/24 [120/1] via 192.168.4.1, 00:00:26, Serial0/0/1
R 192.168.6.0/24 [120/1] via 192.168.2.1, 00:00:24, Serial0/0/0
                 [120/1] via 192.168.4.1, 00:00:26, Serial0/0/1
R 192.168.7.0/24 [120/1] via 192.168.4.1, 00:00:26, Serial0/0/1
R 192.168.8.0/24 [120/2] via 192.168.4.1, 00:00:26, Serial0/0/1
```

NOTE: Although the Routing Information Protocol (RIP) is no longer included as a CCENT or CCNA exam topic, using RIP to explain routing concepts is still a valid use of the deprecated routing protocol.

Notice in the output that one network, 192.168.6.0/24, has two routes. RIP will load-balance between these equal-cost routes. All the other routing protocols are capable of automatically load-balancing traffic for up to four equal-cost routes by default. EIGRP is also capable of load-balancing across unequal-cost paths.

Administrative Distance

There can be times when a router learns a route to a remote network from more than one routing source. For example, a static route might have been configured for the same network/subnet mask that was learned dynamically by a dynamic routing protocol, such as RIP. The router must choose which route to install.

Although less common, more than one dynamic routing protocol can be deployed in the same network. In some situations, it might be necessary to route the same network address using multiple routing protocols such as RIP and OSPF. Because different routing protocols use different metrics—RIP uses hop count and OSPF uses bandwidth—it is not possible to compare metrics to determine the best path.

Administrative distance (AD) defines the preference of a routing source. Each routing source—including specific routing protocols, static routes, and even directly connected networks—is prioritized in order of most to least preferable using an AD value. Cisco routers use the AD feature to select the best path when they learn about the same destination network from two or more different routing sources.

The AD value is an integer value from 0 to 255. The lower the value, the more preferred the route source. An administrative distance of 0 is the most preferred. Only a directly connected network has an AD of 0, which cannot be changed. An AD of 255 means that the router will not believe the source of that route and it will not be installed in the routing table.

In the routing table shown in Example 19-1, the AD value is the first value listed in the brackets. You can see that the AD value for RIP routes is 120. You can also verify the AD value with the **show ip protocols** command, as demonstrated in Example 19-2.

Example 19-2   Verifying the AD Value with the show ip protocols Command

```
R2# show ip protocols

Routing Protocol is "rip"
  Sending updates every 30 seconds, next due in 12 seconds
  Invalid after 180 seconds, hold down 180, flushed after 240
  Outgoing update filter list for all interfaces is not set
  Incoming update filter list for all interfaces is not set
  Redistributing: rip
  Default version control: send version 1, receive any version
    Interface          Send  Recv  Triggered RIP  Key-chain
    Serial0/0/1          1    2 1
    FastEthernet0/0      1    2 1
  Automatic network summarization is in effect
  Maximum path: 4
  Routing for Networks:
    192.168.3.0
    192.168.4.0
Passive Interface(s):
Routing Information Sources:
    Gateway         Distance       Last Update
    192.168.4.1          120
Distance: (default is 120)
```

Table 19-1 shows a chart of the different administrative distance values for various routing protocols.

Table 19-1   Default Administrative Distances

Route Source	AD
Connected	0
Static	1
EIGRP summary route	5
External BGP	20
Internal EIGRP	90
IGRP	100
OSPF	110
IS-IS	115
RIP	120
External EIGRP	170
Internal BGP	200

IGP Comparison Summary

Table 19-2 compares several features of the currently most popular IGPs: RIPv2, OSPF, and EIGRP.

Table 19-2   Comparing Features of IGPs: RIPv2, OSPF, and EIGRP

Features	RIPv2	OSPF	EIGRP
Metric	Hop count	Bandwidth	Function of band-width, delay
Sends periodic updates	Yes (30 seconds)	No	No
Full or partial routing updates	Full	Partial	Partial
Where updates are sent	(224.0.0.9)	(224.0.0.5, 224.0.0.6)	(224.0.0.10)
Route considered to be unreachable	16 hops	Depends on MaxAge of LSA, which is never incremented past 3600 seconds	A delay of all 1s
Supports unequal-cost load balancing	No	No	Yes

Routing Loop Prevention

Without preventive measures, distance vector routing protocols could cause severe routing loops in the network. A routing loop is a condition in which a packet is continuously transmitted within a series of routers without ever reaching its intended destination network. A routing loop can occur when two or more routers have inaccurate routing information to a destination network.

A number of mechanisms are available to eliminate routing loops, primarily with distance vector routing protocols. These mechanisms include the following:

- **Defining a maximum metric to prevent count to infinity:** To eventually stop the incrementing of a metric during a routing loop, "infinity" is defined by setting a maximum metric value. For example, RIP defines infinity as 16 hops—an "unreachable" metric. When the routers "count to infinity," they mark the route as unreachable.

- **Hold-down timers:** Used to instruct routers to hold any changes that might affect routes for a specified period of time. If a route is identified as down or possibly down, any other information for that route containing the same status, or worse, is ignored for a predetermined amount of time (the hold-down period) so that the network has time to converge.

- **Split horizon:** Used to prevent a routing loop by not allowing advertisements to be sent back through the interface they originated from. The split horizon rule stops a router from incrementing a metric and then sending the route back to its source.

- **Route poisoning or poison reverse:** Used to mark the route as unreachable in a routing update that is sent to other routers. Unreachable is interpreted as a metric that is set to the maximum.

- **Triggered updates:** A routing table update that is sent immediately in response to a routing change. Triggered updates do not wait for update timers to expire. The detecting router immediately sends an update message to adjacent routers.

- **TTL field in the IP header:** The purpose of the Time to Live (TTL) field is to avoid a situation in which an undeliverable packet keeps circulating on the network endlessly. With TTL, the 8-bit field is set with a value by the source device of the packet. The TTL is decreased by 1 by every router on the route to its destination. If the TTL field reaches 0 before the packet arrives at its destination, the packet is discarded and the router sends an ICMP error message back to the source of the IP packet.

Link-State Routing Protocol Features

Like distance vector protocols that send routing updates to their neighbors, link-state protocols send link-state updates to neighboring routers, which in turn forward that information to their neighbors, and so on. At the end of the process, like distance vector protocols, routers that use link-state protocols add the best routes to their routing tables, based on metrics. However, beyond this level of explanation, these two types of routing protocol algorithms have little in common.

Building the LSDB

Link-state routers flood detailed information about the internetwork to all the other routers so that every router has the same information about the internetwork. Routers use this link-state database (LSDB) to calculate the currently best routes to each subnet.

OSPF, the most popular link-state IP routing protocol, advertises information in routing update messages of various types, with the updates containing information called link-state advertisements (LSA).

Figure 19-1 shows the general idea of the flooding process, with R8 creating and flooding its router LSA. Note that Figure 19-1 shows only a subset of the information in R8's router LSA.

Figure 19-1 shows the rather basic flooding process, with R8 sending the original LSA for itself and the other routers flooding the LSA by forwarding it until every router has a copy.

After the LSA has been flooded, even if the LSAs do not change, link-state protocols do require periodic reflooding of the LSAs by default every 30 minutes. However, if an LSA changes, the router immediately floods the changed LSA. For example, if Router R8's LAN interface failed, R8 would need to reflood the R8 LSA, stating that the interface is now down.

Figure 19-1   Flooding LSAs Using a Link-State Routing Protocol

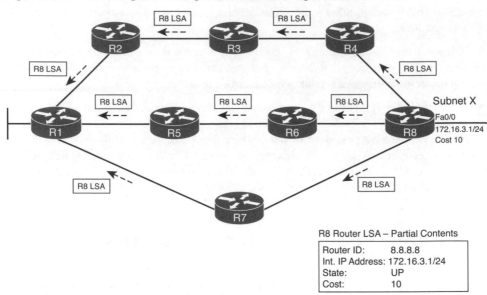

R8 Router LSA – Partial Contents

Router ID:	8.8.8.8
Int. IP Address:	172.16.3.1/24
State:	UP
Cost:	10

Calculating the Dijkstra Algorithm

The flooding process alone does not cause a router to learn what routes to add to the IP routing table. Link-state protocols must then find and add routes to the IP routing table using the Dijkstra Shortest Path First (SPF) algorithm.

The SPF algorithm is run on the LSDB to create the SPF tree. The LSDB holds all the information about all the possible routers and links. Each router must view itself as the starting point, and each subnet as the destination, and use the SPF algorithm to build its own SPF tree to pick the best route to each subnet.

Figure 19-2 shows a graphical view of the results of the SPF algorithm run by Router R1 when trying to find the best route to reach subnet 172.16.3.0/24 (based on Figure 19-1).

To pick the best route, a router's SPF algorithm adds the cost associated with each link between itself and the destination subnet, over each possible route. Figure 19-2 shows the costs associated with each route beside the links, with the dashed lines showing the three routes R1 finds between itself and subnet X (172.16.3.0/24).

Table 19-3 lists the three routes shown in Figure 19-2, with their cumulative costs, showing that R1's best route to 172.16.3.0/24 starts by going through R5.

Table 19-3   Comparing R1's Three Alternatives for the Route to 172.16.3.0/24

Route	Location in Figure 19-2	Cumulative Cost
R1–R7–R8	Left	10 + 180 + 10 = 200
R1–R5–R6–R8	Middle	20 + 30 + 40 + 10 = 100
R1–R2–R3–R4–R8	Right	30 + 60 + 20 + 5 + 10 = 125

Figure 19-2   SPF Tree to Find R1's Route to 172.16.3.0/24

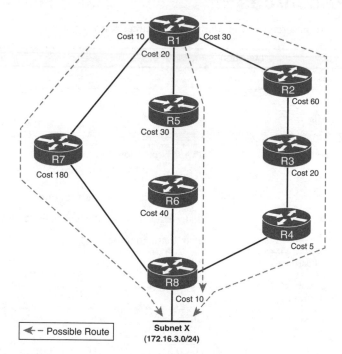

As a result of the SPF algorithm's analysis of the LSDB, R1 adds a route to subnet 172.16.3.0/24 to its routing table, with the next-hop router of R5.

Convergence with Link-State Protocols

Remember, when an LSA changes, link-state protocols react swiftly, converging the network and using the currently best routes as quickly as possible. For example, imagine that the link between R5 and R6 fails in the internetwork of Figures 19-1 and 19-2. The following list explains the process R1 uses to switch to a different route:

1. R5 and R6 flood LSAs that state that their interfaces are now in a "down" state.

2. All routers run the SPF algorithm again to see whether any routes have changed.

3. All routers replace routes, as needed, based on the results of SPF. For example, R1 changes its route for subnet X (172.16.3.0/24) to use R2 as the next-hop router.

These steps allow the link-state routing protocol to converge quickly—much more quickly than distance vector routing protocols.

Study Resources

For today's exam topics, refer to the following resources for more study.

Resource	Location	Topic
Primary Resources		
Routing Concepts	3	All
Routing and Switching Essentials	7	All
ICND1 Official Cert Guide	4	IPv4 Routing Protocols
	16	IP Routing
	17	Comparing Dynamic Routing Protocol Features
		Understanding the OSPF Link-State Routing Protocol
	25	IPv6 Routing Protocols
ICND1 Foundation Learning Guide	14	All
Supplemental Resources		
CCENT Practice and Study Guide	18	All
Flash Cards	11	Questions 1–10

Basic Router Configuration: IPv4

CCENT 100-101 ICND1 Exam Topics

- Configure and verify utilizing the CLI to set basic router configuration.
- Configure and verify operation status of an Ethernet interface.
- Verify router configuration and network connectivity.

Key Topic

Today and tomorrow we review basic router configuration. Today's focus is on configuring and verifying initial settings, including IPv4 addressing. Tomorrow, we will review IPv6 addressing and network connectivity verification. Most of this should be very familiar to you at this point in your studies because these skills are fundamental to all other router configuration tasks.

Basic Router Configuration with IPv4

Figure 18-1 shows the topology and IPv4 addressing scheme that we will use to review basic router configuration and verification tasks.

When configuring a router, certain basic tasks are performed, including the following:

- Naming the router
- Setting passwords
- Configuring interfaces
- Configuring a banner
- Saving changes on a router
- Verifying basic configuration and router operations

Figure 18-1   IPv4 Example Topology

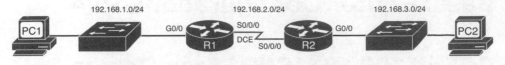

Device	Interface	IP Address	Subnet Mask	Default Gateway
R1	G0/0	192.168.1.1	255.255.255.0	N/A
	S0/0/0	192.168.2.1	255.255.255.0	N/A
R2	G0/0	192.168.3.1	255.255.255.0	N/A
	S0/0/0	192.168.2.2	255.255.255.0	N/A
PC1	N/A	192.168.1.10	255.255.255.0	192.168.1.1
PC2	N/A	192.168.3.10	255.255.255.0	192.168.3.1

Table 18-1 shows the basic router configuration command syntax used to configure R1 in the following example.

Table 18-1   Basic Router Configuration Command Syntax

Configuration Task	Commands
Naming the router	`Router(config)# hostname name`
Setting passwords7	`Router(config)# enable secret password`
	`Router(config)# line console 0`
	`Router(config-line)# password password`
	`Router(config-line)# login`
	`Router(config)# line vty 0 15`
	`Router(config-line)# transport input ssh`
	`Router(config-line)# login local`
	`Router(config)# username name password password`
Configuring a message-of-the-day banner	`Router(config)# banner motd # message #`
Configuring an interface	`Router(config)# interface type number`
	`Router(config-if)# ip address address mask`
	`Router(config-if)# description description`
	`Router(config-if)# no shutdown`
Saving changes on a router	`Router# copy running-config startup-config`
Examining the output of **show** commands	`Router# show running-config`
	`Router# show ip route`
	`Router# show ip interface brief`
	`Router# show interfaces`

Let's walk through a basic configuration for R1. First, we enter privileged EXEC mode, and then we enter global configuration mode:

```
Router> enable
Router# config t
```

Next, name the router and enter the encrypted password for entering privileged EXEC mode. This command overrides the older **enable password** *password* command, so we are not entering that one:

```
Router(config)# hostname R1
R1(config)# enable secret class
```

Next, configure the console password and require that it be entered with the login password:

```
R1(config)# line console 0
R1(config-line)# password cisco
R1(config-line)# login
```

Recall from Day 27, "Basic Switch Configuration," that configuring SSH and disabling Telnet are security best practices. So next, configure the vty lines to only use SSH.

NOTE: SSH configuration is not shown here. Assume that it is already configured. To review SSH configuration, refer to Day 27.

```
R1(config)# line vty 0 15
R1(config-line)# transport input ssh
R1(config-line)# login local
R1(config-line)# exit
R1(config)# username admin password cisco
```

Encrypt all the clear-text passwords in the running configuration using the **service-password encryption** command:

```
R1(config)# service-password encryption
```

Configure the message-of-the-day (MOTD) banner. A delimiting character such as a # is used at the beginning and at the end of the message. At a minimum, a banner should warn against unauthorized access. A good security policy would prohibit configuring a banner that "welcomes" an unauthorized user:

```
R1(config)# banner motd #
Enter TEXT message.  End with the character '#'.
*****************************************
WARNING!! Unauthorized Access Prohibited!!
*****************************************
#
```

Now configure the individual router interfaces with IP addresses and other information. First, enter interface configuration mode by specifying the interface type and number. Next, configure the IP address and subnet mask:

```
R1(config)# interface Serial0/0/0
R1(config-if)# ip address 192.168.2.1 255.255.255.0
```

It is good practice to configure a description on each interface to help document the network information:

```
R1(config-if)# description Ciruit#VBN32696-123 (help desk:1-800-555-1234)
```

Activate the interface:

```
R1(config-if)# no shutdown
```

Assuming that the other side of the link is activated on R2, the serial interface will now be up. Finish R1 by configuring the GigabitEthernet 0/0 interface:

```
R1(config-if)# interface GigabitEthernet0/0
R1(config-if)# ip address 192.168.1.1 255.255.255.0
R1(config-if)# description R1 LAN
R1(config-if)# no shutdown
```

Assume that R2 is fully configured and can route back to the 192.168.1.0/24 LAN attached to R1. We need to add a static route to R1 to ensure connectivity to R2's LAN. Static routing is reviewed in more detail on Day 20, "Basic Routing Concepts." For now, enter the following command to configure a directly attached static route to R2's LAN:

```
R1(config)# ip route 192.168.3.0 255.255.255.0 Serial 0/0/0
```

To save the configuration, enter the **copy running-config startup-config** or **copy run start** command.

You can use the **show running-config** command to verify the full current configuration on the router. However, a few other basic commands can help you not only verify your configuration, but also begin troubleshooting any potential problems.

First, make sure that the networks for your interfaces are now in the routing table by using the **show ip route** command, as demonstrated in Example 18-1.

Example 18-1   show ip route Command

```
R1# show ip route
Codes: L - local, C - connected, S - static, R - RIP, M - mobile, B - BGP
       D - EIGRP, EX - EIGRP external, O - OSPF, IA - OSPF inter area
       N1 - OSPF NSSA external type 1, N2 - OSPF NSSA external type 2
       E1 - OSPF external type 1, E2 - OSPF external type 2
       i - IS-IS, su - IS-IS summary, L1 - IS-IS level-1, L2 - IS-IS level-2
```

```
        ia - IS-IS inter area, * - candidate default, U - per-user static route
        o - ODR, P - periodic downloaded static route, H - NHRP, l - LISP
        + - replicated route, % - next hop override

Gateway of last resort is not set

     192.168.1.0/24 is variably subnetted, 2 subnets, 2 masks
C        192.168.1.0/24 is directly connected, GigabitEthernet0/0
L        192.168.1.1/32 is directly connected, GigabitEthernet0/0
     192.168.2.0/24 is variably subnetted, 2 subnets, 2 masks
C        192.168.2.0/24 is directly connected, Serial0/0/0
L        192.168.2.1/32 is directly connected, Serial0/0/0
S    192.168.3.0/24 is directly connected, Serial0/0/0
R1#
```

If a network is missing, check your interface status with the **show ip interface brief** command, as demonstrated in Example 18-2.

Example 18-2   show ip interface brief Command

```
R1# show ip interface brief
Interface                  IP-Address      OK? Method Status                Protocol
Embedded-Service-Engine0/0 unassigned      YES unset  administratively down down
GigabitEthernet0/0         192.168.1.1     YES manual up                    up
GigabitEthernet0/1         unassigned      YES unset  administratively down down
Serial0/0/0                192.168.2.1     YES manual up                    up
Serial0/0/1                unassigned      YES unset  administratively down down
R1#
```

The output from the **show ip interface brief** command provides you with three important pieces of information:

- IP address
- Line Status (column 5)
- Protocol Status (column 6)

The IP address should be correct, and the interface status should be "up" and "up." Table 18-2 summarizes the two status codes and their meanings.

Table 18-2   Interface Status Codes

Name	Location	General Meaning
Line status	First status code	Refers to the Layer 1 status—for example, is the cable installed, is it the right/wrong cable, is the device on the other end powered on?
Protocol status	Second status code	Refers generally to the Layer 2 status. It is always down if the line status is down. If the line status is up, a protocol status of down is usually caused by mismatched data link layer configuration.

Four combinations of settings exist for the status codes when troubleshooting a network. Table 18-3 lists the four combinations, along with an explanation of the typical reasons of why an interface would be in that state.

Table 18-3   Combinations of Interface Status Codes

Line and Protocol Status	Typical Reasons
Administratively down, down	The interface has a **shutdown** command configured on it.
down, down	The interface has a **no shutdown** command configured, but the physical layer has a problem. For example, no cable has been attached to the interface (or with Ethernet), the switch interface on the other end of the cable is shut down, or the switch is powered off.
up, down	Almost always refers to data link layer problems, most often configuration problems. For example, serial links have this combination when one router was configured to use PPP and the other defaults to use HDLC. However, there could also be a clocking or hardware issue.
up, up	All is well, interface is functioning.

If necessary, use the more verbose **show interface** command if you need to track down a problem with an interface, which will give you output for every physical and virtual interface. You can also specify one interface. Example 18-3 shows the output for GigabitEthernet 0/0.

Example 18-3   show interface gigabitethernet 0/0 Command

```
R1# show interface gigabitethernet 0/0
GigabitEthernet0/0 is up, line protocol is up
  Hardware is CN Gigabit Ethernet, address is 30f7.0da3.0da0 (bia 30f7.0da3.0da0)
  Description: R1 LAN
  Internet address is 192.168.1.1/24
  MTU 1500 bytes, BW 100000 Kbit/sec, DLY 100 usec,
     reliability 255/255, txload 1/255, rxload 1/255
  Encapsulation ARPA, loopback not set
```

```
Keepalive set (10 sec)
Full Duplex, 100Mbps, media type is RJ45
output flow-control is unsupported, input flow-control is unsupported
ARP type: ARPA, ARP Timeout 04:00:00
Last input 00:00:00, output 00:00:01, output hang never
Last clearing of "show interface" counters never
Input queue: 0/75/0/0 (size/max/drops/flushes); Total output drops: 0
Queueing strategy: fifo
Output queue: 0/40 (size/max)
5 minute input rate 0 bits/sec, 0 packets/sec
5 minute output rate 0 bits/sec, 0 packets/sec
    387 packets input, 59897 bytes, 0 no buffer
    Received 252 broadcasts (0 IP multicasts)
    0 runts, 0 giants, 0 throttles
    0 input errors, 0 CRC, 0 frame, 0 overrun, 0 ignored
    0 watchdog, 86 multicast, 0 pause input
    281 packets output, 35537 bytes, 0 underruns
    0 output errors, 0 collisions, 1 interface resets
    56 unknown protocol drops
    0 babbles, 0 late collision, 0 deferred
    0 lost carrier, 0 no carrier, 0 pause output
    0 output buffer failures, 0 output buffers swapped out
R1#
```

This command has a lot of output. However, sometimes this is the only way to find a problem. Therefore, Table 18-4 parses and explains each important part of the **show interface** output.

Table 18-4   show interface Output Explanation

Output	Description
GigabitEthernet...is {up | down | administratively down}	Indicates whether the interface hardware is currently active or down, or whether an administrator has taken it down.
line protocol is {up | down}	Indicates whether the software processes that handle the line protocol consider the interface usable (that is, whether keepalives are successful). If the interface misses three consecutive keepalives, the line protocol is marked as down.
Hardware	Hardware type (for example, MCI Ethernet, serial communications interface [SCI], cBus Ethernet) and address.
Description	Text string description configured for the interface (max 240 characters).
Internet address	IP address followed by the prefix length (subnet mask).
MTU	Maximum transmission unit (MTU) of the interface.

Output	Description
BW	Bandwidth of the interface, in kilobits per second. The bandwidth parameter is used to compute routing protocol metrics and other calculations.
DLY	Delay of the interface, in microseconds.
rely	Reliability of the interface as a fraction of 255 (255/255 is 100 percent reliability), calculated as an exponential average over 5 minutes.
load	Load on the interface as a fraction of 255 (255/255 is completely saturated), calculated as an exponential average over 5 minutes.
Encapsulation	Encapsulation method assigned to an interface.
loopback	Indicates whether loopback is set and can indicate a problem with the carrier.
keepalive	Indicates whether keepalives are set.
ARP type:	Type of Address Resolution Protocol (ARP) assigned.
Last input	Number of hours, minutes, and seconds since the last packet was successfully received by an interface. Useful for knowing when a dead interface failed.
output	Number of hours, minutes, and seconds since the last packet was successfully transmitted by an interface. Useful for knowing when a dead interface failed.
output hang	Number of hours, minutes, and seconds (or never) since the interface was last reset because of a transmission that took too long. When the number of hours in any of the previous fields exceeds 24 hours, the number of days and hours is printed. If that field overflows, asterisks are printed.
Last clearing	Time at which the counters that measure cumulative statistics shown in this report (such as number of bytes transmitted and received) were last reset to 0. Note that variables that might affect routing (for example, load and reliability) are not cleared when the counters are cleared. Asterisks indicate elapsed time too large to be displayed. Reset the counters with the **clear interface** command.
Output queue, input queue, drops queue	Number of packets in output and input queues. Each number is followed by a slash (/), the maximum size of the queue, and the number of packets dropped because of a full queue.
Five minute input rate, Five minute output rate	Average number of bits and packets transmitted per second in the last 5 minutes. If the interface is not in promiscuous mode, it senses network traffic that it sends and receives (rather than all network traffic). The 5-minute input and output rates should be used only as an approximation of traffic per second during a given 5-minute period. These rates are exponentially weighted averages with a time constant of 5 minutes. A period of four time constants must pass before the average will be within 2 percent of the instantaneous rate of a uniform stream of traffic over that period.
packets input	Total number of error-free packets received by the system.

Output	Description
bytes input	Total number of bytes, including data and MAC encapsulation, in the error-free packets received by the system.
no buffers	Number of received packets discarded because there was no buffer space in the main system. Compare with "ignored count." Broadcast storms on Ethernet are often responsible for no input buffer events.
Received...broadcasts	Total number of broadcast or multicast packets received by the interface. The number of broadcasts should be kept as low as practicable. An approximate threshold is less than 20 percent of the total number of input packets.
runts	Number of Ethernet frames that are discarded because they are smaller than the minimum Ethernet frame size. Any Ethernet frame that is less than 64 bytes is considered a runt. Runts are usually caused by collisions. If there is more than one runt per million bytes received, it should be investigated.
giants	Number of Ethernet frames that are discarded because they exceed the maximum Ethernet frame size. Any Ethernet frame that is larger than 1518 bytes is considered a giant.
input error	Includes runts, giants, no buffer, cyclic redundancy check (CRC), frame, overrun, and ignored counts. Other input-related errors can also cause the input error count to be increased, and some datagrams can have more than one error. Therefore, this sum might not balance with the sum of enumerated input error counts.
CRC	CRC generated by the originating LAN station or far-end device not matching the checksum calculated from the data received. On a LAN, this usually indicates noise or transmission problems on the LAN interface or the LAN bus itself. A high number of CRCs is usually the result of collisions or a station transmitting bad data.
frame	Number of packets received incorrectly having a CRC error and a non-integer number of octets. On a LAN, this is usually the result of collisions or a malfunctioning Ethernet device.
overrun	Number of times the receiver hardware was unable to hand-receive data to a hardware buffer because the input rate exceeded the ability of the receiver to handle the data.
ignored	Number of received packets ignored by the interface because the interface hardware ran low on internal buffers. These buffers are different from the system buffers mentioned in the buffer description. Broadcast storms and bursts of noise can cause the ignored count to be increased.
input packets with dribble condition detected	Dribble bit error indicates that a frame is slightly too long. This frame error counter is incremented just for informational purposes; the router accepts the frame.
packets output	Total number of messages transmitted by the system.
bytes	Total number of bytes, including data and MAC encapsulation, transmitted by the system.

Output	Description
underruns	Number of times that the transmitter has been running faster than the router can handle. This might never be reported on some interfaces.
output errors	Sum of all errors that prevented the final transmission of datagrams out of the interface being examined. Note that this might not balance with the sum of the enumerated output errors because some datagrams might have more than one error and others might have errors that do not fall into any of the specifically tabulated categories.
collisions	Number of messages retransmitted because of an Ethernet collision. This is usually the result of an overextended LAN (Ethernet or transceiver cable too long, more than two repeaters between stations, or too many cascaded multiport transceivers). A packet that collides is counted only once in output packets.
interface resets	Number of times an interface has been completely reset. This can happen if packets queued for transmission were not sent within several seconds. On a serial line, this can be caused by a malfunctioning modem that is not supplying the transmit clock signal, or it can be caused by a cable problem. If the system notices that the carrier detect line of a serial interface is up but the line protocol is down, it periodically resets the interface in an effort to restart it. Interface resets can also occur when an interface is looped back or shut down.

Study Resources

For today's exam topics, refer to the following resources for more study.

Resource	Location	Topic
Primary Resources		
Network Basics	6	Configuring a Cisco Router
Introduction to Networks	6	Configuring a Cisco Router
Routing Protocols	1	Basic Settings on a Router
Routing and Switching Essentials	4	Basic Settings on a Router
ICND1 Official Cert Guide	15	Enabling IPv4 Support on Cisco Routers
	16	Configuring Connected Routes
ICND1 Foundation Learning Guide	12	All
Supplemental Resources		
CCENT Practice and Study Guide	6	Configuring a Cisco Router
	15	Initial Configuration of a Router
Flash Cards	5	Questions 11–25

Resource	Location	Topic
Network Simulator	12	Interface Status V
	15	Interface Status VI
		Router CLI Configuration Process
		Router CLI Exec Mode I–II
		Setting Router Passwords
		Rebuild a Configuration
	16	Configuring IP Addresses III–IV
		Configuring Router IP Settings
		Connected Routes
		New Job I
CCNA R&S Portable Companion Guide	6	All

Basic Router Configuration: IPv6

CCENT 100-101 ICND1 Exam Topics

- Configure and verify utilizing the CLI to set basic router configuration.
- Configure and verify operation status of an Ethernet interface.
- Verify router configuration and network connectivity.

Key Topic

Today we review addressing a router with IPv6 and testing network connectivity for both IPv4 and IPv6.

Basic Router Configuration with IPv6

In this section, we will use the topology shown in Figure 17-1 to review the basic commands for enabling IPv6 on a router.

Figure 17-1   IPv6 Example Topology

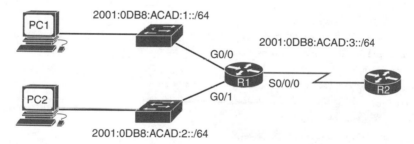

First, you must enable IPv6 routing using the following command in global configuration mode:

```
R1(config)# ipv6 unicast-routing
```

This command will, among other things, configure the router to begin listening for and responding to Neighbor Discovery (ND) messages on all active IPv6 interfaces.

To configure an IPv6 address on a router's interface, you have one of several options:

- Configure the interface to use the EUI-64 method of addressing.

    ```
    Router(config)# ipv6 address ipv6-prefix/prefix-length eui-64
    ```

- Configure the full global unicast address. To manually configure a full IPv6 address, use the following command syntax:

  ```
  Router(config)# ipv6 address ipv6-address/prefix-length
  ```

- Configure the interface as unnumbered (see Day 22, "IPv6 Addressing Concepts").

- Configure the interface as a DHCPv6 client (see Day 12, "DHCP Configuration")

NOTE: To manually configure an interface's link-local address, use the following command syntax:

```
Router(config)# ipv6 address ipv6-address/prefix-length link-local
```

Often, the preferred method is to manually configure the full IPv6 address because you can control the number of hexadecimal digits you must type when testing connectivity or troubleshooting a problem. We can see this by comparing the EUI-64 method to a full configuration. In Example 17-1, the interfaces on R1 are all configured using the EUI-64 method.

Example 17-1   Configuring Interfaces Using the EUI-64 Method

```
R1(config)# interface g0/0
R1(config-if)# ipv6 address 2001:db8:acad:1::/64 eui-64
R1(config-if)# interface g0/1
R1(config-if)# ipv6 address 2001:db8:acad:2::/64 eui-64
R1(config-if)# interface s0/0/0
R1(config-if)# ipv6 address 2001:db8:acad:3::/64 eui-64
R1(config-if)# do show ipv6 interface brief
GigabitEthernet0/0          [up/up]
    FE80::2D0:97FF:FE20:A101
    2001:DB8:ACAD:1:2D0:97FF:FE20:A101
GigabitEthernet0/1          [up/up]
    FE80::2D0:97FF:FE20:A102
    2001:DB8:ACAD:2:2D0:97FF:FE20:A102
Serial0/0/0                 [down/down]
    FE80::20C:CFFF:FE77:A401
    2001:DB8:ACAD:3:20C:CFFF:FE77:A401
<output omitted>
```

Notice the number of hexadecimal digits in the IPv6 addresses highlighted in the output from the **show ipv6 interface brief** command. Imagine having to ping the GigabitEthernet 0/0 address 2001:DB8:ACAD:1:2D0:97FF:FE20:A101.

Furthermore, notice that the link-local addresses are also rather complex. To reduce the complexity of the router's configuration, verification, and troubleshooting, it is a good practice to manually configure the link-local address as well as the IPv6 global unicast address. In Example 17-2, R1 is reconfigured with simpler IPv6 addresses and with FE80::1 as the link-local address on all interfaces. Remember, the link-local address only needs to be unique on that interface's link.

Example 17-2   Full IPv6 Address and Link-Local Address Configuration

```
R1(config-if)# interface g0/0
R1(config-if)# no ipv6 address 2001:db8:acad:1::/64 eui-64
R1(config-if)# ipv6 address 2001:db8:acad:1::1/64
R1(config-if)# ipv6 address fe80::1 link-local
R1(config-if)# interface g0/1
R1(config-if)# no ipv6 address 2001:db8:acad:2::/64 eui-64
R1(config-if)# ipv6 address 2001:db8:acad:2::1/64
R1(config-if)# ipv6 address fe80::1 link-local
R1(config-if)# interface s0/0/0
R1(config-if)# no ipv6 address 2001:db8:acad:3::/64 eui-64
R1(config-if)# ipv6 address 2001:db8:acad:3::1/64
R1(config-if)# ipv6 address fe80::1 link-local
R1(config-if)# do show ipv6 interface brief
GigabitEthernet0/0         [up/up]
    FE80::1
    2001:DB8:ACAD:1::1
GigabitEthernet0/1         [up/up]
    FE80::1
    2001:DB8:ACAD:2::1
Serial0/0/0                [down/down]
    FE80::1
    2001:DB8:ACAD:3::1
<output omitted>
```

NOTE: If you do not remove the previous IPv6 address configuration, each interface will have two IPv6 global unicast addresses. This is different than IPv4, where simply configuring another IPv4 address with the **ip address** command overwrites any previous configuration. However, there can only be one link-local address per interface.

Compare the highlighted output from the **show ipv6 interface brief** command in Example 17-2 with the output in Example 17-1. You can see that simplifying the IPv6 addressing implementation can make your verification and troubleshooting job much easier.

To verify the full configuration of an interface, use the **show ipv6 interface** command. Example 17-3 shows the output for R1's GigabitEthernet 0/0 interface.

Example 17-3   show ipv6 interface gigabitethernet 0/0 Command

```
R1# show ipv6 interface gigabitethernet 0/0
GigabitEthernet0/0 is up, line protocol is up
  IPv6 is enabled, link-local address is FE80::1
  No Virtual link-local address(es):
  Global unicast address(es):
    2001:DB8:ACAD:1::1, subnet is 2001:DB8:ACAD:1::/64
```

```
Joined group address(es):
  FF02::1
  FF02::1:FF00:1
MTU is 1500 bytes
ICMP error messages limited to one every 100 milliseconds
ICMP redirects are enabled
ICMP unreachables are sent
ND DAD is enabled, number of DAD attempts: 1
ND reachable time is 30000 milliseconds
ND advertised reachable time is 0 milliseconds
ND advertised retransmit interval is 0 milliseconds
ND router advertisements are sent every 200 seconds
ND router advertisements live for 1800 seconds
ND advertised default router preference is Medium
Hosts use stateless autoconfig for addresses.
```

Focus on the highlighted output. IPv6 is enabled on this interface with a nice, short link-local address. The global unicast address and its subnet are listed as well as the address of multicast groups that this interface automatically joined. Do you remember what the FF02::1 and FF02::1:FF00:1 addresses are used for? If not, revisit Day 22, "IPv6 Addressing Concepts."

That's all the IPv6 configurations for today. As we continue to review the exam topics in the upcoming days, we will incorporate IPv6 topics.

Verifying IPv4 and IPv6 Network Connectivity

As reviewed on Day 27, "Basic Switch Configuration," ping and traceroute are helpful tools for verifying network connectivity. Example 17-4 demonstrates successful ping output on the router.

Example 17-4   Ping Output on a Router

```
R1# ping 192.168.3.10

Type escape sequence to abort.
Sending 5, 100-byte ICMP Echos to 192.168.3.10, timeout is 2 seconds:
!!!!!
Success rate is 100 percent (5/5), round-trip min/avg/max = 1/2/4 ms
!Pinging an IPv6 destination
R1# ping 2001:db8:acad:1:290:dff:fee5:8095

Type escape sequence to abort.
```

```
Sending 5, 100-byte ICMP Echos to 2001:DB8:ACAD:1:290:CFF:FEE5:8095, timeout is 2
  seconds:
!!!!!
Success rate is 100 percent (5/5), round-trip min/avg/max = 0/9/46 ms

R1#
```

Unsuccessful ping output shows periods (.) instead of exclamation points (!), as demonstrated in Example 17-5. The output would be the same for IPv6.

Example 17-5   Unsuccessful Ping Output on a Router

```
R1# ping 192.168.3.2

Type escape sequence to abort.
Sending 5, 100-byte ICMP Echos to 192.168.3.2, timeout is 2 seconds:
.....
Success rate is 0 percent (0/5)
R1#
```

Example 17-6 shows output from a successful **traceroute** command.

Example 17-6   traceroute Output on a Router

```
R1# traceroute 192.168.3.10
Type escape sequence to abort.
Tracing the route to 192.168.3.10

  1    192.168.2.2      71 msec    70 msec    72 msec
  2    192.168.3.10     111 msec  133 msec   115 msec
R1#
!Tracing to an IPv6 destination.
R2# traceroute 2001:db8:acad:1:290:cff:fee5:8095
Type escape sequence to abort.
Tracing the route to 2001:DB8:ACAD:1:290:CFF:FEE5:8095

  1    2001:DB8:ACAD:3::11 msec    1 msec    1 msec
  2    2001:DB8:ACAD:1:290:CFF:FEE5:80951 msec    1 msec    0 msec
R2#
```

Unsuccessful traces will show the last successful hop and the asterisks for each attempt until the user cancels. To cancel the **traceroute** command on a router, press the key combination **Ctrl-Shift-6** and then the **x** key. Example 17-7 shows unsuccessful **traceroute** output. The output would be the same for IPv6.

Example 17-7   Unsuccessful traceroute Output on a Router

```
R1# traceroute 192.168.3.2
Type escape sequence to abort.
Tracing the route to 192.168.3.2

  1   192.168.2.2      71 msec    70 msec    72 msec
  2   *       *       *
  3   *       *       *
  4   *       *       *
  5   *
R1#
```

Using Telnet or SSH to remotely access another device also tests connectivity. More importantly, these remote access methods will test whether a device has been correctly configured so that you can access it for management purposes. This can be very important when a device is truly remote (for example, across town or in another city). Day 27 reviews SSH configuration and verification in greater detail.

During our basic configuration tasks earlier, we entered the commands to properly configure the vty lines for SSH remote access. If accessing a device configured with SSH from a PC, you use the SSH setting in your terminal client. However, you can use the **ssh** command on a router or switch to access another device configured with SSH. Example 17-8 shows how to use SSH to remotely access R2 from R1.

Example 17-8   Remote Access Using SSH

```
R1# ssh ?
  -c    Select encryption algorithm
  -l    Log in using this user name
  -m    Select HMAC algorithm
  -o    Specify options
  -p    Connect to this port
  -v    Specify SSH Protocol Version
  -vrf  Specify vrf name
  WORD  IP address or hostname of a remote system

R1# ssh -l ?
  WORD  Login name

R1# ssh -l admin ?
  -c    Select encryption algorithm
  -m    Select HMAC algorithm
  -o    Specify options
  -p    Connect to this port
  -v    Specify SSH Protocol Version
```

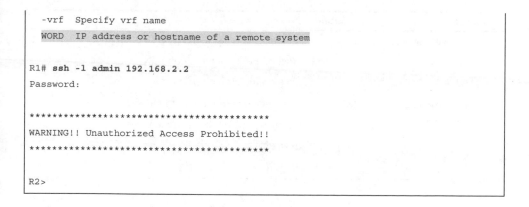

```
  -vrf   Specify vrf name
  WORD   IP address or hostname of a remote system

R1# ssh -l admin 192.168.2.2
Password:


*********************************************
WARNING!! Unauthorized Access Prohibited!!
*********************************************


R2>
```

NOTE: During your CCENT studies and lab practice, you more than likely used a Telnet configuration to remotely access your lab equipment. Although Telnet is easier to use than SSH, remember that SSH is considered best practice. Therefore during the CCENT exam, be ready to use SSH to remotely access devices on simulation questions as Telnet might not be configured or allowed.

Study Resources

For today's exam topics, refer to the following resources for more study.

Resource	Location	Topic
Primary Resources		
Network Basics	7	IPv6 Unicast Addresses
Introduction to Networks	8	IPv6 Unicast Addresses
Routing Protocols	1	Basic Settings on a Router
Routing and Switching Essentials	4	Basic Settings on a Router
ICND1 Official Cert Guide	18	Testing Connectivity with ping, traceroute, and telnet
	27	All
ICND1 Foundation Learning Guide	20	IPv6 Routing
Supplemental Resources		
CCENT Practice and Study Guide	8	IPv6 Unicast Addresses
	15	Initial Configuration of a Router
Flash Cards	12	Questions 27–29

Resource	Location	Topic
Network Simulator	27	Configuring IPv6 Addresses I–III
		IPv6 Address Configuration I–IX
		IPv6 Configuration I–II
CCNA R&S Portable Command Guide	16	Assigning IPv6 Addresses to Interfaces
		Verifying and Troubleshooting IPv6
		IPv6 Ping
		IPv6 Traceroute

Static and Default Route Configuration

CCENT 100-101 ICND1 Exam Topics

- Configure and verify routing configuration for a static or default route given specific routing requirements.

Key Topics

Today we focus on static and default routing for IPv4 and IPv6. Static routes are a common part of an enterprise's routing policy. Static routes can be used to force traffic to use a specific path or to establish a default route out of the enterprise. Static routes are hard-coded into the routing table by the network administrator. Thus, a network administrator must monitor and maintain static routes to ensure connectivity.

Static and Default Routing Overview

When a router configured with a dynamic routing protocol can learn routes from other routers without any additional input from the network administrator, why would you use static routing? Situations vary and there can be other reasons unique to a particular implementation, but in general:

- Use static routes:
    - In a small network that requires only simple routing
    - In a hub-and-spoke network topology
    - When you want to create a quick ad hoc route
    - As a backup when there is failure on the primary route
- Do not use static routes:
    - In a large network
    - When the network is expected to scale

Static routes are commonly used when you are routing from a larger network to a stub network (a network that is accessed by a single link). Static routes can also be useful for specifying a default route or "gateway of last resort." For example, in Figure 16-1, R2 is attached to a stub network.

Figure 16-1   Example of a Stub Network

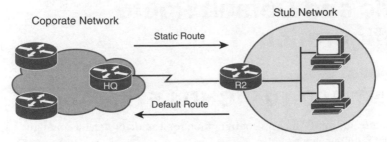

In Figure 16-1, there is no other route out of the stub network except to send packets to HQ. So it makes sense to configure R2 with a default route pointing out the interface attached to HQ. Similarly, there is only one way for HQ to route packets destined for the stub network attached to R2. So it makes sense to configure HQ with a static route pointing out the interface attached to R2. Yes, you could configure both routers with a dynamic routing protocol. But it can introduce a level of complexity that might not be necessary in a stub network situation.

IPv4 Static Route Configuration

To configure a static route, use the **ip route** command with the following relevant syntax:

```
Router(config)# ip route network-address subnet-mask {ip-address | exit-interface}}
    [administrative-distance]
```

The explanation for each parameter is as follows:

- *network-address*: The destination network address of the remote network to be added to the routing table.

- *subnet-mask*: The subnet mask of the remote network to be added to the routing table. The subnet mask can be modified to summarize a group of networks.

One or both of the following parameters are used:

- *ip-address*: Commonly referred to as the next-hop router's IP address

- *exit-interface*: Outgoing interface that would be used in forwarding packets to the destination network

Also shown is the *administrative-distance* optional parameter. This is used when configuring a floating static route, as we will see later in today's review.

Figure 16-2 shows the topology we will use today to review static and default routing.

Figure 16-2   Static and Default Routing IPv4 Topology

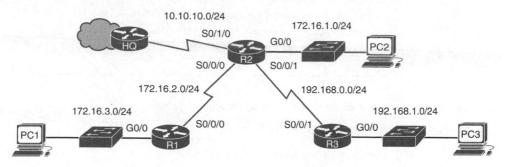

Table 16-1 shows the IPv4 addressing scheme we will use with the topology shown in Figure 16-2.

Table 16-1   IPv4 Addressing Scheme

Device	Interface	IP Address	Subnet Mask	Default Gateway
HQ	S0/0/0	10.10.10.1	255.255.255.0	—
R1	G0/0	172.16.3.1	255.255.255.0	—
	S0/0/0	172.16.2.2	255.255.255.0	—
R2	G0/0	172.16.1.1	255.255.255.0	—
	S0/0/0	172.16.2.1	255.255.255.0	—
	S0/0/1	192.168.0.1	255.255.255.0	—
	S0/1/0	10.10.10.2	255.255.255.0	—
R3	G0/0	192.168.1.1	255.255.255.0	—
	S0/0/1	192.168.0.2	255.255.255.0	—
PC1	NIC	172.16.3.10	255.255.255.0	172.16.3.1
PC2	NIC	172.16.1.10	255.255.255.0	172.16.1.1
PC3	NIC	192.168.2.10	255.255.255.0	192.168.2.1

Assume that R1 is configured and knows about its own directly connected networks. Example 16-1 shows the routing table for R1 before any static routing is configured.

Example 16-1   R1 Routing Table Before Static Routes Are Configured

```
R1# show ip route
<output omitted>


Gateway of last resort is not set

    172.16.0.0/16 is variably subnetted, 4 subnets, 2 masks
```

```
C        172.16.2.0/24 is directly connected, Serial0/0/0
L        172.16.2.2/32 is directly connected, Serial0/0/0
C        172.16.3.0/24 is directly connected, GigabitEthernet0/0
L        172.16.3.1/32 is directly connected, GigabitEthernet0/0
R1#
```

The remote networks that R1 does not know about are as follows:

- 172.16.1.0/24: The LAN on R2

- 192.168.0.0/24: The serial network between R2 and R3

- 192.168.1.0/24: The LAN on R3

- 10.10.10.0/24: The serial network between R2 and HQ

- 0.0.0.0/0: All other networks accessible through HQ

IPv4 Static Routes Using the "Next-Hop" Parameter

Using the "next-hop" parameter, R1 can be configured with three static routes—one for each of the networks R1 does not yet know about. Example 16-2 shows the command syntax.

Example 16-2   Static Route Configuration with "Next-Hop" Parameter

```
R1(config)# ip route 172.16.1.0 255.255.255.0 172.16.2.1
R1(config)# ip route 192.168.0.0 255.255.255.0 172.16.2.1
R1(config)# ip route 192.168.1.0 255.255.255.0 172.16.2.1
R1(config)# ip route 10.10.10.0 255.255.255.0 172.16.2.1
```

The interface that routes to the next hop must be "up" and "up" before the static routes can be entered in the routing table. Example 16-3 verifies that the static routes are now in the routing table.

Example 16-3   R1 Routing Table After Static Routes Are Configured

```
R1# show ip route
<output omitted>

Gateway of last resort is not set

     10.0.0.0/24 is subnetted, 1 subnets
S       10.10.10.0/24 [1/0] via 172.16.2.1
     172.16.0.0/16 is variably subnetted, 5 subnets, 2 masks
S       172.16.1.0/24 [1/0] via 172.16.2.1
```

```
C        172.16.2.0/24 is directly connected, Serial0/0/0
L        172.16.2.2/32 is directly connected, Serial0/0/0
C        172.16.3.0/24 is directly connected, GigabitEthernet0/0
L        172.16.3.1/32 is directly connected, GigabitEthernet0/0
S     192.168.0.0/24 [1/0] via 172.16.2.1
S     192.168.1.0/24 [1/0] via 172.16.2.1
R1#
```

With using the next-hop parameter, the router must have a route in the table to the network that the next-hop address belongs to. Highlighted in Example 16-3, we see that R1 does indeed have a route to the 172.16.2.0/24 network, which includes the next-hop address 172.16.2.1. However, configuring a next-hop address requires the router to perform a recursive lookup to find the exit interface before it can send the packet out the Serial 0/0/0 interface.

IPv4 Static Routes Using the Exit Interface Parameter

To avoid a recursive lookup and have a router immediately send packets to the exit interface, configure the static route using the exit-interface parameter instead of the next-hop (*ip-address*) parameter.

For example, on R2, we can configure static routes to the R1 and R3 LANs by specifying the exit interface:

```
R2(config)# ip route 172.16.3.0 255.255.255.0 serial 0/0/0
R2(config)# ip route 192.168.1.0 255.255.255.0 serial 0/0/1
```

Any previous static routes to this network using a next-hop IP address should be removed. R2 now has two static routes in its routing table, as shown in Example 16-4, that it can use immediately to route to the 172.16.3.0/24 and 192.168.1.0/24 networks without having to do a recursive route lookup.

Example 16-4   R2 Routing Table After Static Route Is Configured

```
R2# show ip route
<output omitted>


Gateway of last resort is not set


     10.0.0.0/8 is variably subnetted, 2 subnets, 2 masks
C        10.10.10.0/24 is directly connected, Serial0/1/0
L        10.10.10.2/32 is directly connected, Serial0/1/0
     172.16.0.0/16 is variably subnetted, 5 subnets, 2 masks
```

```
C        172.16.1.0/24 is directly connected, GigabitEthernet0/0
L        172.16.1.1/32 is directly connected, GigabitEthernet0/0
C        172.16.2.0/24 is directly connected, Serial0/0/0
L        172.16.2.1/32 is directly connected, Serial0/0/0
S        172.16.3.0/24 is directly connected, Serial0/0/0
      192.168.0.0/24 is variably subnetted, 2 subnets, 2 masks
C        192.168.0.0/24 is directly connected, Serial0/0/1
L        192.168.0.1/32 is directly connected, Serial0/0/1
S     192.168.1.0/24 is directly connected, Serial0/0/1
R2#
```

NOTE: Although the highlighted output in Example 16-4 shows that the routes are "direct-ly connected," technically that is not true. However, as far as R2 is concerned, the exit inter-face is the way to get to the destination, much like truly directly connected routes. Another benefit to using the exit interface configuration as opposed to the next-hop address con-figuration is that the static route does not depend upon the IP address stability of the next hop. Most of the time, using the exit interface configuration is the best practice. And so we will use the exit interface configuration for all static and default routes as we continue with today's and the remaining days' reviews.

IPv4 Default Route Configuration

A default route is a special kind of static route used to represent all routes with zero or no bits matching. In other words, when there are no routes that have a more specific match in the routing table, the default route will be a match.

The destination IP address of a packet can match multiple routes in the routing table. For example, consider having the following two static routes in the routing table:

```
172.16.0.0/24 is subnetted, 3 subnets
S        172.16.1.0 is directly connected, Serial0/0/0
S        172.16.0.0/16 is directly connected, Serial0/0/1
```

A packet destined for 172.16.1.10, the packet's destination IP address, matches both routes. However, the 172.16.1.0 route is the more specific route because the destination matches the first 24 bits, whereas the destination matches only the first 16 bits of the 172.16.0.0 route. Therefore, the router will use the route with the most specific match.

A default route is a route that will match all packets. Commonly called a quad-zero route, a default route uses 0.0.0.0 (thus, the term *quad-zero*) for both the network-address and subnet-mask parameter, as shown in this syntax:

```
Router(config)# ip route 0.0.0.0 0.0.0.0 {ip-address | exit-interface}
```

Referring to the topology shown in Figure 16-2, assume that HQ has a connection to the Internet. From the perspective of R2, all default traffic can be sent to HQ for routing out-side the domain known to R2.

The following command configures R2 with a default route pointing to HQ:

```
R2(config)# ip route 0.0.0.0 0.0.0.0 serial 0/1/0
```

R2 now has a "gateway of last resort" listed in the routing table—a candidate default route indicated by the asterisk (*) next to the S code, as shown in Example 16-5.

Example 16-5   R2 Routing Table After Default Route Is Configured

```
R2# show ip route
<some codes omitted>
        * - candidate default, U - per-user static route, o - ODR
        P - periodic downloaded static route

Gateway of last resort is 0.0.0.0 to network 0.0.0.0

     10.0.0.0/8 is variably subnetted, 2 subnets, 2 masks
C       10.10.10.0/24 is directly connected, Serial0/1/0
L       10.10.10.2/32 is directly connected, Serial0/1/0
     172.16.0.0/16 is variably subnetted, 5 subnets, 2 masks
C       172.16.1.0/24 is directly connected, GigabitEthernet0/0
L       172.16.1.1/32 is directly connected, GigabitEthernet0/0
C       172.16.2.0/24 is directly connected, Serial0/0/0
L       172.16.2.1/32 is directly connected, Serial0/0/0
S       172.16.3.0/24 is directly connected, Serial0/0/0
     192.168.0.0/24 is variably subnetted, 2 subnets, 2 masks
C       192.168.0.0/24 is directly connected, Serial0/0/1
L       192.168.0.1/32 is directly connected, Serial0/0/1
S    192.168.1.0/24 is directly connected, Serial0/0/1
S*   0.0.0.0/0 is directly connected, Serial0/1/0
R2#
```

From R1 and R3's perspective, R2 is the default route. The following commands configure R1 and R3 with a default route pointing to R2:

```
R1(config)# ip route 0.0.0.0 0.0.0.0 serial 0/0/0
!
R3(config)# ip route 0.0.0.0 0.0.0.0 serial 0/0/1
```

Again, we can verify that the default route is now in the routing table for R1, as shown in Example 16-6.

Example 16-6   R1 and R3 Routing Tables After Default Route Is Configured

```
!R1!!!!!!!!!!!!
R1# show ip route
<some codes omitted>
       * - candidate default, U - per-user static route, o - ODR
       P - periodic downloaded static route


Gateway of last resort is 0.0.0.0 to network 0.0.0.0


    172.16.0.0/16 is variably subnetted, 4 subnets, 2 masks
C       172.16.2.0/24 is directly connected, Serial0/0/0
L       172.16.2.2/32 is directly connected, Serial0/0/0
C       172.16.3.0/24 is directly connected, GigabitEthernet0/0
L       172.16.3.1/32 is directly connected, GigabitEthernet0/0
S*   0.0.0.0/0 is directly connected, Serial0/0/0
R1#
!
!R3!!!!!!!!!!!!
R3# show ip route
<some codes omitted>
       * - candidate default, U - per-user static route, o - ODR
       P - periodic downloaded static route


Gateway of last resort is 0.0.0.0 to network 0.0.0.0


    192.168.0.0/24 is variably subnetted, 2 subnets, 2 masks
C       192.168.0.0/24 is directly connected, Serial0/0/1
L       192.168.0.2/32 is directly connected, Serial0/0/1
    192.168.1.0/24 is variably subnetted, 2 subnets, 2 masks
C       192.168.1.0/24 is directly connected, GigabitEthernet0/0
L       192.168.1.1/32 is directly connected, GigabitEthernet0/0
S*   0.0.0.0/0 is directly connected, Serial0/0/1
R3#
```

After evaluating the complete routing tables for R1, R2, and R3 shown in Examples 16-5 and 16-6, you can see that R1 and R3 only need one route out—a default route. R2 acts as a hub router to the R1 and R3 spokes. Therefore, it needs two static routes pointing to the R1 and R3 LANs. R2 also has a route out to HQ for any destinations it does not know about. But what about HQ? Currently, HQ does not have routes back to any of the networks accessible through R2. So any traffic from PC1, PC2, and PC3 is currently confined to the R1, R2, and R3 networks. None of these PCs can ping the HQ interface address 10.10.10.1. In the traceroute output shown in Example 16-7, failure occurs after R2 responds. This is because HQ receives the ICMP requests from PC1 but does not have a route back to the 172.16.3.0/24 network. Therefore, HQ is dropping the packets.

Example 16-7   traceroute from PC1 to HQ Fails

```
C:\> tracert 10.10.10.1


Tracing route to 10.10.10.1 over a maximum of 30 hops:

  1    0 ms       0 ms       1 ms      172.16.3.1
  2    0 ms       0 ms       1 ms      172.16.2.1
  3    *          *          *         Request timed out.
  4    ^C
C:\>
```

Let's configure HQ with static routes to complete the static route configuration for the topology shown in Figure 16-2.

IPv4 Summary Static Route Configuration

Before configuring five separate static routes for each of the networks shown in Figure 16-2, notice that the 172.16 networks can be summarized into one route and that the 192.168 networks can be summarized into one route. We reviewed summary routes on Day 23, "IPv4 Subnetting and VLSM," so we will not detail the process here. Example 16-8 shows the five routes in binary with the bits in common highlighted.

Example 16-8   Summary Route Calculation for HQ Static Routes

```
Summary calculation for the 172.16 networks:
10101100.00010000.00000001.00000000
10101100.00010000.00000010.00000000
10101100.00010000.00000011.00000000
Summary calculation for the 192.168 networks:
11000000.10101000.00000000.00000000
11000000.10101000.00000001.00000000
```

So, the summary route for the 172.16 networks is 172.16.0.0/22 because the three network addresses have 22 bits in common. Although not part of the current addressing scheme, this summary static route would also include the route 172.16.0.0/24. The summary route for the 192.168 networks is 192.168.0.0/23 because the two network addresses have 23 bits in common.

You can now configure HQ with two summary static routes instead of five individual static routes:

```
HQ(config)# ip route 172.16.0.0 255.255.252.0 serial 0/0/0
HQ(config)# ip route 192.168.0.0 255.255.254.0 Serial0/0/0
```

Now PC1 can successfully trace a route to the HQ interface, as shown in Example 16-9.

Example 16-9   traceroute from PC1 to HQ Succeeds

```
C:\> tracert 10.10.10.1

Tracing route to 10.10.10.1 over a maximum of 30 hops:

  1   1 ms       0 ms       0 ms       172.16.3.1
  2   0 ms       1 ms       2 ms       172.16.2.1
  3   1 ms       2 ms       1 ms       10.10.10.1

Trace complete.

C:\>
```

The trace is successful because HQ now has a route back to PC1's network, as shown in Example 16-10.

Example 16-10 HQ Routing Table with IPv4 Summary Static Routes

```
HQ# show ip route
<output omitted>

Gateway of last resort is not set

     10.0.0.0/8 is variably subnetted, 2 subnets, 2 masks
C       10.10.10.0/24 is directly connected, Serial0/0/0
L       10.10.10.1/32 is directly connected, Serial0/0/0
     172.16.0.0/22 is subnetted, 1 subnets
S        172.16.0.0/22 is directly connected, Serial0/0/0
S    192.168.0.0/23 is directly connected, Serial0/0/
HQ#
```

IPv6 Static Routing

Static routing with IPv6 is very similar to IPv4. We will use the same topology but change the addressing to IPv6, as shown in Figure 16-3.

Table 16-2 shows the IPv6 addressing scheme we will use with the topology shown in Figure 16-3.

Figure 16-3   Static and Default Routing IPv6 Topology

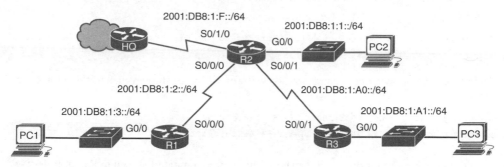

Table 16-2   IPv6 Addressing Scheme

Device	Interface	IPv6 Address/Prefix	Default Gateway
HQ	S0/0/0	2001:DB8:1:F::1/64	—
	Link-local	FE80::F	
R1	G0/0	2001:DB8:1:3::1/64	—
	S0/0/0	2001:DB8:1:2::2/64	—
		FE80::1	
R2	G0/0	2001:DB8:1:1::1/64	—
	S0/0/0	2001:DB8:1:2::1/64	—
	S0/0/1	2001:DB8:1:A0::1/64	—
	S0/1/0	2001:DB8:1:F::2/64	—
	Link-local	FE80::2	
R3	G0/0	2001:DB8:1:A1::1/64	—
	S0/0/1	2001:DB8:1:A0::2/64	—
	Link-local	FE80::3	—
PC1	NIC	2001:DB8:1:3:209:7CFF:FE9A:1A87/64	FE80::1
PC2	NIC	2001:DB8:1:1:204:9AFF:FEE3:C943/64	FE80::2
PC3	NIC	2001:DB8:1:A1:201:C9FF:FEE5:D3A/64	FE80::3

NOTE: The IPv6 addressing for the PCs is set to autoconfiguration. Pinging from PC to PC would not really be much fun. However, the IPv6 addresses are not manually set so that you can practice your knowledge of how EUI-64 works. Can you figure out what the MAC address is for each PC? If not, review Day 21, "Implementing IPv6 Addressing." (Hint: FFFE and flip the bit.) Then, if you are following along using a simulator, you might want to consider manually configuring the PCs with easier IPv6 addresses—2001:DB8:1:3::A/64 on PC1, for example. This will greatly improve your pinging experience.

IPv6 Static Route Configuration

The command syntax for IPv6 static routing is similar to IPv4:

```
Router(config)# ipv6 route ipv6-prefix/prefix-length {ipv6-address | exit-interface}
  [administrative-distance]
```

Therefore, the following commands would configure R2 with static routes to the R1 and R3 LANs:

```
R2(config)# ipv6 route 2001:DB8:1:3::/64 Serial0/0/0
R2(config)# ipv6 route 2001:DB8:1:A1::/64 Serial0/0/1
```

As highlighted in the output from the **show ipv6 route** command shown in Example 16-11, R2 now has routes in the routing table to the R1 and R3 LANs.

Example 16-11 R2 IPv6 Routing Table After Static Routes Are Configured

```
R2# show ipv6 route
IPv6 Routing Table - 11 entries
<code output omitted>
C   2001:DB8:1:1::/64 [0/0]
     via ::, GigabitEthernet0/0
L   2001:DB8:1:1::1/128 [0/0]
     via ::, GigabitEthernet0/0
C   2001:DB8:1:2::/64 [0/0]
     via ::, Serial0/0/0
L   2001:DB8:1:2::1/128 [0/0]
     via ::, Serial0/0/0
S   2001:DB8:1:3::/64 [1/0]
     via ::, Serial0/0/0
C   2001:DB8:1:F::/64 [0/0]
     via ::, Serial0/1/0
L   2001:DB8:1:F::2/128 [0/0]
     via ::, Serial0/1/0
C   2001:DB8:1:A0::/64 [0/0]
     via ::, Serial0/0/1
L   2001:DB8:1:A0::1/128 [0/0]
     via ::, Serial0/0/1
S   2001:DB8:1:A1::/64 [1/0]
     via ::, Serial0/0/1
L   FF00::/8 [0/0]
     via ::, Null0
```

IPv6 Default Route Configuration

The following is the command syntax for an IPv6 default route:

```
Router(config)# ipv6 route ::/0 {ipv6-address | exit-interface}
```

Just like the quad-zero in IPv4, the double colon (::) means all 0s or any address and the /0 means any prefix length.

Continuing with our example in Figure 16-3, we would configure R1, R2, and R3 with the following default routes:

```
R1(config)# ipv6 route ::/0 serial 0/0/0
R2(config)# ipv6 route ::/0 serial 0/1/0
R3(config)# ipv6 route ::/0 serial 0/0/1
```

The highlights in Example 16-12 show the default routes for R1, R2, and R3.

Example 16-12 Default Routes in the Routing Tables for R1, R2, and R3

```
!R1!!!!!!!!!!!!
R1# show ipv6 route
IPv6 Routing Table - 6 entries
<code output omitted>
S    ::/0 [1/0]
     via ::, Serial0/0/0
<output for connected and local routes omitted>


!R2!!!!!!!!!!!!
R2# show ipv6 route
IPv6 Routing Table - 12 entries
<code output omitted>
S    ::/0 [1/0]
     via ::, Serial0/1/0
S    2001:DB8:1:3::/64 [1/0]
     via ::, Serial0/0/0
S    2001:DB8:1:A1::/64 [1/0]
     via ::, Serial0/0/1
<output for connected and local routes omitted>


!R3!!!!!!!!!!!!
R3# show ipv6 route
IPv6 Routing Table - 6 entries
<code output omitted>
S    ::/0 [1/0]
     via ::, Serial0/0/1
<output for connected and local routes omitted>
```

IPv6 Summary Static Route Configuration

Similar to the IPv4 static routing scenario, HQ can be configured with two summary static routes to the R1, R2, and R3 LANs. Example 16-13 shows the first four hextet (64 bits) of the five routes in binary with the bits in common highlighted.

Example 16-13 Summary Route Calculation for HQ Static Routes

```
Summary calculation for the first four hextets of 2001:DB8:1:1::/64,
  2001:DB8:1:2::/64, and 2001:DB8:1:3::/64 networks:
0010000000000001:0000110110111000:0000000000000001: 0000000000000001:<4 all-0s
  hextets>
0010000000000001:0000110110111000:0000000000000001: 0000000000000010:<4 all-0s
  hextets>
0010000000000001:0000110110111000:0000000000000001: 0000000000000011:<4 all-0s
  hextets>
Summary calculation for the first four hextets of 2001:DB8:1:A0::/64 and
  2001:DB8:1:A1::/64 networks:
0010000000000001:0000110110111000:0000000000000001: 000000001010 0000:<4 all-0s
  hextets>
0010000000000001:0000110110111000:0000000000000001: 000000001010 0001:<4 all-0s
  hextets>
```

So, the first summary route is 2001:DB8:1::/62 because the three network addresses have 62 bits in common. Although not part of the current addressing scheme, this summary static route would also include the network 2001:DB8:1::/64. The second summary route is 2001:DB8:1:A0::/63 because the two network addresses have 63 bits in common.

You can now configure HQ with the following two summary static routes:

```
HQ(config)# ipv6 route 2001:DB8:1::/62 Serial0/0/0
HQ(config)# ipv6 route 2001:DB8:1:A0::/63 Serial0/0/0
```

Now HQ has two summary routes, as shown in the highlighted entries in Example 16-14.

Example 16-14 HQ Routing Table with IPv6 Summary Static Routes

```
HQ# show ipv6 route
IPv6 Routing Table - 5 entries
<output omitted>
S    2001:DB8:1::/62 [1/0]
     via ::, Serial0/0/0
C    2001:DB8:1:F::/64 [0/0]
     via ::, Serial0/0/0
L    2001:DB8:1:F::1/128 [0/0]
     via ::, Serial0/0/0
S    2001:DB8:1:A0::/63 [1/0]
     via ::, Serial0/0/0
```

```
L    FF00::/8 [0/0]
     via ::, Null0
HQ#
```

Study Resources

For today's exam topics, refer to the following resources for more study.

Resource	Chapter	Section or Topic
Primary Resources		
Routing Protocols	2	All
Routing and Switching Essentials	6	All
IPv6 Fundamentals	7	Configuring IPv6 Static Routes
ICND1 Official Cert Guide	16	Configuring Static Routes
	29	Static IPv6 Routes
ICND1 Foundation Learning Guide	13	All
	20	IPv6 Routing
Supplemental Resources		
CCENT Practice and Study Guide	17	All
Flash Cards	5	Questions 43–47
Network Simulator	16	Default Routes I–II
		Static Routes I–V
		Static Routing I–II
CCNA R&S Portable Companion Guide	7	All (IPv4)
	16	Static Routes (IPv6)
		Floating Static Routes (IPv6)
		Default Routes (IPv6)

Single-Area OSPFv2

CCENT 100-101 ICND1 Exam Topics

- Configure and verify OSPF (single-area).

Key Topics

Open Shortest Path First (OSPF) is a link-state routing protocol that was developed as a replacement for Routing Information Protocol (RIP). OSPF's major advantages over RIP are its fast convergence and its scalability to much larger network implementations. Today we review the operation, configuration, verification, and troubleshooting of basic OSPF.

OSPF Operation

The Internet Engineering Task Force (IETF) chose OSPF over Intermediate System–to–Intermediate System (IS-IS) as its recommended interior gateway protocol (IGP). In 1998, the OSPFv2 specification was updated in RFC 2328 and is the current RFC for OSPF. RFC 2328, "OSPF Version 2," is on the IETF website at www.ietf.org/rfc/rfc2328. Cisco IOS Software will choose OSPF routes over RIP routes because OSPF has an administrative distance of 110 versus RIP's AD of 120.

OSPF Message Format

The data portion of an OSPF message is encapsulated in a packet. This data field can include one of five OSPF packet types. Figure 15-1 shows an encapsulated OSPF message in an Ethernet frame.

The OSPF packet header is included with every OSPF packet, regardless of its type. The OSPF packet header and packet type-specific data are then encapsulated in an IP packet. In the IP packet header, the protocol field is set to 89 to indicate OSPF, and the destination address is typically set to one of two multicast addresses: 224.0.0.5 or 224.0.0.6. If the OSPF packet is encapsulated in an Ethernet frame, the destination MAC address is also a multicast address: 01-00-5E-00-00-05 or 01-00-5E-00-00-06.

Figure 15-1   Encapsulated OSPF Message

Data Link Frame Header	IP Packet Header	OSPF Packet Header	OSPF Packet Type-Specific Data

Data Link Frame (Ethernet Fields Shown Here)

MAC Source Address = Address of Sending Interface
MAC Destination Address = Multicast: 01-00-5E-00-00-05 or 01-00-5E-00-00-06

IP Packet

IP Source Address = Address of Sending Interface
IP Destination Address = Multicast: 224.0.0.5 or 224.0.0.6
Protocol Field = 89 for OSPF

OSPF Packet Header

Type Code for OSPF Packet Type
Router ID and Area ID

OSPF Packet Types

0x01 Hello
0x02 Database Description
0x03 Link State Request
0x04 Link State Update
0x05 Link State Acknowledgment

OSPF Packet Types

These five OSPF packet types each serve a specific purpose in the routing process:

- **Hello:** Hello packets are used to establish and maintain adjacency with other OSPF routers.

- **DBD:** The database description (DBD) packet contains an abbreviated list of the sending router's link-state database and is used by receiving routers to check against the local link-state database.

- **LSR:** Receiving routers can then request more information about any entry in the DBD by sending a link-state request (LSR).

- **LSU:** Link-state update (LSU) packets are used to reply to LSRs and to announce new information. LSUs contain 11 types of link-state advertisements (LSA).

- **LSAck:** When an LSU is received, the router sends a link-state acknowledgment (LSAck) to confirm receipt of the LSU.

Neighbor Establishment

Hello packets are exchanged between OSPF neighbors to establish adjacency. Figure 15-2 shows the OSPF header and Hello packet.

Figure 15-2   OSPF Packet Header and Hello Packet

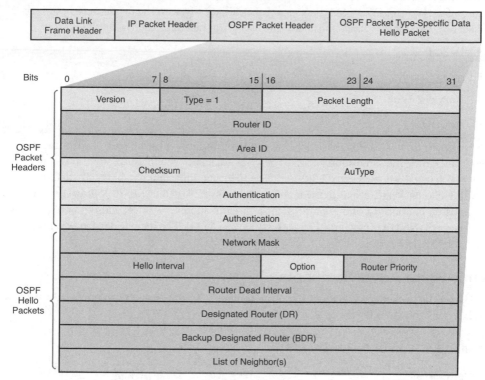

Important fields shown in the figure include the following:

- **Type:** OSPF packet type: Hello (Type 1), DBD (Type 2), LS Request (Type 3), LS Update (Type 4), LS ACK (Type 5)

- **Router ID:** ID of the originating router

- **Area ID:** Area from which the packet originated

- **Network Mask:** Subnet mask associated with the sending interface

- **Hello Interval:** Number of seconds between the sending router's Hellos

- **Router Priority:** Used in DR/BDR election

- **Designated Router (DR):** Router ID of the DR, if any

- **Backup Designated Router (BDR):** Router ID of the BDR, if any

- **List of Neighbors:** Lists the OSPF Router ID of the neighboring router(s)

Hello packets are used to do the following:

- Discover OSPF neighbors and establish neighbor adjacencies

- Advertise parameters on which two routers must agree to become neighbors

- Elect the DR and BDR on multiaccess networks such as Ethernet and Frame Relay

Receiving an OSPF Hello packet on an interface confirms for a router that another OSPF router exists on this link. OSPF then establishes adjacency with the neighbor. To establish adjacency, two OSPF routers must have the following matching interface values:

- Hello Interval
- Dead Interval
- Network Type
- Area ID

Before both routers can establish adjacency, both interfaces must be part of the same network, including the same subnet mask. Then full adjacency will happen after both routers have exchanged any necessary LSUs and have identical link-state databases. By default, OSPF Hello packets are sent to the multicast address 224.0.0.5 (*ALLSPFRouters*) every 10 seconds on multiaccess and point-to-point segments and every 30 seconds on nonbroadcast multiaccess (NBMA) segments (Frame Relay, X.25, ATM). The default dead interval is four times the Hello interval.

Link-State Advertisements

LSUs are the packets used for OSPF routing updates. An LSU packet can contain 11 types of LSAs, as shown in Figure 15-3.

Figure 15-3   LSUs Contain LSAs

Type	Packet Name	Description
1	Hello	Discovers neighbors and builds adjacencies between them.
2	DBD	Checks for database synchronization between routers.
3	LSR	Requests specific link-state records from router to router.
4	LSU	Sends specifically requested link-state records.
5	LSAck	Acknowledges the other packet types.

The acronyms LSA and LSU are often used interchangeably.

An LSU contains one or more LSAs.

LSAs contain route information for destination networks.

LSA specifics are discussed in CCNP.

LSA Type	Description
1	Router LSAs
2	Network LSAs
3 or 4	Summary LSAs
5	Autonomous System External LSAs
6	Multicast OSPF LSAs
7	Defined for Not-So-Stubby Areas
8	External Attributes LSA for Border Gateway Protocol (BGP)
9, 10, 11	Opaque LSAs

OSPF DR and BDR

Multiaccess networks create two challenges for OSPF regarding the flooding of LSAs:

- Creation of multiple adjacencies, one adjacency for every pair of routers

- Extensive flooding of LSAs

The solution to managing the number of adjacencies and the flooding of LSAs on a multiaccess network is the designated router (DR). To reduce the amount of OSPF traffic on multiaccess networks, OSPF elects a DR and backup DR (BDR). The DR is responsible for updating all other OSPF routers when a change occurs in the multiaccess network. The BDR monitors the DR and takes over as DR if the current DR fails. All other routers become DROTHERs. A DROTHER is a router that is neither the DR nor the BDR.

OSPF Algorithm

Each OSPF router maintains a link-state database containing the LSAs received from all other routers. When a router has received all the LSAs and built its local link-state database, OSPF uses Dijkstra's shortest path first (SPF) algorithm to create an SPF tree. This algorithm accumulates costs along each path, from source to destination. The SPF tree is then used to populate the IP routing table with the best paths to each network.

For example, in Figure 15-4, each path is labeled with an arbitrary value for cost. The cost of the shortest path for R2 to send packets to the LAN attached to R3 is 27 (20 + 5 + 2 = 27). Notice that this cost is not 27 for all routers to reach the LAN attached to R3. Each router determines its own cost to each destination in the topology. In other words, each router uses the SPF algorithm to calculate the cost of each path to a network and determines the best path to that network from its own perspective.

Table 15-1 lists the shortest path to each LAN for R1, along with the cost.

Table 15-1   SPF Tree for R1

Destination	Shortest Path	Cost
R2 LAN	R1 to R2	22
R3 LAN	R1 to R3	7
R4 LAN	R1 to R3 to R4	17
R5 LAN	R1 to R3 to R4 to R5	27

You should be able to create a similar table for each of the other routers in Figure 15-4.

Figure 15-4   Dijkstra's Shortest Path First Algorithm

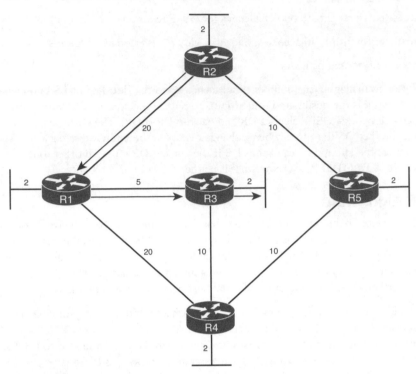

Shortest Path for Host on R2 LAN to Reach Host on R3 LAN:
R2 to R1 (20) + R1 to R3 (5) + R3 to LAN (2) = 27

Link-State Routing Process

The following list summarizes the link-state routing process used by OSPF. All OSPF rout-ers complete the following generic link-state routing process to reach a state of convergence:

1. Each router learns about its own links and its own directly connected networks. This is done by detecting that an interface is in the up state, including a Layer 3 address.

2. Each router is responsible for establishing adjacency with its neighbors on directly con-nected networks by exchanging Hello packets.

3. Each router builds a link-state packet (LSP) containing the state of each directly con-nected link. This is done by recording all the pertinent information about each neigh-bor, including neighbor ID, link type, and bandwidth.

4. Each router floods the LSP to all neighbors, who then store all LSPs received in a data-base. Neighbors then flood the LSPs to their neighbors until all routers in the area have received the LSPs. Each router stores a copy of each LSP received from its neighbors in a local database.

5. Each router uses the database to construct a complete map of the topology and computes the best path to each destination network. The SPF algorithm is used to construct the map of the topology and to determine the best path to each network. All routers will have a common map or tree of the topology, but each router independently determines the best path to each network within that topology.

Single-Area OSPFv2 Configuration

To review the OSPF configuration commands, we will use the topology in Figure 15-5 and the addressing scheme in Table 15-2.

Figure 15-5   OSPFv2 Configuration Topology

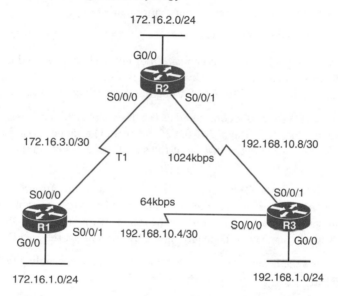

172.16.2.0/24

G0/0

R2

S0/0/0   S0/0/1

172.16.3.0/30   192.168.10.8/30

T1   1024kbps

S0/0/0   S0/0/1

64kbps

R1   S0/0/0   R3

S0/0/1   192.168.10.4/30

G0/0   G0/0

172.16.1.0/24   192.168.1.0/24

Table 15-2   Addressing Scheme for OSPFv2

Device	Interface	IP Address	Subnet Mask
R1	G0/0	172.16.1.1	255.255.255.0
	S0/0/0	172.16.3.1	255.255.255.252
	S0/0/1	192.168.10.5	255.255.255.252
R2	G0/0	172.16.2.1	255.255.255.0
	S0/0/0	172.16.3.2	255.255.255.252
	S0/0/1	192.168.10.9	255.255.255.252
R3	G0/0	192.168.1.1	255.255.255.0
	S0/0/0	192.168.10.6	255.255.255.252
	S0/0/1	192.168.10.10	255.255.255.252

The router ospf Command

OSPF is enabled with the **router ospf** *process-id* global configuration command:

```
R1(config)# router ospf process-id
```

The *process-id* is a number between 1 and 65,535 and is chosen by the network administrator. The process ID is locally significant. It does not have to match other OSPF routers to establish adjacencies with those neighbors. This differs from Enhanced Interior Gateway Routing Protocol (EIGRP). The EIGRP process ID or autonomous system number must match before two EIGRP neighbors will become adjacent.

For our review, we will enable OSPF on all three routers using the same process ID of 10.

The network Command

The **network** command is used in router configuration mode:

```
Router(config-router)# network network-address wildcard-mask area area-id
```

The OSPF **network** command uses a combination of *network-address* and *wildcard-mask*. The network address, along with the wildcard mask, is used to specify the interface or range of interfaces that will be enabled for OSPF using this **network** command.

The wildcard mask is customarily configured as the inverse of a subnet mask. For example, R1's Serial 0/0/0 interface is on the 172.16.3.0/30 network. The subnet mask for this interface is /30 or 255.255.255.252. The inverse of the subnet mask results in the wildcard mask 0.0.0.3.

The **area** *area-id* refers to the OSPF area. An OSPF area is a group of routers that share link-state information. All OSPF routers in the same area must have the same link-state information in their link-state databases. Therefore, all the routers within the same OSPF area must be configured with the same area ID on all routers. By convention, the area ID is 0.

Example 15-1 shows the **network** commands for all three routers, enabling OSPF on all interfaces.

Example 15-1   Configuring OSPF Networks

```
R1(config)# router ospf 10
R1(config-router)# network 172.16.1.0 0.0.0.255 area 0
R1(config-router)# network 172.16.3.0 0.0.0.3 area 0
R1(config-router)# network 192.168.10.4 0.0.0.3 area 0
R2(config)# router ospf 10
R2(config-router)# network 172.16.2.0 0.0.0.255 area 0
R2(config-router)# network 172.16.3.0 0.0.0.3 area 0
R2(config-router)# network 192.168.10.8 0.0.0.3 area 0
R3(config)# router ospf 10
R3(config-router)# network 192.168.1.0 0.0.0.255 area 0
R3(config-router)# network 192.168.10.4 0.0.0.3 area 0
R3(config-router)# network 192.168.10.8 0.0.0.3 area 0
```

Router ID

The router ID plays an important role in OSPF. It is used to uniquely identify each router in the OSPF routing domain. Cisco routers derive the router ID based on three criteria in the following order:

1. Use the IP address configured with the OSPF **router-id** command.

2. If the router ID is not configured, the router chooses the highest IP address of any of its loopback interfaces.

3. If no loopback interfaces are configured, the router chooses the highest active IP address of any of its physical interfaces.

The router ID can be viewed with several commands, including **show ip ospf interfaces**, **show ip protocols**, and **show ip ospf**.

Because the OSPF **router-id** command can be controlled by the network administrator and because loopback interfaces clutter up the routing table, it is a best practice to configure the **router-id** command. The **router-id** command accepts an IPv4 address as its only argument. Example 15-2 shows the router ID configurations for the routers in our topology.

Example 15-2   Router ID Configurations

```
R1(config-router)# router-id 1.1.1.1
R2(config-router)# router-id 2.2.2.2
R3(config-router)# router-id 3.3.3.3
```

The router ID is selected when OSPF is configured with its first OSPF **network** command. So the **router-id** command should already be configured. However, you can force OSPF to release its current ID and use the configured router ID by clearing the OSPF routing process:

```
Router# clear ip ospf process
```

Passive Interfaces

By default, OSPF messages are forwarded out all OSPF-enabled interfaces. However, these messages really only need to be sent out interfaces connecting to other OSPF-enabled routers. Sending out unneeded messages on a LAN affects the network in three ways:

- **Inefficient use of bandwidth:** Available bandwidth is consumed transporting unnecessary messages.

- **Inefficient use of resources:** All devices on the LAN must process the message.

- **Increased security risk:** OSPF messages can be intercepted and routing updates can be modified, corrupting the routing table.

Use the **passive-interface** command to prevent OSPF updates from being sent out unnecessary interfaces. For our topology in Figure 15-5, each router's GigabitEthernet 0/0 interface should be set to passive with the following command:

```
Router(config)# passive-interface gigabitethernet 0/0
```

As an alternative, all interfaces can be made passive using the **passive-interface default** command. Then, interfaces that should not be passive can be reenabled using the **no passive-interface** *interface* command.

Modifying the OSPF Metric

Cisco IOS Software uses the cumulative bandwidths of the outgoing interfaces from the router to the destination network as the cost value. At each router, the cost for an interface is calculated using the following formula:

Cisco IOS Cost for OSPF = 10^8/bandwidth in bps

In this calculation, the value 10^8 is known as the *reference bandwidth*. Table 15-3 shows the default OSPF costs using the default reference bandwidth for several types of interfaces.

Table 15-3   Cisco Default OSPF Cost Values

Interface Type	10^8/bps = Cost	Cost
10 Gigabit Ethernet (10Gbps)	10^8/10,000,000,000 bps = 1	1
Gigabit Ethernet (1Gbps)	10^8/1,000,000,000 bps = 1	1
Fast Ethernet (100Mbps)	10^8/100,000,000 bps = 1	1
Ethernet (10Mbps)	10^8/10,000,000 bps = 10	10
T1 (1.544Mbps)	10^8/1,544,000 bps = 64	64
128kbps	10^8/128,000 bps = 781	781
64kbps	10^8/64,000 bps = 1562	1562

In Table 15-3, 10GigE, Gigabit Ethernet, and Fast Ethernet all have the same cost. That's because the OSPF cost value must be an integer. This was not an issue prior to the introduction of gigabit and higher data rates.

However, today's networks are certainly running at gigabit speeds. Therefore, as a matter of policy, you should change the reference bandwidth to accommodate networks with links faster than 100,000,000 bps (100Mbps). Use the following command to change the reference bandwidth:

```
Router(config-router)# auto-cost reference-bandwidth Mbps
```

Because the value entered is in Mbps, changing the reference bandwidth 10000 will ensure that all OSPF routers are ready to accurately calculate cost for 10GigE networks. When used, this command should be entered on all routers so that the OSPF routing metric remains consistent. In fact, the IOS will reply with the follow syslog message when you con-figure the **auto-cost reference-bandwidth** command:

```
% OSPF: Reference bandwidth is changed.
        Please ensure reference bandwidth is consistent across all routers.
```

So, for our topology in Figure 15-5, we would enter the commands shown in Example 15-3.

Example 15-3   Changing the OSPF Reference Bandwidth

```
R1(config-router)# auto-cost reference-bandwidth 10000
```
```
R2(config-router)# auto-cost reference-bandwidth 10000
```
```
R3(config-router)# auto-cost reference-bandwidth 10000
```

Table 15-4 shows the modified cost values with the new reference bandwidth of 10,000,000,000 bps, or 10^{10}.

Table 15-4   OSPF Cost Values with Modified Reference Bandwidth = 10000

Interface Type	10^{10}/bps = Cost	Cost
10 Gigabit Ethernet (10Gbps)	10^{10}/10,000,000,000 bps = 1	1
Gigabit Ethernet (1Gbps)	10^{10}/1,000,000,000 bps = 1	10
Fast Ethernet (100Mbps)	10^{10}/100,000,000 bps = 1	100
Ethernet (10Mbps)	10^{10}/10,000,000 bps = 10	1000
T1 (1.544Mbps)	10^{10}/1,544,000 bps = 64	6477
128kbps	10^{10}/128,000 bps = 781	78125
64kbps	10^{10}/64,000 bps = 1562	156250 (see note)

NOTE: Although the cost for a 64kbps speed calculates to 156250, the maximum OSPF cost for a Cisco router interface is 65535.

But we are not done. There is still one more adjustment we need to make to ensure that OSPF is using accurate costs. On Cisco routers, the default bandwidth on most serial inter-faces is set to T1 speed, or 1.544Mbps. But in our topology in Figure 15-5, we have the fol-lowing actual speeds:

- Link between R1 and R2 is running at 1544kbps (default value).

- Link between R2 and R3 is running at 1024kbps.

- Link between R1 and R3 is running at 64kbps.

You can modify the OSPF metric in two ways:

- Use the **bandwidth** command to modify the bandwidth value used by the Cisco IOS Software in calculating the OSPF cost metric.

■ Use the **ip ospf cost** command, which allows you to directly specify the cost of an interface.

An advantage of configuring a cost over setting the interface bandwidth is that the router does not have to calculate the metric when the cost is manually configured. Also, the **ip ospf cost** command is useful in multivendor environments, where non-Cisco routers can use a metric other than bandwidth to calculate the OSPF costs.

Table 15-5 shows the two alternatives that can be used in modifying the costs of the serial links in the topology in Figure 15-5. The right side of the figure shows the **ip ospf cost** command equivalents of the **bandwidth** commands on the left.

Table 15-5   Comparing the bandwidth and ip ospf cost Commands

Adjusting the Interface Bandwidth	=	Manually Setting the OSPF Cost
R1(config)# **interface S0/0/1** R1(config-if)# **bandwidth 64**	=	R1(config)# **interface S0/0/1** R1(config-if)# **ip ospf cost 65535**
R2(config)# **interface S0/0/1** R2(config-if)# **bandwidth 1024**	=	R2(config)# **interface S0/0/1** R2(config-if)#)# **ip ospf cost 9765**
R3(config)# **interface S0/0/0** R3(config-if)# **bandwidth 64**	=	R3(config)# interface S0/0/0 R3(config-if)# **ip ospf cost 65535**
R3(config)# **interface S0/0/1** R3(config-if)# **bandwidth 1024**	=	R3(config)# **interface S0/0/1** R3(config-if)# ip ospf cost 9765

NOTE: The 64kbps interface is set to the maximum cost of 65535.

Verifying OSPFv2

To verify any routing configuration, you will most likely depend on the **show ip interface brief**, **show ip route**, and **show ip protocols** commands. All the expected interfaces should be "up" and "up" and configured with the correct IP address. The routing table should have all the expected routes. The protocol status should show routing for all expected networks as well as show all expected routing sources. Example 15-4 shows R1's output from these three basic commands.

Example 15-4   R1 Basic Routing Verification Commands

```
R1# show ip route
<output omitted>

Gateway of last resort is not set

      172.16.0.0/16 is variably subnetted, 5 subnets, 3 masks
C        172.16.1.0/24 is directly connected, GigabitEthernet0/0
```

```
L        172.16.1.1/32 is directly connected, GigabitEthernet0/0
O        172.16.2.0/24 [110/6576] via 172.16.3.2, 00:04:57, Serial0/0/0
C        172.16.3.0/30 is directly connected, Serial0/0/0
L        172.16.3.1/32 is directly connected, Serial0/0/0
O     192.168.1.0/24 [110/16341] via 172.16.3.2, 00:00:41, Serial0/0/0
      192.168.10.0/24 is variably subnetted, 3 subnets, 2 masks
C        192.168.10.4/30 is directly connected, Serial0/0/1
L        192.168.10.5/32 is directly connected, Serial0/0/1
O        192.168.10.8/30 [110/16241] via 172.16.3.2, 00:00:41, Serial0/0/0
R1# show ip interface brief
Interface                      IP-Address      OK? Method Status                Protocol
Embedded-Service-Engine0/0 unassigned          YES unset  administratively down down
GigabitEthernet0/0             172.16.1.1      YES manual up                     up
GigabitEthernet0/1             unassigned      YES unset  administratively down down
Serial0/0/0                    172.16.3.1      YES manual up                     up
Serial0/0/1                    192.168.10.5    YES manual up                     up
R1# show ip protocols
*** IP Routing is NSF aware ***

Routing Protocol is "ospf 10"
  Outgoing update filter list for all interfaces is not set
  Incoming update filter list for all interfaces is not set
  Router ID 1.1.1.1
  Number of areas in this router is 1. 1 normal 0 stub 0 nssa
  Maximum path: 4
  Routing for Networks:
    172.16.1.0 0.0.0.255 area 0
    172.16.3.0 0.0.0.3 area 0
    192.168.10.4 0.0.0.3 area 0
  Passive Interface(s):
    GigabitEthernet0/0
  Routing Information Sources:
    Gateway         Distance      Last Update
    3.3.3.3              110      00:09:00
    2.2.2.2              110      00:09:00
  Distance: (default is 110)
```

You can verify that expected neighbors have established adjacency with the **show ip ospf neighbor** command. Example 15-5 shows the neighbor tables for all three routers.

Example 15-5   Verifying Neighbor Adjacency with the show ip ospf neighbor Command

```
R1# show ip ospf neighbor

Neighbor ID     Pri   State        Dead Time   Address        Interface
3.3.3.3           0   FULL/  -     00:00:37    192.168.10.6   Serial0/0/1
2.2.2.2           0   FULL/  -     00:00:37    172.16.3.2     Serial0/0/0
R2# show ip ospf neighbor

Neighbor ID     Pri   State        Dead Time   Address        Interface
3.3.3.3           0   FULL/  -     00:00:38    192.168.10.10  Serial0/0/1
1.1.1.1           0   FULL/  -     00:00:37    172.16.3.1     Serial0/0/0
R3# show ip ospf neighbor

Neighbor ID     Pri   State        Dead Time   Address        Interface
2.2.2.2           0   FULL/  -     00:00:37    192.168.10.9   Serial0/0/1
1.1.1.1           0   FULL/  -     00:00:30    192.168.10.5   Serial0/0/0
```

For each neighbor, this command displays the following output:

- **Neighbor ID:** The router ID of the neighboring router.

- **Pri:** The OSPF priority of the interface. These all show 0 because point-to-point links do not elect a DR or BDR.

- **State:** The OSPF state of the interface. FULL state means that the router's interface is fully adjacent with its neighbor and they have identical OSPF link-state databases.

- **Dead Time:** The amount of time remaining that the router will wait to receive an OSPF Hello packet from the neighbor before declaring the neighbor down. This value is reset when the interface receives a Hello packet.

- **Address:** The IP address of the neighbor's interface to which this router is directly connected.

- **Interface:** The interface on which this router has formed adjacency with the neighbor.

The **show ip ospf** command shown in Example 15-6 for R1 can also be used to examine the OSPF process ID and router ID. In addition, this command displays the OSPF area information and the last time that the SPF algorithm was calculated.

Example 15-6   show ip ospf Command

```
R1# show ip ospf
Routing Process "ospf 10" with ID 1.1.1.1
  Start time: 00:29:52.316, Time elapsed: 00:45:15.760
  Supports only single TOS(TOS0) routes
  Supports opaque LSA
  Supports Link-local Signaling (LLS)
```

```
Supports area transit capability
Supports NSSA (compatible with RFC 3101)
Event-log enabled, Maximum number of events: 1000, Mode: cyclic
Router is not originating router-LSAs with maximum metric
Initial SPF schedule delay 5000 msecs
Minimum hold time between two consecutive SPFs 10000 msecs
Maximum wait time between two consecutive SPFs 10000 msecs
Incremental-SPF disabled
Minimum LSA interval 5 secs
Minimum LSA arrival 1000 msecs
LSA group pacing timer 240 secs
Interface flood pacing timer 33 msecs
Retransmission pacing timer 66 msecs
Number of external LSA 0. Checksum Sum 0x000000
Number of opaque AS LSA 0. Checksum Sum 0x000000
Number of DCbitless external and opaque AS LSA 0
Number of DoNotAge external and opaque AS LSA 0
Number of areas in this router is 1. 1 normal 0 stub 0 nssa
Number of areas transit capable is 0
External flood list length 0
IETF NSF helper support enabled
Cisco NSF helper support enabled
Reference bandwidth unit is 10000 mbps
    Area BACKBONE(0)
        Number of interfaces in this area is 3
        Area has no authentication
        SPF algorithm last executed 00:18:32.788 ago
        SPF algorithm executed 7 times
        Area ranges are
        Number of LSA 3. Checksum Sum 0x01BB59
        Number of opaque link LSA 0. Checksum Sum 0x000000
        Number of DCbitless LSA 0
        Number of indication LSA 0
        Number of DoNotAge LSA 0
        Flood list length 0
```

The quickest way to verify OSPF interface settings is to use the **show ip ospf interface brief** command. As shown in the output for R1 in Example 15-7, this command provides a detailed list for every OSPF-enabled interface. The command is also useful to determine whether the network statements were correctly configured.

Example 15-7   show ip ospf interface brief Command

```
R1# show ip ospf interface brief
Interface    PID   Area              IP Address/Mask    Cost   State Nbrs F/C
Se0/0/1      10    0                 192.168.10.5/30    65535  P2P   1/1
Se0/0/0      10    0                 172.16.3.1/30      6476   P2P   1/1
Gi0/0        10    0                 172.16.1.1/24      100    DR    0/0
```

Tomorrow, we will continue with OSPF, comparing OSPFv2 to OSPFv3 and configuring OSPFv3.

Study Resources

For today's exam topics, refer to the following resources for more study.

Resource	Chapter	Section or Topic
Primary Resources		
Routing Protocols	6	Characteristics of OSPF
		Configuring Single-Area OSPFv2
Routing and Switching Essentials	8	Characteristics of OSPF
		Configuring Single-Area OSPFv2
ICND1 Official Cert Guide	17	Understanding the OSPF Link-State Routing Protocol
		OSPF Configuration
ICND1 Foundation Learning Guide	15	All
Supplemental Resources		
CCENT Practice and Study Guide	19	Characteristics of OSPF
		Configuring Single-Area OSPFv2
Flash Cards	11	All
Network Simulator	17	Loopback Interfaces
		OSPF Neighbors I–V
		OSPF Serial Configuration I–VI
		OSPF Configuration I–III
	18	PC IP Commands I
CCNA R&S Portable Command Guide	9	Configuring OSPF
		Using Wildcard Masks with OSPF Areas
		Loopback Interfaces
		DR/BDR Elections
		Modifying Cost Metrics
		OSPF auto-cost reference-bandwidth

Single-Area OSPFv3

CCENT 100-101 ICND1 Exam Topics

- Configure and verify OSPF (single-area).

Key Topics

Today we review the differences between OSPFv2 and OSPFv3. Then we review the commands necessary to configure and verify an OSPFv3 implementation. The review content for the day is light. So this is a good day to practice configuring OSPFv2 and OSPFv3, possibly dual-stacking them on the same topology so that you can easily compare the two.

OSPFv2 Versus OSPFv3

In 1999, OSPFv3 for IPv6 was published in RFC 2740. In 2008, OSPFv3 was updated in RFC 5340 as OSPF for IPv6. However, it's still referred to as OSPFv3.

OSPFv3 has the same functionality as OSPFv2 but uses IPv6 as the network layer transport, communicating with OSPFv3 peers and advertising IPv6 routes. OSPFv3 also uses the shortest path first (SPF) algorithm as the computation engine to determine the best paths throughout the routing domain.

As with all IPv6 routing protocols, OSPFv3 has separate processes from its IPv4 counterpart. OSPFv2 and OSPFv3 each have separate adjacency tables, OSPF topology tables, and IP routing tables.

Similarities Between OSPFv2 and OSPFv3

OSPFv3 operates very much like OSPFv2. Table 14-1 summarizes the operational features that OSPFv2 and OSPFv3 share in common.

Table 14-1   OSPFv2 and OSPFv3 Similarities

Feature	OSPFv2 and OSPFv3
Link-State	Yes
Routing algorithm	SPF
Metric	Cost
Areas	Supports the same two-level hierarchy
Packet types	Same Hello, DBD, LSR, LSU, and LSAck packets

Feature	OSPFv2 and OSPFv3
Neighbor discovery	Transitions through the same states using Hello packets
LSDB synchronization	Exchange contents of their LSDB between two neighbors
DR and BDR	Function and election process are the same
Router ID	32-bit router ID and the process in determining the 32-bit Router ID are the same in both protocols

Differences Between OSPFv2 and OSPFv3

The major differences between OSPFv2 and OSPFv3 are listed in Table 14-2.

Table 14-2   OSPFv2 and OSPFv3 Differences

Feature	OSPFv2	OSPFv3
Advertises	IPv4 networks.	IPv6 prefixes.
Source address	IPv4 source address.	IPv6 link-local address.
Destination address	Choice of:	Choice of:
	Neighbor IPv4 unicast address	Neighbor IPv6 link-local address
	224.0.0.5 all-OSPF-routers multicast address	FF02::5 all-OSPFv3-routers multicast address
	224.0.0.6 DR/BDR multicast address	FF02::6 DR/BDR multicast address
Advertise networks	Configured using the **network** router configuration command.	Configured using the **ipv6 ospf area** interface configuration command.
IP unicast routing	IPv4 unicast routing is enabled by default.	The **ipv6 unicast-routing** global configuration command must be configured.
Authentication	Plain text and MD5.	IPsec.

Single-Area OSPFv3 Configuration

OSPFv3 configuration requires the same basic steps as OSPFv2: pick and configure a process ID, and enable the process on each interface, while assigning the correct OSPF area to each interface. However, the way in which these steps are implemented is quite different.

Figure 14-1 shows the topology we will use to review the OSPFv3 configuration steps.

Figure 14-1   OSPFv3 Configuration Topology

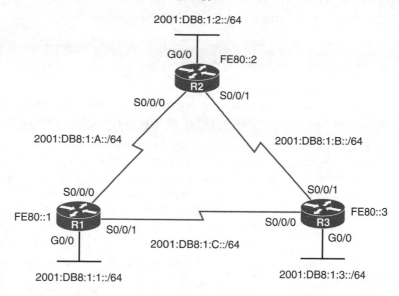

To ease our configuration and verification steps, we will use the simplified IPv6 addressing scheme shown in Table 14-3.

Table 14-3   Addressing Scheme for OSPFv3

Device	Interface	IPv6 Address/Prefix
R1	G0/0	2001:DB8:1:1::1/64
	S0/0/0	2001:DB8:1:A::1/64
	S0/0/1	2001:DB8:1:C::1/64
	Link-local	FE80::1
R2	G0/0	2001:DB8:1:2::1/64
	S0/0/0	2001:DB8:1:A::2/64
	S0/0/1	2001:DB8:1:B::1/64
	Link-local	FE80::2
R3	G0/0	2001:DB8:1:3::1/64
	S0/0/0	2001:DB8:1:C::2/64
	S0/0/1	2001:DB8:1:B::2/64
	Link-local	FE80::3

The Router ID in OSPFv3

Like OSPFv2, OSPFv3 chooses the router ID in the following order:

1. If the **router-id** command is configured, use the manually configured IPv4 router ID.

2. If the router ID is not configured, use the highest configured loopback interface IPv4 address.

3. If no loopback IPv4 address is configured, use the highest configured interface IPv4 address. The interface can be either in the up/up state or the up/down state.

Also like OSPFv2, you configure the router ID with the **router-id** command in router configuration mode. However, notice that both OSPFv2 and OSPFv3 use an IPv4 address for the router ID. This means that, before a router can start an OSPFv3 routing process, there must be an IPv4 address configured—either an interface or a router ID. If not, the router will return the following syslog message when you attempt to enable the OSPFv3 routing process with the **ipv6 router ospf** command:

```
R1(config)# ipv6 router ospf 10
*Jun  3 13:06:06.579: %OSPFv3-4-NORTRID: Process OSPFv3-10-IPv6 could not pick a
  router-id, please configure manually
```

So the next step on R1 is to configure the router ID. It can be any IPv4 address. For simplicity, we will use 1.1.1.1:

```
R1(config-rtr)# router-id 1.1.1.1
```

To make sure that costs are accurately calculated for the Gigabit interfaces, we will change the reference bandwidth to 1,000,000,000 bps or 1000 Mbps, with the **auto-cost reference-bandwidth** command:

```
R1(config-rtr)# auto-cost reference-bandwidth 1000
% OSPFv3-10-IPv6:  Reference bandwidth is changed.
        Please ensure reference bandwidth is consistent across all routers.
```

A syslog message reminds us to do this on every router. Like OSPFv2, we can stop sending updates out the GigabitEthernet 0/0 interface with the **passive-interface** command:

```
R1(config-rtr)# passive-interface g0/0
```

That's it for router configuration commands. Next, we simply enable OSPFv3 on each of the active interfaces as shown in Example 14-1.

Example 14-1   Enable OSPFv3 on Interfaces

```
R1(config-rtr)# exit
R1(config)# interface GigabitEthernet 0/0
R1(config-if)# ipv6 ospf 10 area 0
R1(config-if)# interface Serial0/0/0
R1(config-if)# ipv6 ospf 10 area 0
R1(config-if)# interface Serial0/0/1
R1(config-if)# ipv6 ospf 10 area 0
```

Configure R2 and R3 with similar commands (we can use 2.2.2.2 and 3.3.3.3 for R2 and R3, respectively), and OSPFv3 is fully operational.

Verifying OSPFv3

Wendell Odom, in his book *Cisco CCENT/CCNA ICND1 100-101 Official Cert Guide*, uses a table (repeated as Table 14-4 here) to summarize the verification commands for both OSPFv2 and OSPFv3. Notice that every OSPFv2 command shown is also available for OSPFv3—just substitute **ipv6** for **ip**.

Table 14-4   OSPFv2 and Matching OSPFv3 show Commands

To Display Details About...	OSPFv2	OSPFv3
OSPF process	`show ip ospf`	`show ipv6 ospf`
All sources of routing information	`show ip protocols`	`show ipv6 protocols`
Details about OSPF-enabled interfaces	`show ip ospf interface`	`show ipv6 ospf interface`
Concise info about OSPF-enabled interfaces	`show ip ospf interface brief`	`show ipv6 ospf interface brief`
List of neighbors	`show ip ospf neighbor`	`show ipv6 ospf neighbor`
Summary of LSDB	`show ip ospf database`	`show ipv6 ospf database`
OSPF-learned routes	`show ip route ospf`	`show ipv6 route ospf`

Examples 14-2–14-8 show the output from R1 for the OSPFv3 verification commands shown in Table 14-4.

Example 14-2   Verify the OSPF Process

```
R1# show ipv6 ospf
 Routing Process "ospfv3 10" with ID 1.1.1.1
 Event-log enabled, Maximum number of events: 1000, Mode: cyclic
 Router is not originating router-LSAs with maximum metric
 Initial SPF schedule delay 5000 msecs
 Minimum hold time between two consecutive SPFs 10000 msecs
 Maximum wait time between two consecutive SPFs 10000 msecs
 Minimum LSA interval 5 secs
 Minimum LSA arrival 1000 msecs
 LSA group pacing timer 240 secs
 Interface flood pacing timer 33 msecs
 Retransmission pacing timer 66 msecs
 Number of external LSA 0. Checksum Sum 0x000000
```

```
Number of areas in this router is 1. 1 normal 0 stub 0 nssa
Graceful restart helper support enabled
Reference bandwidth unit is 1000 mbps
RFC1583 compatibility enabled
    Area BACKBONE(0)
        Number of interfaces in this area is 3
        SPF algorithm executed 4 times
        Number of LSA 11. Checksum Sum 0x05AD44
        Number of DCbitless LSA 0
        Number of indication LSA 0
        Number of DoNotAge LSA 0
        Flood list length 0
R1#
```

Example 14-3   Verify Sources of Routing Information

```
R1# show ipv6 protocols
IPv6 Routing Protocol is "connected"
IPv6 Routing Protocol is "ND"
IPv6 Routing Protocol is "ospf 10"
  Router ID 1.1.1.1
  Number of areas: 1 normal, 0 stub, 0 nssa
  Interfaces (Area 0):
    Serial0/0/1
    Serial0/0/0
    GigabitEthernet0/0
  Redistribution:
    None
R1#
```

Example 14-4   Verify Details of an OSPF-Enabled Interface

```
R1# show ipv6 ospf interface serial 0/0/0
Serial0/0/0 is up, line protocol is up
  Link Local Address FE80::1, Interface ID 6
  Area 0, Process ID 10, Instance ID 0, Router ID 1.1.1.1
  Network Type POINT_TO_POINT, Cost: 647
  Transmit Delay is 1 sec, State POINT_TO_POINT
  Timer intervals configured, Hello 10, Dead 40, Wait 40, Retransmit 5
    Hello due in 00:00:07
  Graceful restart helper support enabled
  Index 1/2/2, flood queue length 0
  Next 0x0(0)/0x0(0)/0x0(0)
  Last flood scan length is 3, maximum is 3
```

```
  Last flood scan time is 0 msec, maximum is 0 msec
  Neighbor Count is 1, Adjacent neighbor count is 1
    Adjacent with neighbor 2.2.2.2
  Suppress hello for 0 neighbor(s)
R1#
```

Example 14-5   Verify OSPF Interface Status

```
R1# show ipv6 ospf interface brief
Interface    PID   Area          Intf ID    Cost  State Nbrs F/C
Se0/0/1      10    0             7          647   P2P   1/1
Se0/0/0      10    0             6          647   P2P   1/1
Gi0/0        10    0             3          100   DR    0/0
R1#
```

Example 14-6   Verify OSPF Neighbor Table

```
R1# show ipv6 ospf neighbor

              OSPFv3 Router with ID (1.1.1.1) (Process ID 10)

Neighbor ID     Pri   State         Dead Time   Interface ID   Interface
3.3.3.3           0   FULL/  -      00:00:31    6              Serial0/0/1
2.2.2.2           0   FULL/  -      00:00:38    6              Serial0/0/0
R1#
```

Example 14-7   Verify the OSPF Link-State Database

```
R1# show ipv6 ospf database

            OSPFv3 Router with ID (1.1.1.1) (Process ID 10)

                Router Link States (Area 0)

ADV Router      Age        Seq#          Fragment ID  Link count  Bits
  1.1.1.1       1042       0x80000004    0            2           None
  2.2.2.2       1264       0x80000002    0            2           None
  3.3.3.3       1260       0x80000002    0            2           None

              Link (Type-8) Link States (Area 0)

ADV Router      Age        Seq#          Link ID   Interface
  1.1.1.1       1042       0x80000002    7         Se0/0/1
```

```
3.3.3.3          1265        0x80000001  6          Se0/0/1
1.1.1.1          1042        0x80000002  6          Se0/0/0
2.2.2.2          1313        0x80000001  6          Se0/0/0
1.1.1.1          1042        0x80000002  3          Gi0/0


                Intra Area Prefix Link States (Area 0)

ADV Router       Age         Seq#        Link ID    Ref-lstype  Ref-LSID
1.1.1.1          1042        0x80000003  0          0x2001      0
2.2.2.2          1308        0x80000002  0          0x2001      0
3.3.3.3          1260        0x80000002  0          0x2001      0
R1#
```

Example 14-8   Verify OSPF Routes in the Routing Table

```
R1# show ipv6 route ospf
IPv6 Routing Table - default - 10 entries
<output omitted>
O    2001:DB8:1:2::/64 [110/747]
     via FE80::2, Serial0/0/0
O    2001:DB8:1:3::/64 [110/747]
     via FE80::3, Serial0/0/1
O    2001:DB8:1:B::/64 [110/1294]
     via FE80::2, Serial0/0/0
     via FE80::3, Serial0/0/1
R1#
```

Study Resources

For today's exam topics, refer to the following resources for more study.

Resource	Chapter	Section or Topic
Primary Resources		
Routing Protocols	6	Configure Single-Area OSPFv3
Routing and Switching Essentials	8	Configure Single-Area OSPFv3
IPv6 Fundamentals	8	OSPFv3
ICND1 Official Cert Guide	29	Dynamic Routes with OSPFv3
ICND1 Foundation Learning Guide	20	IPv6 Routing
Supplemental Resources		
CCENT Practice and Study Guide	19	Configure Single-Area OSPFv3

Resource	Chapter	Section or Topic
Flash Cards	12	Questions 30–32
Network Simulator	29	IPv6 OSPF Metric Tuning
		IPv6 OSPF Neighbors I–VI
		IPv6 OSPF Router ID
		IPv6 OSPF Serial Configuration I–III
		IPv6 OSPF Troubleshooting I
CCNA R&S Portable Command Guide	17	All

Inter-VLAN Routing Configuration

CCENT 100-101 ICND1 Exam Topics

- Configure and verify inter-VLAN routing (router on a stick).

Key Topics

Because Layer 2 switches cannot perform the routing function, it is necessary to implement a Layer 3 device to route between VLANs. Today, we review inter-VLAN routing concepts and configurations.

Inter-VLAN Routing Concepts

Inter-VLAN communications cannot occur without a Layer 3 device. There are three options for implementing inter-VLAN routing:

- Traditional or legacy inter-VLAN routing
- Router on a stick
- Multilayer switch

Let's briefly review the concept of each method.

Legacy Inter-VLAN Routing

Legacy inter-VLAN routing requires multiple physical interfaces on both the router and the switch. When using a router to facilitate inter-VLAN routing, the router interfaces can be connected to separate VLANs. Devices on those VLANs send traffic through the router to reach other VLANs. For example, in Figure 13-1, each S2 interface connected to R1 is assigned to a VLAN. The router is already configured with the appropriate IP addressing on each of its interfaces, so no additional configuration is required. However, you can see that if you used a separate interface for each VLAN on a router, you would quickly run out of interfaces.

Figure 13-1   Legacy Inter-VLAN Routing

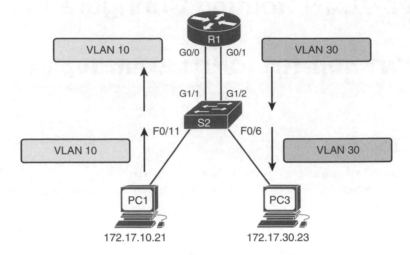

Router on a Stick

Today, router software permits configuring one router interface as multiple trunks using subinterfaces. In Figure 13-2, the physical GigabitEthernet 0/0 interface is logically subdivided into two logical interfaces. The one switch trunk is configured to trunk both VLAN 10 and VLAN 30, and each subinterface on the router is assigned a separate VLAN. The router performs inter-VLAN routing by accepting VLAN-tagged traffic on the trunk interface coming from the adjacent switch. The router then forwards the routed traffic, VLAN-tagged for the destination VLAN, out the same physical interface as it used to receive the traffic.

Figure 13-2   Router on a Stick

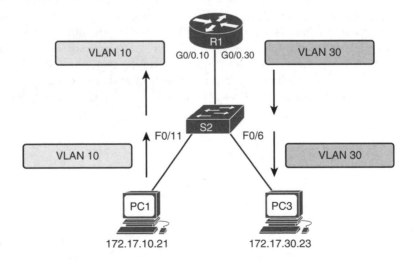

Multilayer Switch

Router on a stick works fine in a small business with one or two routers. But the most scalable solution in enterprise networks today is to use a multilayer switch to replace both the router and the switch, as shown in Figure 13-3. A multilayer switch will perform both functions: switching traffic within the same VLAN and routing traffic between VLANs.

Figure 13-3   Multilayer Switch

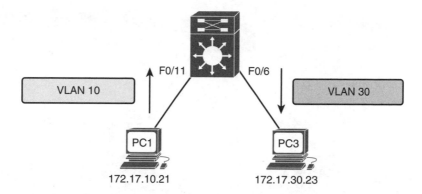

Multilayer switching is more scalable than any other inter-VLAN routing implementation because

- Routers have a limited number of available interfaces to connect to networks.

- Limited amounts of traffic can be accommodated on the physical link at one time.

With a multilayer switch, packets are forwarded down a single trunk line to obtain new VLAN-tagging information. A multilayer switch does not completely replace the functionality of a router but can be thought of as a Layer 2 device that is upgraded to have some routing capabilities.

Router on a Stick Configuration and Verification

When configuring inter-VLAN routing using the router on a stick model, the physical interface of the router must be connected to a trunk link on the adjacent switch. On the router, subinterfaces are created for each unique VLAN on the network. Each subinterface is assigned an IP address specific to its subnet/VLAN and is also configured to tag frames for that VLAN. This way, the router can keep the traffic from each subinterface separated as it traverses the trunk link back to the switch.

Configuring inter-VLAN routing is pretty straightforward. Refer to the sample topology shown in Figure 13-4 to review the commands.

Figure 13-4   Topology for Inter-VLAN Routing

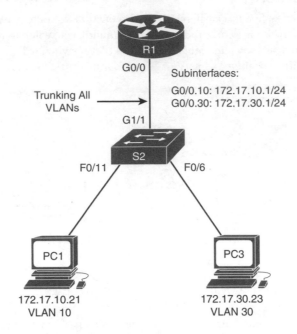

This router on a stick topology is configured using the following steps on the router:

Step 1.   Activate the physical interface that is trunking with the switch using the **no shutdown** command.

Step 2.   Enter subinterface configuration mode for the first VLAN that needs routing. One convention is to use the VLAN number as the subinterface number. For example, the **interface g0/1.10** command enters subinterface configuration mode for VLAN 10.

Step 3.   Configure the trunking encapsulation type using the subinterface configuration command **encapsulation** {**dot1q** | **isl**} *vlan-number* [**native**]. Set the encapsulation to **dot1q**.

- Inter-switch link (ISL) encapsulation—a Cisco-proprietary trunking method—existed prior to the IEEE 802.1Q standard, which is now the recommended best practice. However, older switches that are still in use might only support ISL. In those cases, you would substitute the **dot1q** keyword for **isl**.

- On some routers, the optional keyword **native** must be configured for the native VLAN before the router will route native VLAN traffic. Native VLAN routing is not shown in the following examples. Refer to your Study Resources for more on the native VLAN.

Step 4.   Configure the IP address and subnet mask.

Step 5.   Repeat Steps 2–4 for each additional VLAN that needs routing.

Assuming that the switch is already configured with VLANs and trunking, Example 13-1 shows the commands to configure R1 to provide routing between VLAN 10 and VLAN 30.

Example 13-1   Configuring R1 to Route Between VLANs

```
R1(config)# interface g0/0
R1(config-if)# no shutdown
R1(config-if)# interface g0/1.10
R1(config-subif)# encapsulation dot1q 10
R1(config-subif)# ip add 172.17.10.1 255.255.255.0
R1(config-subif)# interface g0/1.30
R1(config-subif)# encapsulation dot1q 30
R1(config-subif)# ip add 172.17.30.1 255.255.255.0
```

To verify the configuration, use the **show vlans**, **show ip route**, and **show ip interface brief** commands to make sure that the new networks are in the routing table and that the subinterfaces are "up" and "up," as shown in Example 13-2.

Example 13-2   Verifying the Inter-VLAN Routing Configuration

```
R1# show vlans
<output omitted>
Virtual LAN ID:  10 (IEEE 802.1Q Encapsulation)
   vLAN Trunk Interface:   GigabitEthernet0/0.10
   Protocols Configured:  Address:              Received:          Transmitted:
          IP               172.17.10.1               0                  0
<output omitted>
Virtual LAN ID:  30 (IEEE 802.1Q Encapsulation)
   vLAN Trunk Interface:   GigabitEthernet0/0.30
   Protocols Configured:  Address:              Received:          Transmitted:
          IP               172.17.30.1               0                  0
<output omitted>
R1# show ip route
<output omitted>

Gateway of last resort is not set

     172.17.0.0/16 is variably subnetted, 4 subnets, 2 masks
C        172.17.10.0/24 is directly connected, GigabitEthernet0/0.10
L        172.17.10.1/32 is directly connected, GigabitEthernet0/0.10
C        172.17.30.0/24 is directly connected, GigabitEthernet0/0.30
L        172.17.30.1/32 is directly connected, GigabitEthernet0/0.30
```

```
R1# show ip interface brief
Interface            IP-Address      OK? Method Status                 Protocol
GigabitEthernet0/0   unassigned      YES unset  up                     up
GigabitEthernet0/0.10 172.17.10.1    YES manual up                     up
GigabitEthernet0/0.30 172.17.30.1    YES manual up                     up
GigabitEthernet0/1   unassigned      YES unset  administratively down  down
Serial0/0/0          unassigned      YES manual administratively down  down
Serial0/0/1          unassigned      YES manual administratively down  down
Vlan1                unassigned      YES manual administratively down  down
R1#
```

Assuming that the switch and PCs are configured correctly, the two PCs should now be able to ping each other. R1 will route the traffic between VLAN 10 and VLAN 30.

Multilayer Switch Inter-VLAN Routing Configuration and Verification

Most enterprise networks use multilayer switches to achieve high-packet processing rates using hardware-based switching. All Catalyst multilayer switches support the following types of Layer 3 interfaces:

- **Routed port:** Similar to a physical interface on a Cisco IOS router

- **Switch virtual interface (SVI):** Virtual VLAN interface used for inter-VLAN routing

All Layer 3 Cisco Catalyst switches support routing protocols (3500, 4500, and 6500 series). Catalyst 2960 Series switches running IOS Release 12.2(55) or later support static routing.

Creating Additional SVIs

The SVI for the default VLAN (VLAN1) already exists to permit remote switch administration. For a topology like the one shown in Figure 13-5, additional SVIs must be explicitly created.

Create an SVI using the **interface vlan** *vlan-id* command. The *vlan-id* used corresponds to the VLAN tag associated with data frames coming from that VLAN. For example, when creating an SVI as a gateway for VLAN 10, use the **interface VLAN 10** command. Assign an IP address and enable the new SVI with the **no shutdown** command.

Figure 13-5   Switched Virtual Interfaces

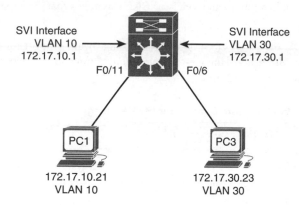

The following are some of the advantages of SVIs (the only disadvantage is that multilayer switches are more expensive):

- They are much faster than routers on a stick because everything is hardware switched and routed.

- There is no need for external links from the switch to the router for routing.

- They are not limited to one link. Layer 2 EtherChannels can be used between the switches to get more bandwidth.

- Latency is much lower because it does not need to leave the switch.

Configuring a 2960 to Route Between VLANs

The Catalyst 2960 switch shown in Figure 13-6 can function as a Layer 3 device and route between VLANs by enabling the Cisco Switch Database Manager (SDM) template for LAN-based routing.

Figure 13-6   2960 Catalyst Switch Routing Between VLANs

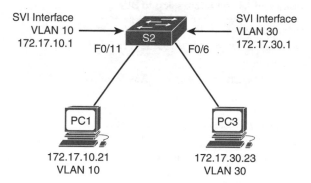

The following steps show how to configure a 2960 to do Layer 3 switching. The rest of the steps after Step 1 would apply to all models of Cisco switches that are capable of doing Layer 3 switching.

Step 1. With IOS Release 12.2(55) or later, enable hardware support for IPv4 routing with the **sdm prefer lanbase-routing** global command and reload the switch, as shown in Example 13-3.

Example 13-3   Enable Hardware Support for IPv4 Routing

```
S2(config)# sdm prefer lanbase-routing
Changes to the running SDM preferences have been stored, but cannot take effect
until the next reload.
Use 'show sdm prefer' to see what SDM preference is currently active.
Switch(config)# do reload

System configuration has been modified. Save? [yes/no]: yes
Building configuration...
[OK]
Proceed with reload? [confirm]

S2# show sdm prefer
 The current template is "lanbase-routing" template.
<output omitted>
```

Step 2. Create VLAN interfaces for each VLAN for which the Layer 3 switch is routing packets (**interface vlan** *vlan_id*), as shown in Example 13-3.

Step 3. Configure an IP address and mask on the VLAN interface.

Step 4. If the switch defaults to place the VLAN interface in a disabled (**shutdown**) state, enable the interface (**no shutdown**). Steps 2–4 are shown in Example 13-4.

Example 13-4   Create and Assign Addressing to SVIs

```
S2(config-if)# interface vlan 30
S2(config-if)# ip address 172.17.30.1 255.255.255.0
S2(config-if)# no shutdown
Mar 20 01:00:25.021: %LINEPROTO-5-UPDOWN: Line protocol on Interface Vlan30,
  changed state to up
S2(config-if)# interface vlan 10
S2(config-if)# ip address 172.17.10.1 255.255.255.0
S2(config-if)# no shutdown
Mar 20 01:00:25.021: %LINEPROTO-5-UPDOWN: Line protocol on Interface Vlan10,
  changed state to up
S2(config-if)#
```

Step 5.   Enable IPv4 routing globally (**ip routing**), verify that the switch now has a routing table, and test connectivity between PCs in different VLANS, as shown in
Example 13-5.

Example 13-5   Enable Routing and Verify Connectivity

```
S2(config-if)# do show ip route
<output omitted>
Gateway of last resort is not set


     172.17.0.0/16 is variably subnetted, 4 subnets, 2 masks
C         172.17.10.0/24 is directly connected, Vlan10
L         172.17.10.1/32 is directly connected, Vlan10
C         172.17.30.0/24 is directly connected, Vlan30
L         172.17.30.1/32 is directly connected, Vlan30
S2(config)#
!Ping PC1 from PC3
C:\> ping 172.17.10.21


Pinging 172.17.10.21 with 32 bytes of data:
Reply from 172.17.10.21: bytes=32 time=5ms TTL=127
Reply from 172.17.10.21: bytes=32 time=1ms TTL=127
Reply from 172.17.10.21: bytes=32 time=<1ms TTL=127
Reply from 172.17.10.21: bytes=32 time=<1ms TTL=127


Ping statistics for 172.17.10.21:
    Packets: Sent = 4, Received = 4, Lost = 0 (0% loss),
Approximate round trip times in milli-seconds:
    Minimum = 19ms, Maximum = 5ms, Average = 19ms


C:\>
```

NOTE: The CCENT exam topics about inter-VLAN routing mention "upstream routing,"
which simply means that even if a router or switch can route between VLANs, it will still
need to be able to route most traffic "upstream" to other areas of the enterprise and to the
Internet.

Study Resources

For today's exam topics, refer to the following resources for more study.

Resource	Location	Topic
Primary Resources		
Switched Networks	6	Inter-VLAN Routing Configuration
		Layer 3 Switching Operation and Configuration
Routing and Switching Essentials	5	Inter-VLAN Routing Configuration
		Layer 3 Switching Operation and Configuration
ICND1 Official Cert Guide	16	Routing Between Subnets on VLANs
ICND1 Foundation Learning Guide	6	Routing Between VLANs
Supplemental Resources		
CCENT Practice and Study Guide	16	Inter-VLAN Routing Configuration
		Layer 3 Switching
Flash Cards	9	Questions 25–28
Network Simulator		VLAN Configuration V
		VLAN Trunking II
CCNA R&S Portable Command Guide	13	Inter-VLAN Communication Using an External Router: Router on a Stick
		Inter-VLAN Communication on a Multilayer Switch Through a Switch Virtual Interface
		Inter-VLAN Communication Tips
		Configuration Example: Inter-VLAN Communication

DHCP Configuration

CCENT 100-101 ICND1 Exam Topics

- Configure and verify DHCP (IOS router).

Key Topics

Fortunately, we normally don't have to statically configure host devices with IP addressing. The Dynamic Host Configuration Protocol (DHCP) does the work for us. Today, we review the commands to configure a Cisco router as a DHCP server and as a DHCP client for both IPv4 and IPv6.

DHCPv4

DHCPv4 allows a host to obtain an IP address dynamically when it connects to the network. The DHCPv4 server is contacted by sending a request, and an IP address is requested. The DHCPv4 server chooses an address from a configured range of addresses called a pool and assigns it to the host client for a set period. Figure 12-1 graphically shows the process for how a DHCPv4 server fulfills a request from a DHCPv4 client.

Figure 12-1   **Allocating IP Addressing Information Using DHCPv4**

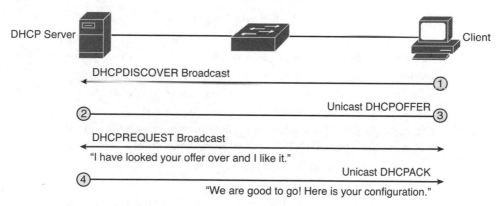

When a DHCPv4-configured device boots up or connects to the network, the client broadcasts a DHCPDISCOVER packet to identify any available DHCPv4 servers on the network. A DHCPv4 server replies with a DHCPOFFER, which is a lease offer message with an assigned IP address, subnet mask, DNS server, and default gateway information, as well as the duration of the lease.

The client can receive multiple DHCPOFFER packets if the local network has more than one DHCPv4 server. The client must choose between them and broadcast a DHCPREQUEST packet that identifies the explicit server and lease offer that it is accepting.

Assuming that the IP address is still valid, the chosen server returns a DHCPACK (acknowledgment) message finalizing the lease. If the offer is no longer valid for some reason, the chosen server responds to the client with a DHCPNAK (negative acknowledgment) message. After it is leased, the client will renew prior to the lease expiration through another DHCPREQUEST. If the client is powered down or taken off the network, the address is returned to the pool for reuse.

DHCPv4 Configuration Options

A Cisco router can be configured to handle DHCP requests in two ways: as a DHCP server and as a DHCP relay agent. A Cisco router can also be configured as a DHCP client, requesting an IPv4 address from a DHCP server for one or more of its interfaces. All of these options can be configured at the same time on the same device. For example, a router might be the DHCP server for a directly connected LAN while at the same time forwarding DHCP server requests to another DHCP server for other LANs. In addition, the router could also have one or more of its interfaces configured to request DHCP addressing from a remote server.

Configuring a Router as a DHCPv4 Server

A Cisco router running Cisco IOS Software can be configured to act as a DHCPv4 server. The Cisco IOS DHCPv4 server assigns and manages IPv4 addresses from specified address pools within the router to DHCPv4 clients.

The steps to configure a router as a DHCPv4 server are as follows:

Step 1. Use the **ip dhcp excluded-address** *low-address* [*high-address*] command to identify an address or range of addresses to exclude from the DHCPv4 pool. For example:

```
R1(config)# ip dhcp excluded-address 192.168.10.1 192.168.10.9
R1(config)# ip dhcp excluded-address 192.168.10.254
```

Step 2. Create the DHCPv4 pool using the **ip dhcp pool** *pool-name* command, which will then place you in DHCP config mode, as demonstrated here:

```
R1(config)# ip dhcp pool LAN-POOL-10
R1(dhcp-config)#
```

Step 3. Configure the IP addressing parameter you need to automatically assign to requesting clients. Table 12-1 lists the required commands.

Table 12-1   Required DHCPv4 Configuration Commands

Required Task	Command
Define the address pool	`network network-number [mask	/prefix-length]`
Define the default router or gateway	`default-router address [address2...address8]`

Table 12-2 lists some of the more common optional DHCPv4 tasks.

Table 12-2   Optional DHCPv4 Configuration Commands

Optional Task	Command
Define a DNS server	`dns-server address [address2...address8]`
Define the domain name	`domain-name domain`
Define the duration of the DHCPv4 lease	`lease {days [hours] [minutes]	infinite}`
Define the NetBIOS WINS server	`netbios-name-server address [address2...address8]`

Figure 12-2 shows a sample DHCPv4 topology.

Figure 12-2   DHCPv4 Sample Topology

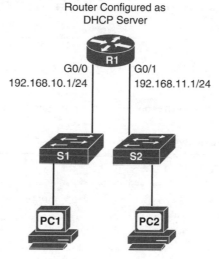

Router Configured as
DHCP Server

R1

G0/0   G0/1
192.168.10.1/24   192.168.11.1/24

S1   S2

PC1   PC2

PCs Configured to Automatically
Obtain IP Addressing

Example 12-1 shows DHCPv4 required and optional commands to configure R1 as the DHCPv4 server for both LANs.

Example 12-1   DHCPv4 Configuration Example

```
!Configure IP addresses that you want excluded from the DHCPv4 pool of addresses
R1(config)# ip dhcp excluded-address 192.168.10.1 192.168.10.9
R1(config)# ip dhcp excluded-address 192.168.10.254
R1(config)# ip dhcp excluded-address 192.168.11.1 192.168.11.9
R1(config)# ip dhcp excluded-address 192.168.11.254
!R1 needs two DHCPv4 pools for the two LANs. Each pool is configured with required
  and optional commands.
R1(config)# ip dhcp pool LAN-POOL-10
R1(dhcp-config)# network 192.168.10.0 255.255.255.0
R1(dhcp-config)# default-router 192.168.10.1
R1(dhcp-config)# dns-server 192.168.50.195 209.165.202.158
R1(dhcp-config)# domain-name cisco.com
R1(dhcp-config)# lease 2
R1(dhcp-config)# netbios-name-server 192.168.10.254
R1(dhcp-config)# ip dhcp pool LAN-POOL-11
R1(dhcp-config)# network 192.168.11.0 255.255.255.0
R1(dhcp-config)# default-router 192.168.11.1
R1(dhcp-config)# dns-server 192.168.50.195 209.165.202.158
R1(dhcp-config)# domain-name cisco.com
R1(dhcp-config)# lease 2
R1(dhcp-config)# netbios-name-server 192.168.11.254
R1(dhcp-config)# end
```

Cisco IOS Software supports DHCPv4 service by default. To disable it, use the global command **no service dhcp**.

To verify DHCPv4 operations on the router, use the commands shown in Example 12-2.

Example 12-2   Verifying DHCPv4 Operation

```
R1# show ip dhcp binding
Bindings from all pools not associated with VRF:
IP address            Client-ID/              Lease expiration       Type
                      Hardware address/
                      User name
192.168.10.10         0100.1641.aea5.a7       Jul 18 2008 08:17 AM   Automatic
192.168.11.10         0100.e018.5bdd.35       Jul 18 2008 08:17 AM   Automatic


R1# show ip dhcp server statistics
Memory usage          26455
Address pools         2
Database agents       0
Automatic bindings    2
```

```
Manual bindings        0
Expired bindings       0
Malformed messages     0
Secure arp entries     0


Message                Received
BOOTREQUEST            0
DHCPDISCOVER           2
DHCPREQUEST            2
DHCPDECLINE            0
DHCPRELEASE            0
DHCPINFORM             0


Message                Sent
BOOTREPLY              0
DHCPOFFER              2
DHCPACK               2
DHCPNAK               0
R1#
```

Because PC1 and PC2 are connected to the LANs, each automatically receives its IP addressing information from the router's DHCPv4 server. Example 12-3 shows the output from the **ipconfig/all** command on PC1.

Example 12-3   DHCPv4 Client Configuration

```
C:\> ipconfig/all


Windows IP Configuration


        Host Name . . . . . . . . . . . : ciscolab
        Primary Dns Suffix  . . . . . . . :
        Node Type . . . . . . . . . . . : Hybrid
        IP Routing Enabled. . . . . . . . : No
        WINS Proxy Enabled. . . . . . . . : No


Ethernet adapter Local Area Connection:


        Connection-specific DNS Suffix  . : cisco.com
        Description . . . . . . . . . . . : Intel(R) PRO/1000 PL
        Physical Address. . . . . . . . . : 00-12-41-AE-A5-A7
        Dhcp Enabled. . . . . . . . . . . : Yes
        Autoconfiguration Enabled . . . . : Yes
```

```
IP Address. . . . . . . . . . . . : 192.168.10.11
Subnet Mask . . . . . . . . . . . : 255.255.255.0
Default Gateway . . . . . . . . . : 192.168.10.1
DHCP Server . . . . . . . . . . . : 192.168.10.1
DNS Servers . . . . . . . . . . . : 192.168.50.195
                                    209.165.202.158
Primary WINS Server . . . . . . . : 192.168.10.254
Lease Obtained. . . . . . . . . . : Wednesday, July 16, 2008 8:16:59 AM
Lease Expires . . . . . . . . . . : Friday, July 18, 2008 8:16:59 AM

C:\>
```

To release the DHCPv4 configuration on a Windows-based client, enter the **ipconfig/release** command. To renew the DHCPv4 configuration, enter the **ipconfig/renew** command.

Configuring a Router to Relay DHCPv4 Requests

In a complex network, the DHCPv4 servers are usually contained in a server farm. Therefore, clients typically are not on the same subnet as the DHCPv4 server, as shown in the previous example. To ensure that broadcasted DHCPDISCOVER messages are sent to the remote DHCPv4 server, use the **ip helper-address address** command.

For example, in Figure 12-3, the DHCPv4 server is located on the 192.168.11.0/24 LAN and is serving IP addressing information for both LANs.

Figure 12-3   DHCPv4 Relay Topology

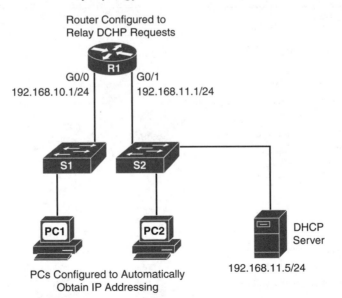

Without the **ip helper-address command**, R1 would discard any broadcasts from PC1 requesting DHCPv4 services. To configure R1 to relay DHCPDISCOVER messages, enter the following commands:

```
R1(config)# interface gigabitethernet 0/0
R1(config-if)# ip helper-address 192.168.11.5
```

Notice that the command is entered on the interface that will receive DHCPv4 broadcasts. R1 then forwards DHCPv4 broadcast messages as a unicast to 192.168.11.5. The **ip helper-address** command by default forwards the following eight UDP services:

- **Port 37:** Time

- **Port 49:** TACACS

- **Port 53:** DNS

- **Port 67:** DHCP/BOOTP client

- **Port 68:** DHCP/BOOTP server

- **Port 69:** TFTP

- **Port 137:** NetBIOS name service

- **Port 138:** NetBIOS datagram service

To specify additional ports, use the global command **ip forward-protocol udp** [*port-number | protocol*]. To disable broadcasts of a particular protocol, use the **no** form of the command.

Configuring a Router as a DHCPv4 Client

Cisco routers in small offices or branch sites are often configured as DHCPv4 clients. The method used depends on the ISP. However, in its simplest configuration, the interface used to connect to a cable or DSL modem is configured with the **ip address dhcp** interface configuration command.

For example, in Figure 12-4, the BRANCH router's GigabitEthernet 0/1 interface can be configured to request addressing from the ISP router.

Figure 12-4   Router as a DHCP Client

BRANCH
DHCP Client
ISP
G0/1

Example 12-4 shows the configuration and verification of DHCP addressing on BRANCH.

Example 12-4   Configuring a Router as a DHCP Client

```
BRANCH(config)# interface g0/1
BRANCH(config-if)# ip address dhcp
BRANCH(config-if)# no shutdown
*Mar 15 08:45:34.632: %DHCP-6-ADDRESS_ASSIGN: Interface GigabitEthernet0/1 assigned
  DHCP address 209.165.201.12, mask 255.255.255.224, hostname BRANCH
BRANCH(config-if)# end
BRANCH# show ip interface g0/1
GigabitEthernet0/1 is up, line protocol is up
  Internet address is 209.165.201.12/27
  Broadcast address is 255.255.255.255
  Address determined by DHCP
  <output omitted>
BRANCH#
```

DHCPv6

There are two methods in IPv6 to automatically obtain a global unicast address:

- SLAAC (Stateless Address Autoconfiguration)
- Stateful DHCPv6 (Dynamic Host Configuration Protocol for IPv6)

SLAAC

As we reviewed in Day 23, "IPv4 Subnetting and VLSM," SLAAC uses ICMPv6 Router Solicitation (RS) and Router Advertisement (RA) messages to provide addressing and other configuration information. A client then uses the RA information to build an IPv6 address and verify it with a special type of Neighbor Solicitation (NS) known as Duplicate Address Detection (DAD). These three message types—RA, RS, and NS—belong to the Neighbor Discovery Protocol:

- **Router Solicitation (RS) message:** When a client is configured to obtain its addressing information automatically using SLAAC, the client will send an RS message to the router. The RS message is sent to the IPv6 all-routers multicast address, FF02::2.

- **Router Advertisement (RA) message:** A client will use this information to create its own IPv6 global unicast address. A router will send an RA message periodically or in response to an RS message. The RA message includes the prefix and prefix length of the local segment. By default, Cisco routers send RA messages every 200 seconds. RA messages are sent to the IPv6 all-nodes multicast address, FF02::1.

- **Neighbor Solicitation (NS) message:** An NS message is normally used to learn the data link layer address of a neighbor on the same network. In the SLAAC process, a host uses Duplicate Address Detection (DAD) by inserting its own IPv6 address as the destination address in an NS. The NS is sent out on the network to verify that a newly minted IPv6 address is unique. If a Neighbor Advertisement is received, the host knows that the IPv6 address is not unique.

Figure 12-5 shows the SLAAC process using three messages of the Neighbor Discovery Protocol (NDP).

Figure 12-5   Neighbor Discovery and the SLAAC Process

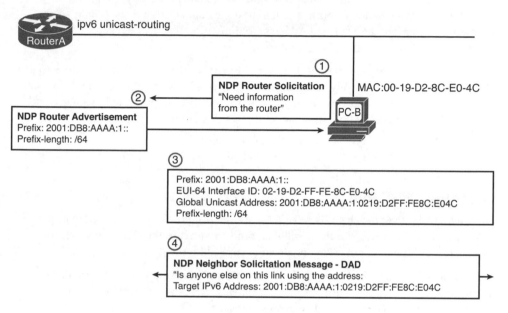

Let's briefly review the steps shown in Figure 12-5.

Step 1.   PC-B sends an RS message to the all-routers multicast address, FF02::2, to inform the local IPv6 router that it needs an RA.

Step 2.   RouterA receives the RS message and responds with an RA message. Included in the RA message are the prefix and prefix length of the network. The RA message is sent to the IPv6 all-nodes multicast address, FF02::1, with the link-local address of the router as the IPv6 source address.

Step 3.   PC-B uses this information to create its own IPv6 global unicast address. It appends the 64-bit prefix address to its own locally generated 64-bit interface ID, which it creates either using the EUI-process (as shown in Figure 12-5) or a random number generator. It uses RouterA's link-local address as the default gateway.

Step 4.   Before PC-B can use this newly created IPv6 address, it uses the Duplicate Address Detection (DAD) process, sending out an NS to verify that the address is unique.

NOTE: A client's operating system can be configured to ignore RA messages, opting always to use the services of a DHCPv6 server.

An RA message informs a client on how to obtain automatic IPv6 addressing: SLAAC, DHCPv6, or a combination of both. The RA message contains two flags to indicate the configuration option: the Managed Address Configuration flag (M flag) and the Other Configuration flag (O flag).

The default setting for these flags is 0, or both bits off. To the client, that means it is to use the SLAAC process exclusively to obtain all of its IPv6 addressing information. If for some reason, either of these flags is set to 1, you can use the **no** form of the following **ipv6 nd** commands in interface configuration mode to reset them to 0.

```
Router(config-if)# no ipv6 nd managed-config-flag
Router(config-if)# no ipv6 nd other-config-flag
```

Stateless DHCPv6

In stateless DHCPv6, the client uses the RA message from the router to generate its global unicast address. However, the client will then send a request to the DHCPv6 server to obtain any additional information not already supplied by the RA.

For stateless DHCPv6, the O flag is set to 1 so that the client is informed that additional configuration information is available from a stateless DHCPv6 server. Use the following command on the interface to modify the RA message.

```
Router(config-if)# ipv6 nd other-config-flag
```

Stateful DHCPv6

For stateful DHCPv6, the RA message informs the client to obtain all of its addressing information from a DHCPv6 server. The M flag must be set on the interface with the following command:

```
Router(config-if)# ipv6 nd managed-config-flag
```

Stateless and Stateful DHCPv6 Operation

Figure 12-6 shows the full operation of DHCPv6 regardless of the method used: SLAAC, stateless DHCPv6, or stateful DHCPv6.

Figure 12-6   DHCPv6 Operations

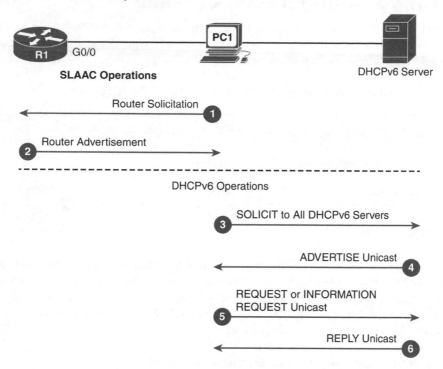

The following steps summarize Figure 12-6:

Step 1. PC1 sends an RS on bootup to begin the process of obtaining IPv6 addressing.

Step 2. R1 replies with an RA. If the M and O flags are not set, PC1 uses SLAAC. If either the M or O flag is set, PC1 begins the DHCPv6 process.

Step 3. PC1 sends a DHCPv6 SOLICIT message to the all-DHCPv6-servers address, FF02::1:2—a link-local multicast address that will not be forwarded by routers.

Step 4. A DHCPv6 server responds with a DHCPv6 ADVERTISE unicast message informing the client of its presence.

Step 5. The client then sends either a unicast DHCPv6 REQUEST (M flag was set and the client is using stateful DHCPv6) or a unicast DHCPv6 INFORMATION-REQUEST (O flag was set and the client is using stateless DHCPv6).

Step 6. The server replies with the information requested.

DHCPv6 Configuration Options

A router can be configured as a stateless DHCPv6 server, a stateful DHCPv6 server, and a DHCPv6 client. Like DHCPv4, the router can be configured with all three, depending on what role it plays for its various interfaces.

Configuring a Router as a Stateless DHCPv6 Server

We will use Figure 12-7 for all our examples in this section. R1 is the DHCPv6 server and R3 is the DHCPv6 client.

Figure 12-7   DHCPv6 Server and Client Topology

DHCPv6 Server   G0/1   DHCPv6 Client

To configure R1 as a stateless DHCP server, you need to make sure that **ipv6 unicast-routing** is enabled. Then, in global configuration mode, configure the pool name, DNS server, and domain name. Finally, enable the DHCPv6 pool on the appropriate interface and set the O flag so that clients on that interface know to request DHCPv6 services from the router. Example 12-5 shows the configuration for R1.

Example 12-5   Configuring a Router as a Stateless DHCPv6 Server

```
R1(config)# ipv6 unicast-routing
R1(config)# ipv6 dhcp pool O-FLAG-SET
R1(config-dhcpv6)# dns-server 2001:db8:acad:1::5
R1(config-dhcpv6)# domain-name cisco.com
R1(config-dhcpv6)# exit
R1(config)# interface g0/1
R1(config-if)# ipv6 address 2001:db8:1:1::1/64
R1(config-if)# ipv6 dhcp server O-FLAG-SET
R1(config-if)# ipv6 nd other-config-flag
R1(config-if)# end
R1# show ipv6 dhcp pool
DHCPv6 pool: O-FLAG-SET
  DNS server: 2001:DB8:ACAD:1::5
  Domain name: cisco.com
  Active clients: 0
R1#
```

To configure a router interface as a DHCPv6 client, enable IPv6 on the interface and enter the **ipv6 address autoconfig** command, as shown in Example 12-6. Verify the configuration with the **show ipv6 interface** command.

Example 12-6   Configuring an Interface as a DHCPv6 Client

```
R3(config)# interface g0/1
R3(config-if)# ipv6 enable
R3(config-if)# ipv6 address autoconfig
R3(config-if)# end
R3# show ipv6 interface g0/1
GigabitEthernet0/1 is up, line protocol is up
  IPv6 is enabled, link-local address is FE80::32F7:DFF:FE25:2DE1
  No Virtual link-local address(es):
  Stateless address autoconfig enabled
  Global unicast address(es):
    2001:DB8:1:1:32F7:DFF:FE25:2DE1, subnet is 2001:DB8:1:1::/64 [EUI/CAL/PRE]
      valid lifetime 2591935 preferred lifetime 604735
  Joined group address(es):
    FF02::1
    FF02::1:FF25:2DE1
  MTU is 1500 bytes
  ICMP error messages limited to one every 100 milliseconds
  ICMP redirects are enabled
  ICMP unreachables are sent
  ND DAD is enabled, number of DAD attempts: 1
  ND reachable time is 30000 milliseconds (using 30000)
  ND NS retransmit interval is 1000 milliseconds
  Default router is FE80::D68C:B5FF:FECE:A0C1 on GigabitEthernet0/1
R3#
```

Configuring a Router as a Stateful DHCPv6 Server

The main difference between a stateless configuration and a stateful configuration is that a stateful server also includes IPv6 addressing information and keeps a record of the IPv6 addresses that are leased out. Also, for the client side, the **ipv6 address dhcp** command is used instead of the **ipv6 address autoconfig** command. Example 12-7 shows the stateful DHCPv6 server configuration with stateful address information added and the M bit set, instead of the O bit.

Example 12-7   Configuring a Router as a Stateful DHCPv6 Server

```
R1(config)# ipv6 unicast-routing
R1(config)# ipv6 dhcp pool M-FLAG-SET
R1(config-dhcpv6)# address prefix 2001:db8:1:1::/64 lifetime infinite infinite
R1(config-dhcpv6)# dns-server 2001:db8:acad:1::5
R1(config-dhcpv6)# domain-name cisco.com
R1(config-dhcpv6)# exit
R1(config)# interface g0/1
R1(config-if)# ipv6 address 2001:db8:1:1::1/64
R1(config-if)# ipv6 nd managed-config-flag
R1(config-if)# end
!After R3 is configured as a DHCP client, verify DHCP with the following commands:
R1# show ipv6 dhcp pool
DHCPv6 pool: M-FLAG-SET
  Address allocation prefix: 2001:DB8:1:1::/64 valid 4294967295 preferred
4294967295 (1 in use, 0 conflicts)
  DNS server: 2001:DB8:ACAD:1::5
  Domain name: cisco.com
  Active clients: 1
R1# show ipv6 dhcp binding
Client: FE80::32F7:DFF:FEA3:1640
  DUID: 0003000130F70DA31640
  Username : unassigned
  IA NA: IA ID 0x00060001, T1 43200, T2 69120
    Address: 2001:DB8:1:1:8902:60D6:E76:6C16
          preferred lifetime INFINITY, , valid lifetime INFINITY,
      R1#
```

Study Resources

For today's exam topics, refer to the following resources for more study.

Resource	Location	Topic
Primary Resources		
Switched Networks	7	All
Routing & Switching Essentials	10	All
IPv6 Fundamentals	9	All
ICND1 Official Cert Guide	18	Configuring Routers to Support DHCP
	28	Dynamic Configuration of Host IPv6 Settings

Resource	Location	Topic
ICND1 Foundation Learning Guide	16	Using a Cisco Router as a DHCP Server
Supplemental Resources		
CCENT Practice and Study Guide	21	All
Flash Cards	9	Questions 29–32
Network Simulator	12	DHCP Server Configuration I–V
		Complete DHCP Server Configuration
CCNA R&S Portable Command Guide	28	All

ACL Concepts

CCENT 100-101 ICND1 Exam Topics

- Describe the types, features, and applications of ACLs.

Key Topics

One of the most important skills a network administrator needs is mastery of access control lists (ACLs). Administrators use ACLs to stop traffic or permit only specified traffic while stopping all other traffic on their networks. Standard and extended ACLs can be used to apply a number of security features, including policy-based routing, quality of service (QoS), Network Address Translation (NAT), and Port Address Translation (PAT).

You can also configure standard and extended ACLs on router interfaces to control the type of traffic that is permitted through a given router. Today, we review ACL concepts, including what they are, how a router uses them to filter traffic, and what types of ACLs are available.

ACL Operation

A router's default operation is to forward all packets as long as a route exists for the packet and the link is up. ACLs can be used to implement a basic level of security. They are not, however, the only security solution a large organization would want to implement. In fact, ACLs increase the latency of routers. So if the organization is very large with routers managing the traffic of hundreds or thousands of users, you more than likely will use a combination of other security implementations that are beyond the CCENT and CCNA scope.

Defining an ACL

An ACL is a router configuration script (a list of statements) that controls whether a router permits or denies packets to pass based on criteria found in the packet header. To determine whether a packet is to be permitted or denied, it is tested against the ACL statements in sequential order. When a statement matches, no more statements are evaluated. The packet is either permitted or denied. There is an implicit deny any statement at the end of the ACL. If a packet does not match any of the statements in the ACL, it is dropped.

Processing Interface ACLs

ACLs can be applied to an interface for inbound and outbound traffic. However, you need a separate ACL for each direction. The flow chart in Figure 11-1 details the steps a router takes when evaluating an ACL on inbound and outbound interfaces.

Figure 11-1   ACL Interface Processing for Inbound and Outbound Traffic

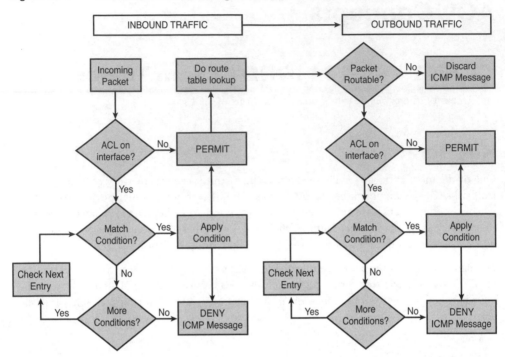

For inbound traffic, the router checks for an inbound ACL applied to the interface before doing a route table lookup. Then, for outbound traffic, the router makes sure that a route exists to the destination before checking for ACLs. Finally, if an ACL statement results in a dropped packet, the router sends an ICMP destination unreachable message.

The choice of using an inbound or outbound ACL is easy to make if first, you place yourself inside the router—be the router. From such a stance, you can visualize processing a packet coming into a router interface (inbound), making a decision on what to do with the packet (Is there an inbound ACL? Is there a route to the destination?), and forwarding the packet (What is the outbound interface? Is there an ACL on the interface?).

List Logic with IP ACLs

An ACL is a list of commands that are processed in order from the first statement in the list to the last statement. Each command has different matching logic that the router must apply to each packet when filtering is enabled. ACLs use first-match logic. After a packet matches one line in the ACL, the router takes the action listed in that line of the ACL and ignores the rest of the ACL statements.

For example, Figure 11-2 shows ACL 1 with three lines of pseudocode. The ACL is applied to R2's S0/0/1 interface, as indicated by the arrow. Inbound traffic from R1 will be filtered using ACL 1.

Figure 11-2   Example of ACL Matching Logic

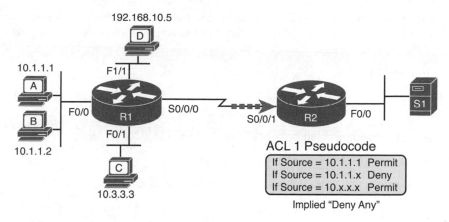

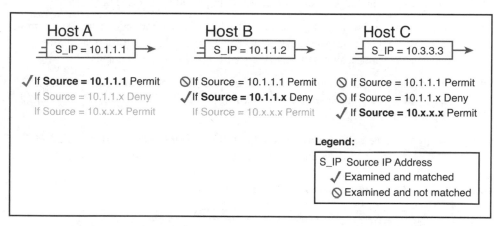

The box below the topology shows the logic for how packets from each host source address (labeled S_IP in the figure) is processed. Notice that after a match is made for Host A and Host B, the condition is applied (Host A is permitted and Host B is denied), and no further statements are evaluated. Host C matches the last statement in the list and is permitted.

Host D does not match any of the items in the ACL, so the packet is discarded. The reason is that every IP ACL has an implied "deny any" at the end of the ACL.

Planning to Use ACLs

Because an ACL can be used to filter traffic, it is important that you thoroughly plan the implementation of an ACL before actually configuring it.

Types of ACLs

ACLs can be configured to filter any type of protocol traffic, including other network layer protocols such as AppleTalk and IPX. For the CCNA exam, we focus on IPv4 ACLs, which come in the following types:

- **Standard ACLs:** Filter traffic based on source address only

- **Extended ACLs:** Can filter traffic based on source and destination address, specific protocols, as well as source and destination TCP and UDP ports

You can use two methods to identify both standard and extended ACLs:

- **Numbered ACLs:** Use a number for identification

- **Named ACLs:** Use a descriptive name or number for identification

Although named ACLs must be used with some types of IOS configurations that are beyond the scope of the CCNA exam topics, they do provide two basic benefits:

- By using a descriptive name (such as BLOCK-HTTP), a network administrator can more quickly determine the purpose of an ACL. This is particularly helpful in larger networks, where a router can have many ACLs with hundreds of statements.

- Reduce the amount of typing you must do to configure each statement in a named ACL, as you will see in the section "Configuring Named ACLs" in Day 10, "Basic ACL Configuration."

Both numbered and named ACLs can be configured for both standard and extended ACL implementations. Figure 11-3 summarizes the categories of IPv4 ACLs.

Figure 11-3   Comparisons of IP ACL Types

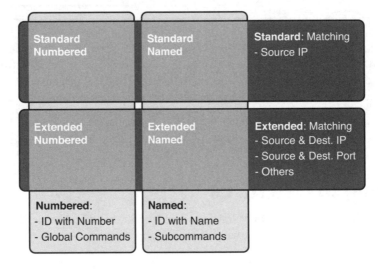

ACL Identification

Table 11-1 lists the different ACL number ranges for the IPv4 protocol. The table is not exhaustive. Other ACL numbers are available for other types of protocols that are either rarely used or beyond CCENT and CCNA scope. IPv6 uses only named ACLs.

Table 11-1   IPv4 ACL Numbers

Protocol	Range
IP	1–99
Extended IP	100–199
Standard IP (expanded)	1300–1999
Extended IP (expanded)	2000–2699

Named IP ACLs give you more flexibility in working with the ACL entries. In addition to using more memorable names, the other major advantage of named ACLs over numbered ACLs is that you can delete individual statements in a named IP access list.

With Cisco IOS Software Release 12.3, IP access list entry sequence numbering was introduced for both numbered and named ACLs. IP access list entry sequence numbering provides the following benefits:

- You can edit the order of ACL statements.

- You can remove individual statements from an ACL.

- You can use the sequence number to insert new statements into the middle of the ACL.

Sequence numbers are automatically added to the ACL if not entered explicitly at the time the ACL is created. No support exists for sequence numbering in software versions earlier than Cisco IOS Software Release 12.3; therefore, all the ACL additions for earlier software versions are placed at the end of the ACL.

ACL Design Guidelines

Well-designed and well-implemented ACLs add an important security component to your network. Follow these general principles to ensure that the ACLs you create have the intended results:

- Based on the test conditions, choose a standard or extended, numbered, or named ACL.

- Only one ACL per protocol, per direction, and per interface is allowed.

- Organize the ACL to enable processing from the top down. Organize your ACL so that the more specific references to a network, subnet, or host appear before ones that are more general. Place conditions that occur more frequently before conditions that occur less frequently.

- All ACLs contain an implicit deny any statement at the end.

- Create the ACL before applying it to an interface.

- Depending on how you apply the ACL, the ACL filters traffic either going through the router or going to and from the router, such as traffic to or from the vty lines.

- You should typically place extended ACLs as close as possible to the source of the traffic that you want to deny. Because standard ACLs do not specify destination addresses, you must put the standard ACL as close as possible to the destination of the traffic you want to deny so that the source can reach intermediary networks.

Study Resources

For today's exam topics, refer to the following resources for more study.

Resource	Location	Topic
Primary Resources		
Routing Protocols	9	IP ACL Operation
Routing & Switching Essentials	9	IP ACL Operation
ICND1 Official Cert Guide	22	IPv4 Access Control List Basics
		List Logic with IP ACLs
ICND1 Foundation Learning Guide	18	Access Control List Operation
Supplemental Resources		
CCENT Practice and Study Guide	20	IP ACL Operation
Flash Cards	6	Questions 1–13

Basic ACL Configuration

CCENT 100-101 ICND1 Exam Topics

- Configure and verify ACLs in a network environment.
- Configure and verify ACLs to filter network traffic (Basic).
- Configure and verify ACLs to limit Telnet and SSH access to the router.

Key Topics

Yesterday, we reviewed ACL concepts. Today, we focus on ACL configurations.

Configuring Standard Numbered ACLs

Standard IPv4 ACLs, which are numbered ACLs in the range of 1 to 99 and 1300 to 1999 or are named ACLs, filter packets based on a source address and mask, and they permit or deny the entire TCP/IP protocol suite. Configuring an ACL requires two steps:

Step 1. Create the ACL.

Step 2. Apply the ACL.

Let's use the simple topology shown in Figure 10-1 to demonstrate how to configure both standard and extended ACLs.

Figure 10-1   ACL Configuration Topology

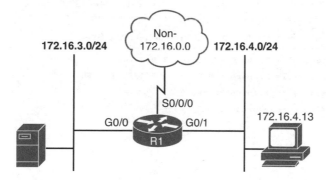

Standard Numbered ACL: Permit Specific Network

Create an ACL to prevent traffic that is not part of the internal networks (172.16.0.0/16) from traveling out either of the Gigabit Ethernet interfaces.

Step 1.   Create the ACL.

Use the **access-list** global configuration command to create an entry in a standard IPv4 ACL:

```
R1(config)# access-list 1 permit 172.16.0.0 0.0.255.255
```

The sample statement matches any address that starts with 172.16.x.x. You can use the **remark** option to add a description to your ACL.

Step 2.   Apply the ACL.

Use the interface configuration command to select an interface to which to apply the ACL. Then use the **ip access-group** interface configuration command to activate the existing ACL on an interface for a specific direction (in or out):

```
R1(config)# interface gigabitethernet 0/0
R1(config-if)# ip access-group 1 out
R1(config-if)# interface gigabitethernet 0/1
R1(config-if)# ip access-group 1 out
```

This step activates the standard IPv4 ACL 1 on both the interfaces as an outbound filter.

This ACL allows only traffic from source network 172.16.0.0 to be forwarded out on G0/0 and G0/1. Traffic from networks other than 172.16.0.0 is blocked with the implied "deny any."

Standard Numbered ACL: Deny a Specific Host

Create an ACL to prevent traffic that originates from host 172.16.4.13 from traveling out G0/0. Create and apply the ACL with the commands shown in Example 10-1.

Example 10-1   ACL Preventing Traffic Originating from a Specific Host

```
R1(config)# access-list 1 deny 172.16.4.13 0.0.0.0
R1(config)# access-list 1 permit 0.0.0.0 255.255.255.255
R1(config)# interface gigabitethernet 0/0
R1(config-if)# ip access-group 1 out
```

This ACL is designed to block traffic from a specific address, 172.16.4.13, and to allow all other traffic to be forwarded on interface G0/0. The first statement can also be written with the keyword **host** replacing the **0.0.0.0** wildcard mask as follows:

```
R1(config)# access-list 1 deny host 172.16.4.13
```

In fact, starting with Cisco IOS Software Release 12.3, you can enter the following:

```
R1(config)# access-list 1 deny 172.16.4.13
```

The second statement can be written with the keyword **any** replacing the source address 0.0.0.0 and wildcard mask 255.255.255.255 as follows:

```
R1(config)# access-list 1 permit any
```

Standard Numbered ACL: Deny a Specific Subnet

Create an ACL to prevent traffic that originates from the subnet 172.16.4.0/24 from traveling out the G0/0 interface. Create and apply the ACL with the commands shown in Example 10-2.

Example 10-2   ACL Preventing Traffic Originating from a Specific Subnet

```
R1(config)# access-list 1 deny 172.16.4.0 0.0.0.255
R1(config)# access-list 1 permit any
R1(config)# interface g0/0
R1(config-if)# ip access-group 1 out
```

This ACL is designed to block traffic from a specific subnet, 172.16.4.0, and to allow all other traffic to be forwarded out G0/0.

Standard Numbered ACL: Deny Telnet or SSH Access to the Router

For traffic into and out of the router (not through the router), filter Telnet or SSH access to the router by applying an ACL to the vty ports. Restricting vty access is primarily a technique for increasing network security and defining which addresses are allowed Telnet access to the router EXEC process. Create and apply the ACL with the commands shown in Example 10-3.

Example 10-3   Access List Allowing One Host Only Remote Access to R1

```
R1(config)# access-list 12 permit host 172.16.4.13
R1(config)# line vty 0 15
R1(config-line)# access-class 12 in
```

In this example, only host 172.16.4.13 is allowed to telnet into R1. All other IP addresses are denied implicitly.

Configuring Extended Numbered ACLs

For more precise traffic-filtering control, use extended IP ACLs, which are numbered ACLs in the range of 100–199 and 2000–2699 or are named ACLs, which check for the source and destination IP address. In addition, at the end of the extended ACL statement, you can specify the protocol and optional TCP or UDP application to filter more precisely. To configure numbered extended IPv4 ACLs on a Cisco router, create an extended IP ACL and activate that ACL on an interface. For CCENT exam purposes, the extended ACL command syntax is as follows:

```
Router(config)# access-list access-list-number {permit | deny} protocol source
   source-wildcard [operator port] destination destination-wildcard [operator port]
   [established] [log]
```

Table 10-1 explains the syntax of the command.

Table 10-1   Command Parameters for a Numbered Extended ACL

Command Parameter	Description
access-list-number	Identifies the list using a number in the range of 100–199 or 2000–2699.
permit | deny	Indicates whether this entry allows or blocks the specified address.
protocol	If **ip** is specified, the entire TCP/IP protocol suite is filtered. Other protocols you can filter include TCP, UDP, ICMP, EIGRP, and OSPF. Use the **?** after the **permit** | **deny** argument to see all the available protocols.
source and destination	Identifies source and destination IP addresses.
source-wildcard and destination-wildcard	Wildcard mask; 0s indicate positions that must match, and 1s indicate "don't care" positions.
operator [port | app_name]	The operator can be **lt** (less than), **gt** (greater than), **eq** (equal to), or **neq** (not equal to). The port number referenced can be either the source port or the destination port, depending on where in the ACL the port number is configured. As an alternative to the port number, well-known application names can be used, such as Telnet, FTP, and SMTP.
established	For inbound TCP only. Allows TCP traffic to pass if the packet is a response to an outbound-initiated session. This type of traffic has the acknowledgment (ACK) bits set.
log	Sends a logging message to the console.

Extended Numbered ACL: Deny FTP from Subnets

For the network in Figure 10-1, create an ACL to prevent FTP traffic originating from the subnet 172.16.4.0/24 and going to the 172.16.3.0/24 subnet from traveling out G0/0. Create and apply the ACL with the commands shown in Example 10-4.

Example 10-4   Access List Preventing FTP Traffic from Specific Subnets

```
R1(config)# access-list 101 deny tcp 172.16.4.0 0.0.0.255 172.16.3.0 0.0.0.255 eq
   21
R1(config)# access-list 101 deny tcp 172.16.4.0 0.0.0.255 172.16.3.0 0.0.0.255 eq
   20
R1(config)# access-list 101 permit ip any any
R1(config)# interface g0/0
R1(config-if)# ip access-group 101 out
```

The **deny** statements block FTP traffic originating from subnet 172.16.4.0 to subnet 172.16.3.0. The **permit** statement allows all other IP traffic out interface G0/0. Two statements must be entered for the FTP application because port 21 is used to establish, maintain, and terminate an FTP session while port 20 is used for the actual file transfer task.

Extended Numbered ACL: Deny Only Telnet from Subnet

Create an ACL to prevent Telnet traffic that originates from the subnet 172.16.4.0/24 from traveling out interface G0/0. Create and apply the ACL with the commands shown in Example 10-5.

Example 10-5   Access List Preventing Telnet Traffic from a Specific Subnet

```
R1(config)# access-list 101 deny tcp 172.16.4.0 0.0.0.255 any eq 23
R1(config)# access-list 101 permit ip any any
R1(config)# interface g0/0
R1(config-if)# ip access-group 101 out
```

This example denies Telnet traffic from 172.16.4.0 that is being sent out interface G0/0. All other IP traffic from any other source to any destination is permitted out G0/0.

Configuring Named ACLs

The named ACL feature allows you to identify standard and extended ACLs with an alphanumeric string (name) instead of the current numeric representations.

Because you can delete individual entries with named ACLs, you can modify your ACL without having to delete and then reconfigure the entire ACL. With Cisco IOS Software Release 12.3 and later, you can insert individual entries using an appropriate sequence number.

Standard Named ACL Steps and Syntax

The following are the steps and syntax used to create a standard named ACL:

Step 1.   Name the ACL.

Starting from global configuration mode, use the **ip access-list standard** *name* command to name the standard ACL. ACL names are alphanumeric and must be unique:

```
Router(config) ip access-list standard name
```

Step 2.   Create the ACL.

From standard named ACL configuration mode, use **permit** or **deny** statements to specify one or more conditions for determining whether a packet is forwarded or dropped. If you do not specify a sequence number, IOS will increment the sequence number by 10 for every statement you enter:

```
Router(config-std-nacl)# [sequence-number] {permit | deny} source
    source-wildcard [log]
```

Step 3.   Apply the ACL.

Activate the named ACL on an interface with the **ip access-group** *name* command:

```
Router(config-if)# ip access-group name [in | out]
```

Standard Named ACL: Deny a Single Host from a Given Subnet

For the network shown previously in Figure 10-1, create a standard ACL named TROUBLEMAKER to prevent traffic that originates from the host 172.16.4.13 from traveling out interface G0/0. Create and apply the ACL with the commands shown in Example 10-6.

Example 10-6   Named ACL Preventing Traffic from a Specific Host

```
R1(config)# ip access-list standard TROUBLEMAKER
R1(config-std-nacl)# deny host 172.16.4.13
R1(config-std-nacl)# permit 172.16.4.0 0.0.0.255
R1(config-std-nacl)# interface e0
R1(config-if)# ip access-group troublemaker out
```

Extended Named ACL Steps and Syntax

The following are the steps and syntax used to create an extended named ACL:

Step 1.   Name the ACL.

Starting from global configuration mode, use the **ip access-list extended** *name* command to name the extended ACL:

```
Router(config)# ip access-list extended name
```

Step 2.   Create the ACL.

From extended named ACL configuration mode, use **permit** or **deny** statements to specify one or more conditions for determining whether a packet is forwarded or dropped:

```
Router(config-ext-nacl)# [sequence-number] {deny | permit} protocol
   source source-wildcard [operator port] destination destination-wildcard
   [operator port] [established] [log]
```

Step 3.   Apply the ACL.

Activate the named ACL on an interface with the **ip access-group** *name* command:

```
Router(config-if)# ip access-group name [in | out]
```

Adding Comments to Named or Numbered ACLs

You can add comments to ACLs using the **remark** argument in place of the permit or deny. Remarks are descriptive statements that you can use to better understand and troubleshoot either named or numbered ACLs.

Example 10-7 shows how to add a comment to a numbered ACL.

Example 10-7   Adding Comments to a Numbered ACL

```
R1(config)# access-list 101 remark Permitting John to Telnet to Server
R1(config)# access-list 101 permit tcp host 172.16.1.13 host 172.16.3.10 eq telnet
```

Example 10-8 shows how to add a comment to a named ACL.

Example 10-8   Adding Comments to a Named ACL

```
R1(config)# ip access-list standard PREVENTION
R1(config-std-nacl)# remark Do not allow Jones subnet through
R1(config-std-nacl)# deny 172.16.4.0 0.0.0.255
```

Verifying ACLs

When you finish configuring an ACL, use **show** commands to verify the configuration. Use the **show access-lists** command to display the contents of all ACLs, as demonstrated in Example 10-9. By entering the ACL name or number as an option for this command, you can display a specific ACL.

Example 10-9 Verifying Access List Configuration

```
R1# show access-lists
Standard IP access list SALES
    10 permit 10.3.3.1
    20 permit 10.4.4.1
    30 permit 10.5.5.1
    40 deny    10.1.1.0, wildcard bits 0.0.0.255
    50 permit any
Extended IP access list ENG
    10 permit tcp host 10.22.22.1 any eq telnet (25 matches)
    20 permit tcp host 10.33.33.1 any eq ftp
    30 permit tcp host 10.33.33.1 any eq ftp-data
```

Notice in the output from the **show access-lists** command in Example 10-9 that sequence numbers are incremented by 10—most likely because the administrator did not enter a sequence number. Also notice that this command tells you how many times IOS has matched a packet to a statement—25 times in the case of the first statement in the named ACL ENG.

The **show ip interface** command displays IP interface information and indicates whether any IP ACLs are set on the interface. In the **show ip interface g0/0** command output shown in Example 10-10, IP ACL 1 has been configured on the G0/0 interface as an inbound ACL. No outbound IP ACL has been configured on the G0/0 interface.

Example 10-10 Verifying Access List Configuration on a Specific Interface

```
R1# show ip interface g0/0
GigabitEthernet0/0 is up, line protocol is up
  Internet address is 10.1.1.11/24
  Broadcast address is 255.255.255.255
  Address determined by setup command
  MTU is 1500 bytes
  Helper address is not set
  Directed broadcast forwarding is disabled
  Outgoing access list is not set
  Inbound access list is 1
  Proxy ARP is enabled
  <output omitted>
```

Finally, you can also verify your ACL creation and application with the **show running-config** command, as shown in Example 10-11.

Example 10-11 Verifying ACL Creation and Application in the Running Configuration

```
R1# show running-config
Building configuration...
!
<output omitted>
!
interface GigabitEthernet0/0
 ip address 10.44.44.1 255.255.255.0
 ip access-group ENG out
!
<output omitted>
!
interface Serial0/0/0
ip address 172.16.2.1 255.255.255.252
 ip access-group SALES in
!
<output omitted>
ip access-list standard SALES
 permit 10.3.3.1
 permit 10.4.4.1
 permit 10.5.5.1
 deny   10.1.1.0 0.0.0.255
 permit any
!
ip access-list extended ENG
 permit tcp host 10.22.22.1 any eq telnet
 permit tcp host 10.33.33.1 any eq ftp
 permit tcp host 10.33.33.1 any eq ftp-data
!
<output omitted>
```

Study Resources

For today's exam topics, refer to the following resources for more study.

Resource	Location	Topic
Primary Resources		
Routing Protocols	9	Standard IPv4 ACLs
		Extended IPv4 ACLs
Routing & Switching Essentials	9	Standard IPv4 ACLs
		Extended IPv4 ACLs
ICND1 Official Cert Guide	22	Standard Numbered IPv4 ACLs
		Practice Applying Standard IP ACLs
	23	Extended Numbered IP Access Control Lists
		Named ACLs and ACL Editing
ICND1 Foundation Learning Guide	18	Configuring ACLs
Supplemental Resources		
CCENT Practice and Study Guide	20	Standard IPv4 ACLs
		Extended IPv4 ACLs
Flash Cards	6	Questions 14–23
Network Simulator	23	Standard ACL
		ACL I–VI
		ACL Analysis I
		Named ACL I–III
		Extended ACL I–II
CCNA R&S Portable Command Guide	33	All

NAT

CCENT 100-101 ICND1 Exam Topics

- Identify the basic operation of NAT.
- Configure and verify NAT for given network requirements.

Key Topics

To cope with the depletion of IPv4 addresses, several short-term solutions were developed. One short-term solution is to use private addresses and Network Address Translation (NAT). NAT enables inside network hosts to borrow a legitimate Internet IPv4 address while accessing Internet resources. When the requested traffic returns, the legitimate IPv4 address is repurposed and available for the next Internet request by an inside host. Using NAT, network administrators need only one or a few IPv4 addresses for the router to provide to the hosts, instead of one unique IPv4 address for every client joining the network. Although IPv6 ultimately solves the problem NAT was created to address—IPv4 address space depletion—it is still in wide use in current network implementation strategies. Today, we review the concepts, configuration, and troubleshooting of NAT.

Network Time Protocol (NTP) is used enterprise-wide to synchronize the clocks of all networking devices. This is important so that syslog messages are stamped with the correct time, thus facilitating accurate problem isolation and troubleshooting as well as guarding against malicious attacks aimed at manipulating the clocks and syslog messages. Today, we review NTP concepts, configuration, and verification tasks.

NAT Concepts

NAT, defined in RFC 3022, has many uses. But its key use is to conserve IPv4 addresses by allowing networks to use private IPv4 addresses. NAT translates nonroutable, private, internal addresses into routable, public addresses. NAT also has the benefit of hiding internal IPv4 addresses from outside networks.

A NAT-enabled device typically operates at the border of a stub network. Figure 9-1 shows the master topology used during today's review. R2 is the border router and will be the device used for today's example configurations.

Figure 9-1   NAT Topology

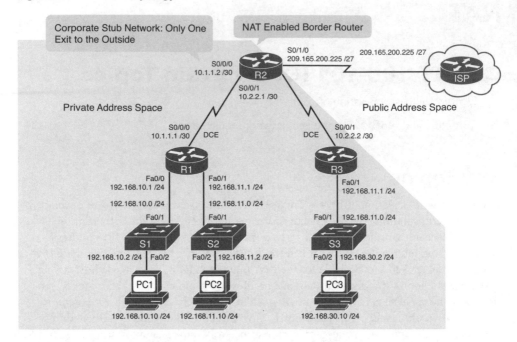

In NAT terminology, the inside network is the set of networks that are subject to translation (every network in the shaded region in Figure 9-1). The outside network refers to all other addresses. Figure 9-2 shows how to refer to the addresses when configuring NAT:

- **Inside local address:** Most likely a private address. In the figure, the IPv4 address 192.168.10.10 assigned to PC1 is an inside local address.

- **Inside global address:** A valid public address that the inside host is given when it exits the NAT router. When traffic from PC1 is destined for the web server at 209.165.201.1, R2 must translate the inside local address to an inside global address, which is 209.165.200.226 in this case.

- **Outside global address:** A reachable IPv4 address assigned to a host on the Internet. For example, the web server can be reached at IPv4 address 209.165.201.1.

- **Outside local address:** The local IPv4 address assigned to a host on the outside network. In most situations, this address is identical to the outside global address of that outside device. (Outside local addresses are beyond CCENT and CCNA scope.)

Figure 9-2   NAT Terminology

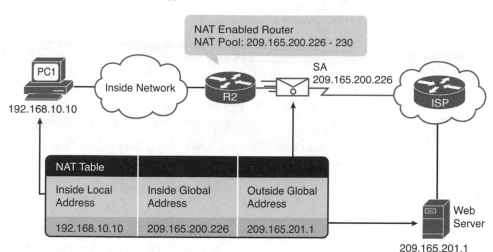

A NAT Example

Referring to Figure 9-1, the following steps illustrate the NAT process when PC1 sends traffic to the Internet:

1. PC1 sends a packet destined for the Internet to R1, the default gateway.

2. R1 forwards the packet to R2, as directed by its routing table.

3. R2 refers to its routing table and identifies the next hop as the ISP router. It then checks to see whether the packet matches the criteria specified for translation. R2 has an ACL that identifies the inside network as a valid host for translation. Therefore, it translates an inside local IPv4 address to an inside global IPv4 address, which in this case is 209.165.200.226. It stores this mapping of the local to global address in the NAT table.

4. R2 modifies the packet with the new source IPv4 address (the inside global address) and sends it to the ISP router.

5. The packet eventually reaches its destination, which then sends its reply to the inside global address 209.165.200.226.

6. When replies from the destination arrive back at R2, it consults the NAT table to match the inside global address to the correct inside local address. R2 then modifies the packet, inserting the inside local address (192.168.10.10) as the destination address and sending it to R1.

7. R1 receives the packet and forwards it to PC1.

Dynamic and Static NAT

The two types of NAT translation are as follows:

- **Dynamic NAT:** Uses a pool of public addresses and assigns them on a first-come, first-served basis or reuses an existing public address configured on an interface. When a host with a private IPv4 address requests access to the Internet, dynamic NAT chooses an IPv4 address from the pool that is not already in use by another host. Instead of using a pool, dynamic NAT can be configured to overload an existing public address configured on an interface.

- **Static NAT:** Uses a one-to-one mapping of local and global addresses, and these mappings remain constant. Static NAT is particularly useful for web servers or hosts that must have a consistent address that is accessible from the Internet.

NAT Overload

NAT overloading (also called Port Address Translation [PAT]) maps multiple private IPv4 addresses to a single public IPv4 address or a few addresses. To do this, each private address is also tracked by a port number. When a response comes back from the outside, source port numbers determine to which client the NAT router translates the packets.

Figure 9-3 and the following steps illustrate the NAT overload process.

Figure 9-3   NAT Overload Example

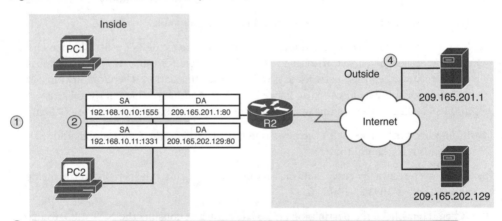

1. PC1 and PC2 send packets destined for the Internet.

2. When the packets arrive at R2, NAT overload changes the source address to the inside global IPv4 address and keeps a record of the assigned source port numbers (1555 and 1331, in this example) to identify the client from which the packets originated.

3. R2 updates its NAT table. Notice the assigned ports. R2 then routes the packets to the Internet.

4. When the web server replies, R2 uses the destination source port to translate the packet to the correct client.

NAT overload attempts to preserve the original source port. However, if this source port is already used, NAT overload assigns the first available port number starting from the beginning of the appropriate port group 0–511, 512–1023, or 1024–65535.

NAT Benefits

The benefits of using NAT include the following:

- NAT conserves registered IPv4 address space because, with NAT overload, internal hosts can share a single public IPv4 address for all external communications.

- NAT increases the flexibility of connections to the public network. Multiple pools, backup pools, and load-balancing pools can be implemented to ensure reliable public network connections.

- NAT allows the existing scheme to remain while supporting a new public addressing scheme. This means that an organization could change ISPs and not need to change any of its inside clients.

- NAT provides a layer of network security because private networks do not advertise their inside local addresses outside the organization. However, the phrase "NAT firewall" is misleading. NAT does not replace firewalls.

NAT Limitations

The limitations of using NAT include the following:

- **Performance is degraded:** NAT increases switching delays because translating each IPv4 address within the packet headers takes time.

- **End-to-end functionality is degraded:** Many Internet protocols and applications depend on end-to-end functionality, with unmodified packets forwarded from the source to the destination.

- **End-to-end IP traceability is lost:** It becomes much more difficult to trace packets that undergo numerous packet address changes over multiple NAT hops, making troubleshooting challenging.

- **Tunneling is more complicated:** Using NAT also complicates tunneling protocols, such as IPsec, because NAT modifies values in the headers that interfere with the integrity checks done by IPsec and other tunneling protocols.

- **Services can be disrupted:** Services that require the initiation of TCP connections from the outside network, or stateless protocols such as those using UDP, can be disrupted.

Configuring Static NAT

Static NAT is a one-to-one mapping between an inside address and an outside address. Static NAT allows connections initiated by external devices to access inside devices. For example, you might want to map an inside global address to a specific inside local address that is assigned to your inside web server. The steps and syntax to configure static NAT are as follows:

Step 1. Configure the static translation of an inside local address to an inside global address:

```
Router(config)# ip nat inside source static local-ip global-ip
```

Step 2. Specify the inside interface:

```
Router(config)# interface type number
Router(config-if)# ip nat inside
```

Step 3. Specify the outside interface:

```
Router(config)# interface type number
Router(config-if)# ip nat outside
```

Figure 9-4 shows a sample static NAT topology.

Figure 9-4   Static NAT Topology

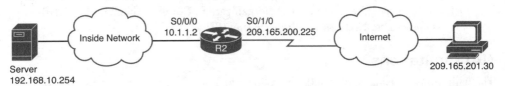

Example 9-1 shows the static NAT configuration.

Example 9-1   Static NAT Configuration

```
R2(config)# ip nat inside source static 192.168.10.254 209.165.200.254
R2(config)# interface serial0/0/0
R2(config-if)# ip nat inside
R2(config-if)# interface serial 0/1/0
R2(config-if)# ip nat outside
```

This configuration statically maps the inside private IPv4 address of 192.168.10.254 to the outside public IPv4 address of 209.165.200.254. This allows outside hosts to access the internal web server using the public IPv4 address 209.165.200.254.

Configuring Dynamic NAT

Dynamic NAT maps private IPv4 addresses to public addresses drawn from a NAT pool. The steps and syntax to configure dynamic NAT are as follows:

Step 1.   Define a pool of global addresses to be allocated:

```
Router(config)# ip nat pool name start-ip end-ip {netmask netmask |
    prefix-length prefix-length}
```

Step 2.   Define a standard access list permitting those addresses that are to be translated:

```
Router(config)# access-list access-list-number source source-wildcard
```

Step 3.   Bind the pool of addresses to the access list:

```
Router(config)# ip nat inside source list access-list-number pool name
```

Step 4.   Specify the inside interface:

```
Router(config)# interface type number
Router(config-if)# ip nat inside
```

Step 5.   Specify the outside interface:

```
Router(config)# interface type number
Router(config-if)# ip nat outside
```

Figure 9-5 shows a sample dynamic NAT topology.

Figure 9-5   **Dynamic NAT Topology**

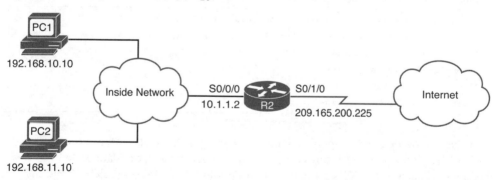

Example 9-2 shows the dynamic NAT configuration.

Example 9-2   Dynamic NAT Configuration

```
R2(config)# ip nat pool NAT-POOL1 209.165.200.226 209.165.200.240 netmask
255.255.255.224
R2(config)# access-list 1 permit 192.168.0.0 0.0.255.255
R2(config)# ip nat inside source list 1 pool NAT-POOL1
R2(config)# interface serial 0/0/0
R2(config-if)# ip nat inside
R2(config-if)# interface serial s0/1/0
R2(config-if)# ip nat outside
```

Configuring NAT Overload

Commonly with home networks and small- to medium-sized businesses, the ISP assigns only one registered IPv4 address to your router. Therefore, it is necessary to overload that one IPv4 address so that multiple inside clients can use it simultaneously.

The configuration is similar to dynamic NAT, except that instead of a pool of addresses, the **interface** keyword is used to identify the outside IPv4 address. The **overload** keyword enables PAT so that source port numbers are tracked during translation.

Example 9-3 shows how R2 in Figure 9-5 would be configured to overload its registered IPv4 address on the serial interface.

Example 9-3   Configuring NAT to Overload an Interface Address

```
R2(config)# access-list 1 permit 192.168.0.0 0.0.255.255
R2(config)# ip nat inside source list 1 interface serial 0/1/0 overload
R2(config)# interface serial 0/0/0
R2(config-if)# ip nat inside
R2(config-if)# interface serial s0/1/0
R2(config-if)# ip nat outside
```

You can also overload a NAT pool of addresses, which might be necessary in organizations that potentially have many clients simultaneously needing translations. In our previous Example 9-2, NAT is configured with a pool of 15 addresses (209.165.200.226– 209.165.200.240). If, at any given moment, R2 is translating all 15 addresses, packets for the 16th client will be queued for processing and possibly time out. To avoid this problem, add the keyword **overload** to the command that binds the access list to the NAT pool as follows:

```
R2(config)# ip nat inside source list 1 pool NAT-POOL1 overload
```

Interestingly, IOS will use the first IPv4 address in the pool until it runs out of available port numbers. Then it will move to the next IPv4 address in the pool.

Verifying NAT

Assume that both the static and dynamic NAT topologies shown in Figures 9-4 and 9-5 are configured on R2 with the inside server statically translated to 209.165.200.254 and the **NAT-POOL1** configured with the **overload** keyword. Further, assume that two inside clients have connected to an outside host. You can use the **show ip nat translations** command to verify the current translations in the R2 NAT table, as shown in Example 9-4.

Example 9-4   Verifying NAT Operations with show ip nat translations

```
R2# show ip nat translations
Pro  Inside global         Inside local         Outside local       Outside global
---  209.165.200.254       192.168.10.254       ---                 ---
tcp 209.165.200.226:47392 192.168.10.10:47392 209.165.201.30:80  209.165.201.30:80
tcp 209.165.200.226:50243 192.168.11.10:50243 209.165.201.30:80  209.165.201.30:80
```

The static entry is always in the table. Currently, there are two dynamic entries. Notice that both inside clients received the same inside global address, but the source port numbers are different (47392 for PC1 and 50243 for PC2).

The **show ip nat statistics** command, shown in Example 9-5, displays information about the total number of active translations, NAT configuration parameters, how many addresses are in the pool, and how many have been allocated.

Example 9-5   Verifying NAT Operations with show ip nat statistics

```
R2# show ip nat statistics
Total translations: 3 (1 static, 2 dynamic, 2 extended)
Outside Interfaces: Serial0/1/0
Inside Interfaces: FastEthernet0/0 , Serial0/0/0 , Serial0/0/1
Hits: 29  Misses: 7
Expired translations: 5
Dynamic mappings:
-- Inside Source
access-list 1 pool NAT-POOL1 refCount 2
 pool NAT-POOL1: netmask 255.255.255.224
      start 209.165.200.226 end 209.165.200.240
      type generic, total addresses 3 , allocated 1 (7%), misses 0
```

Alternatively, use the **show run** command and look for NAT, access command list, interface, or pool-related commands with the required values. Examine the output from these commands carefully to discover any errors.

It is sometimes useful to clear the dynamic entries sooner than the default. This is especially true when testing the NAT configuration. To clear dynamic entries before the timeout has expired, use the **clear ip nat translation *** privileged EXEC command.

Troubleshooting NAT

When you have IP connectivity problems in a NAT environment, it is often difficult to determine the cause of the problem. The first step in solving your problem is to rule out NAT as the cause. Follow these steps to verify that NAT is operating as expected:

Step 1.   Based on the configuration, clearly define what NAT is supposed to achieve. This might reveal a problem with the configuration.

Step 2.   Verify that correct translations exist in the translation table using the **show ip nat translations** command.

Step 3.   Use the **clear** and **debug** commands to verify that NAT is operating as expected. Check to see whether dynamic entries are re-created after they are cleared.

Step 4.   Review in detail what is happening to the packet, and verify that routers have the correct routing information to forward the packet.

Use the **debug ip nat** command to verify the operation of the NAT feature by displaying information about every packet that the router translates, as shown in Example 9-6.

Example 9-6   Troubleshooting NAT with debug ip nat

```
R2# debug ip nat
IP NAT debugging is on
R2#
NAT: s=192.168.10.10->209.165.200.226, d=209.165.201.30[8]
NAT*: s=209.165.201.30, d=209.165.200.226->192.168.10.10[8]
NAT: s=192.168.10.10->209.165.200.226, d=209.165.201.30[8]
NAT: s=192.168.10.10->209.165.200.226, d=209.165.201.30[8]
NAT*: s=209.165.201.30, d=209.165.200.226->192.168.10.10[8]
NAT*: s=209.165.201.30, d=209.165.200.226->192.168.10.10[8]
NAT: s=192.168.10.10->209.165.200.226, d=209.165.201.30[8]
NAT: s=192.168.10.10->209.165.200.226, d=209.165.201.30[8]
NAT*: s=209.165.201.30, d=209.165.200.226->192.168.10.10[8]
NAT*: s=209.165.201.30, d=209.165.200.226->192.168.10.10[8]
NAT: s=192.168.10.10->209.165.200.226, d=209.165.201.30[8]
R2#
```

You can see that inside host 192.168.10.10 initiated traffic to outside host 209.165.201.30 and has been translated into address 209.165.200.226.

When decoding the debug output, note what the following symbols and values indicate:

- *: The asterisk next to NAT indicates that the translation is occurring in the fast-switched path. The first packet in a conversation is always process-switched, which is slower. The remaining packets go through the fast-switched path if a cache entry exists.

- s=: Refers to the source IPv4 address.

- **a.b.c.d->w.x.y.z:** Indicates that source address **a.b.c.d** is translated into **w.x.y.z**.

- **d=:** Refers to the destination IPv4 address.

- **[xxxx]:** The value in brackets is the IP identification number. This information can be useful for debugging because it enables correlation with other packet traces from protocol analyzers.

NAT for IPv6

We finish our NAT review with a quick look at NAT for IPv6. IPv6 was developed with the intention of making NAT for IPv4 unnecessary. However, IPv6 does include its own IPv6 private address space and NAT, which are implemented differently than they are for IPv4.

IPv6 Private Address Space

IPv6 unique local addresses (ULA) are similar to RFC 1918 private addresses in IPv4, but there are significant differences as well. The intent of unique local addresses is to provide IPv6 address space for communications within a local site. It is not meant to provide additional IPv6 address space, nor is it meant to provide a level of security.

As shown in Figure 9-6, unique local addresses have the prefix FC00::/7, which results in a first hextet range of FC00–FDFF.

Figure 9-6   IPv6 Unique Local Address Format

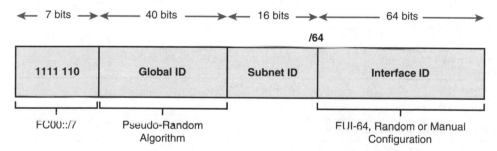

ULAs are also known as local IPv6 addresses (not to be confused with IPv6 link-local addresses). Unlike private IPv4 addresses, it has not been the intention of the Internet Engineering Task Force (IETF) to use a form of NAT to translate between unique local addresses and IPv6 global unicast addresses. The implementation and potential uses for IPv6 unique local addresses are still being examined by the Internet community.

Purpose of NAT for IPv6

NAT for IPv6 is used in a much different context than NAT for IPv4. The varieties of NAT for IPv6 are used to transparently provide access between IPv6-only and IPv4-only networks, as shown in Figure 9-7. It is not used as a form of private IPv6–to–global IPv6 translation.

Figure 9-7   Overview of NAT64 Operation

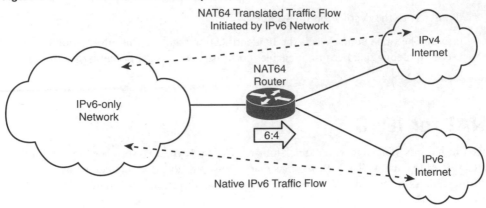

Over the years, there have been several types of NAT for IPv6 including NAT-PT (Network Address Translation – Protocol Translation). NAT-PT has been deprecated by the IETF in favor of its replacement, NAT64 (the **64** stands for IPv6 to IPv4 translation). NAT64 is beyond the CCENT and CCNA scope. However, be prepared to answer questions about the major differences between NAT for IPv4 and NAT for IPv6.

NOTE: If you would like a detailed explanation of NAT64, see Chapter 11 in Rick Graziani's Cisco Press book, *IPv6 Fundamentals*.

Study Resources

For today's exam topics, refer to the following resources for more study.

Resource	Location	Topic
Primary Resources		
Routing & Switching Essentials	11	All
ICND1 Official Cert Guide	24	All
ICND1 Foundation Learning Guide	16	Scaling the Network with NAT and PAT
Supplemental Resources		
CCENT Practice and Study Guide	22	All
Flash Cards	7	Questions 8–21
Network Simulator	24	NAT Configuration I–VII
		Configuring NAT I–III
		NAT
CCNA R&S Portable Command Guide	27	All

Basic Device Security

CCENT 100-101 ICND1 Exam Topics

- Configure and verify network device security features.
- Configure and verify NTP as a client.

Key Topics

More than likely, your CCENT studies had security issues, concerns, and configurations sprinkled throughout your training. This is reflected in the Study Resources section, where you can see a variety of places to read up on network device security. We have already covered some important security configurations including passwords and SSH. Today, we will do a comprehensive review of basic device security. But because we have already reviewed some security configurations (passwords and SSH, for example), this review will also point you to the correct "day" to revisit, when necessary.

Network Security Overview

Computers and networks, if left in their default configurations, are vulnerable. Whether through unintentional or malicious attacks, the damage can be costly. Intruders can gain access to a network through software vulnerabilities, through hardware attacks, or through guessing someone's username and password. Even in small networks, it is necessary to consider security threats and vulnerabilities when planning a network implementation.

Physical Security

Software vulnerabilities are top of mind in today's networks. However, a sound security policy starts with the physical security of devices, including protecting against physical damage to equipment as follows:

- **Environmental threats:** Temperature or humidity extremes
- **Electrical threats:** Voltage spikes, insufficient power, power loss, unconditioned power
- **Maintenance threats:** Poor handling of electrical components, lack of parts, and poor cabling and labeling

In addition, sensitive networking equipment should be secured behind a locked security system—for example, a locked door or a more elaborate security clearance process.

Types of Security Vulnerabilities

There are three primary vulnerabilities or weaknesses shown in the following list with examples of each:

- **Technological:** Vulnerabilities inherent in the software such as the TCP/IP suite, operating system weakness, password protection, lack of authorization, routing protocols, and firewall holes

- **Configuration:** Unsecured user accounts, easy-to-guess passwords, misconfigured services, default settings, misconfigured network equipment

- **Security:** Lack of a written security policy, organizational politics, installation or modifications done "by the book," no disaster recovery policy

Mitigating Network Attacks

The damage from network attacks can be mitigated by following a vigilant policy that includes the following:

- Backing up critical data offsite and maintaining a regular schedule of software upgrades or patches.

- Implementing AAA (authentication, authorization, and accounting) network security can help mitigate internal and external threats.

- Controlling traffic with firewall devices that do multiple levels of packet filtering and stateful packet inspection.

- Securing endpoint devices through well-documented policies and employee training.

Security Best Practices

The following are ten best practices that are a good starting point for securing your network:

- Develop a written security policy.

- Shut down unused services and ports.

- Use strong passwords and change them often.

- Control physical access to devices.

- Use secure HTTPS for login screens.

- Perform backups on a regular basis.

- Educate employees about social engineering attacks.

- Encrypt and password-protect sensitive data.

- Implement security hardware and software.

- Keep software up to date.

Securing the IOS

Part of network security is securing actual devices, including end devices and intermediate devices, such as network devices. When a new operating system is installed on a device, the security settings are set to the default values. In most cases, the level of security provided by the default settings of a device is inadequate. Cisco access switches, like the 2960, are ready to be installed "out of the box" in the network. For both routers and switches, the console port is open and ready for full access with no passwords. Home routers use default passwords that are easily obtained with a quick Internet search. Initial steps to secure the operating system include

- Change the default usernames and passwords immediately.

- Restrict access to authorized personnel only.

- Disable or uninstall unnecessary services.

Passwords, Authentication, Timers, and SSH

We reviewed password and SSH configuration on Day 27, "Basic Switch Configuration," and Day 21, "Implementing IPv6 Addressing," within the context of basic switch and router configuration. As a quick reminder, Figure 8-1 reviews the locations where IOS can require a password.

Figure 8-1   Locations for Passwords: Console, vty, and Enable

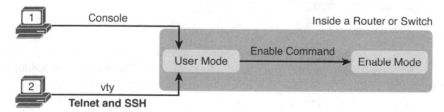

The following list points out the reasons for using the various password options:

- Use the **enable secret** command to override the **enable password** command, which is now deprecated and shouldn't be used.

- Avoid using simple password checking for the console or vtys with the **login** *line-mode* command because this method does not identify individual users.

- Disable support for inbound Telnet connections because Telnet sends the passwords as clear text. Instead, configure SSH and the **transport input ssh** command in vty line mode.

- Authenticate CLI logins using an external authentication server. However, if necessary, use locally configured **username secret** commands, which hide the passwords with a hash, as shown in Example 8-1.

Example 8-1   Strong Encryption with the username secret Command

```
R1(config)# username BobAdmin secret a11-34cT%
R1(config)#
*Jun 10 12:33:33.043: End->Password:yY6nb9c6RgExpgm9VkW7r961XigSmiGMCcS7hNrVsfE
R1(config)# do show run | begin username
username admin password 7 030752180500
username BobAdmin secret 4 yY6nb9c6RgExpgm9VkW7r961XigSmiGMCcS7hNrVsfE
!
```

The password for admin in Example 8-1 is encrypted with the **service password-encryption** text. Search the web for "cisco password decrypt" and you will find out what the password is for 030752180500. Although the secret passwords can also be cracked, it is a much more involved process.

Because passwords are easy to crack, a password policy should at least take into consideration the following guidelines:

- Use a password length of eight to ten characters.

- Make passwords complex, using uppercase, lowercase, numbers, symbols, and spaces.

- Avoid passwords based on easily identifiable pieces of information.

- Deliberately misspell a password.

- Change passwords often.

- Do not write passwords down.

As we've seen, the **service password-encryption** command prevents unauthorized individuals from viewing plain-text passwords in the configuration file. The IOS has two additional commands that can help with the length of passwords and protect against brute-force attacks, as shown in Example 8-2.

Example 8-2   Securing Passwords, Mitigating Brute-Force Attacks, and Lowering Timeout Defaults

```
R1(config)# service password-encryption
R1(config)# security passwords min-length 8
R1(config)# login block-for 120 attempts 2 within 60
R1(config)# line vty 0 15
R1(config-line)# exec-timeout 3 30
R1(config-line)# do show run | begin line vty
line vty 0 4
 exec-timeout 3 30
 password 7 060506324F41
 login local
 transport input ssh
```

```
<output omitted>
!With the login command configured, a syslog message is generated on password
  failures.
*Jun  9 23:22:45.875: %SEC_LOGIN-1-QUIET_MODE_ON: Still timeleft for watching
  failures is 114 secs, [user: admin] [Source: 10.1.1.2] [localport: 22] [Reason:
  Login Authentication Failed - BadPassword] [ACL: sl_def_acl] at 23:22:45 UTC Sun
  Jun 9 2013
!After 120 seconds, the user can attempt to authenticate again.
*Jun  9 23:24:45.875: %SEC_LOGIN-5-QUIET_MODE_OFF: Quiet Mode is OFF, because block
  period timed out at 23:23:15 UTC Sun Jun 9 2013
```

The commands shown in Example 8-2 have the following effect:

- Hopefully, there are no plain-text passwords in the configuration file. But if there are, they will at least be encrypted to prevent someone from "looking over the shoulder" and reading a password.

- Passwords must be at least eight characters long.

- Login attempts are limited to two within 60 seconds. Additional attempts are blocked for 120 seconds.

- After being logged in to a vty line, the session will time out if idle for 3 minutes and 30 seconds. The default **exec-timeout** is 5 minutes.

Notice that SSH is enabled on the vty lines and that the **login local** command is also configured. The **username** *user* **secret** *password* command configured in Example 8-1 would be used to log in remotely. The password under the vty line would only be valid if SSH was disabled and the **login local** command was changed to simply **login**.

Banners

Cisco switches can display a variety of banners depending on what a router or switch administrator is doing. Table 8-1 lists the three most popular banners and their typical uses.

Table 8-1   Banners and Their Uses

Banner	Typical Use
Message of the Day (MOTD)	Shown before the login prompt. Used for temporary messages that can change from time to time, such as "Router1 down for maintenance at midnight."
Login	Shown before the login prompt but after the MOTD banner. Used for permanent messages such as "Unauthorized Access Prohibited."
Exec	Shown after the login prompt. Used to supply information that should be hidden from unauthorized users.

The **banner** global configuration command can be used to configure all three types of these banners. In each case, the type of banner is listed as the first parameter, with MOTD being the default option. The first nonblank character after the banner type is called a beginning delimiter character.

Example 8-3 shows the configuration process for all three types of banners from Table 8-1. The first banner in the example, the MOTD banner, omits the banner type in the **banner** command as a reminder that **motd** is the default banner type. The delimiter is the "$" symbol, but it could be any character as long as it is the same at the beginning and end of the banner text and is not reused inside the banner text.

Example 8-3   Banner Configuration Examples

```
! The "banner" command defaults the "motd" parameter, as shown here.
R1(config)# banner $
Enter TEXT message. End with the character '$'.
Automated backup scheduled for 11PM Today $
R1(config)# banner login $
Enter TEXT message. End with the character '$'.
*******************************************
WARNING: Unauthorized Access Prohibited!!!!
*******************************************
$
R1(config)# banner exec $
Enter TEXT message. End with the character '$'.
Policy Reminder: User password changes scheduled for next week.
$
R1(config)#
```

Banners display at different times depending upon how the user is accessing the device. If the user is accessing it from the console, the user will see the **banner motd** and the **banner login** messages immediately. The **banner exec** text is displayed after successful login, as shown in Example 8-4.

Example 8-4   User Accessing R1 Through the Console Port

```
R1 con0 is now available
Press RETURN to get started.
Automated backup scheduled for 11PM Today
*******************************************
WARNING: Unauthorized Access Prohibited!!!!
*******************************************


User Access Verification


Password:
```

```
Policy Reminder: User password changes scheduled for next week.

R2>
```

If the user is accessing the device remotely, he will only see the **banner login** text when attempting to log in. After a successful login, the **banner motd** and **banner exec** texts display, as shown in Example 8-5.

Example 8-5   User Remotely Accessing R1 from R2

```
R2# ssh -l admin 10.1.1.2

*********************************************
WARNING: Unauthorized Access Prohibited!!!!
*********************************************

Password:

Automated backup scheduled for 11PM Today
Policy Reminder: User password changes scheduled for next week.
R1>
```

Disable Services

In any service that a computer uses for good reason, hackers can use it as a way to attack a network. So, every good security plan looks to change the default settings to minimize security risks. Cisco makes several recommendations about which services to disable and enable. Knowing these specific recommendations is beyond the CCENT and CCNA scope. However, we can quickly highlight some important services to consider.

HTTP Service

Depending on the IOS, HTTP service might be enabled by default. An attacker could enter her default gateway address in a web browser to see whether she is prompted for a username and password. The Cisco recommendation is to disable HTTP service and only enable the HTTPS service if you intend to allow users to connect to the router or switch using a web browser.

CDP

Cisco Discovery Protocol (CDP) allows devices on the same link to learn basic information from each other. However, that basic information can help an attacker learn some useful information about the network. So, as a security recommendation, Cisco suggests disabling CDP on all interfaces connected to untrusted parts of the network. To be even more secure, CDP could be disabled globally.

Small Services

IOS has a set of services that IOS categorizes as small services. For example, the Echo service is one of these small services. It acts a lot like ping, with ICMP Echo Request and Echo Reply messages, but unlike these ICMP messages, the Echo application uses either TCP or UDP. Some IOS versions leave these services enabled by default, while some do not. To be thorough, disable both TCP and UDP small services.

Example 8-6 shows a configuration on R1 disabling the functions mentioned in this section.

Example 8-6   Disabling IOS Services

```
R1(config)# no ip http server
R1(config)# no service tcp-small-servers
R1(config)# no service udp-small-servers
R1(config)# interface gigabitEthernet 0/0
R1(config-if)# no cdp enable
! CDP is only disabled on the specified interface. To disable CDP globally,
! enter the "no cdp run" command in global configuration mode.
R1(config-if)#
```

NOTE: If you are interested in learning more about the Cisco recommendations for disabling services, search for "Guide to Harden Cisco IOS Devices" for more detailed documentation.

Network Time Protocol

As you know, routers and switches issue log messages in response to different events. For example, when an interface fails, the device creates log messages. With default settings, IOS sends these messages to the console port. But it can be configured to also send messages to a Syslog server, where they can be stored for administration review and troubleshooting. Figure 8-2 shows a topology with a Syslog server.

Figure 8-2   Sample Network with a Syslog Server

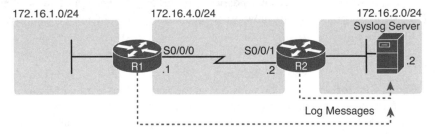

Most log messages list the date and time as part of the message so that when a network engineer looks back at the message, the engineer knows exactly when that message occurred.

Network Time Protocol (NTP) provides a way to synchronize the time-of-day clock so that timestamps will be consistent across devices, making troubleshooting easier.

To configure a router or switch to synchronize its time with an existing NTP server, use the **ntp server** command, as shown in Example 8-7.

Example 8-7   Configuration and Verification of an NTP Client

```
R1(config)# ntp server 172.16.2.2 version 4
R1(config)# ^z
R1#
R1# show ntp status
Clock is synchronized, stratum 8, reference is 172.16.2.2
nominal freq is 250.0000 Hz, actual freq is 250.0000 Hz, precision is 2**21
ntp uptime is 4700 (1/100 of seconds), resolution is 4000
reference time is D42BD899.5FFCE014 (13:48:09.374 UTC Fri Oct 19 2012)
clock offset is -0.0033 msec, root delay is 1.28 msec
root dispersion is 3938.51 msec, peer dispersion is 187.59 msec
loopfilter state is 'CTRL' (Normal Controlled Loop), drift is 0.000000000 s/s
system poll interval is 64, last update was 42 sec ago.
R1# show ntp associations
address ref clock st when poll reach delay offset disp
*172.16.2.2 127.127.1.1 7 36 64 1 1.261 -0.001 7937.5
* sys.peer, # selected, + candidate, - outlyer, x falseticker, configured
```

The output of the **show ntp status** command gives the NTP status in the very first line—R1 is synchronized with the NTP server at 172.16.2.2. The **show ntp associations** command lists a single line of output for each other NTP device with which the router has associated.

Routers and switches can actually be the NTP server with just one command (**ntp master**) as well. And NTP can use authentication so that a router or switch does not get fooled into changing its timestamp.

Study Resources

For today's exam topics, refer to the following resources for more study.

Resource	Location	Topic
Primary Resources		
Network Fundamentals	1	Network Security
	11	Keeping the Network Safe
Introduction to Networks	1	Network Security
	11	Keeping the Network Safe
Routing & Switching Essentials	2	Switch Security: Management and Implementation
ICND1 Official Cert Guide	8	Securing the Switch CLI (includes SSH)
		Encrypting and Hiding Passwords
	23	Router and Switch Security
ICND1 Foundation Learning Guide	17	All
Supplemental Resources		
CCENT Practice and Study Guide	1	Network Security Terminology
	11	Keeping the Network Safe
	13	Switch Security: Management and Implementation
Flash Cards	8	All
Network Simulator	23	NTP Configuration I–III

Switch Security Configuration

CCENT 100-101 ICND1 Exam Topics

- Configure and verify switch port security.

Key Topics

Today we review switch security, including configuring port security, how to restore a disabled port, shutting down unused ports and assigning them to an unused VLAN, and configuring the native VLAN as something other than VLAN 1.

Configuring Port Security

If you know which devices should be cabled and connected to particular interfaces on a switch, you can use port security to restrict that interface so that only the expected devices can use it. This reduces exposure to some types of attacks in which the attacker connects a laptop to the wall socket or uses the cable attached to another end device to gain access to the network.

Port security configuration involves several steps. Basically, you need to make the port an access port, which means that the port is not doing any VLAN trunking. You then need to enable port security and then configure the actual Media Access Control (MAC) addresses of the devices allowed to use that port. The following list outlines the steps, including the configuration commands used:

Step 1. Configure the interface for static access mode using the **switchport mode access** interface subcommand.

Step 2. Enable port security using the **switchport port-security** interface subcommand.

Step 3. (Optional) Override the maximum number of allowed MAC addresses associated with the interface (1) using the **switchport port-security maximum** *number* interface subcommand.

Step 4. (Optional) Override the default action to when there is a security violation (shutdown) using the **switchport port-security violation** {**protect** | **restrict** | **shutdown**} interface subcommand.

Step 5. (Optional) Predefine any allowed source MAC address(es) for this interface using the **switchport port-security mac-address** *mac-address* command. Use the command multiple times to define more than one MAC address.

Step 6. (Optional) Instead of Step 5, configure the interface to dynamically learn and configure the MAC addresses of currently connected hosts by configuring the **switchport port-security mac-address sticky** interface subcommand.

When an unauthorized device attempts to send frames to the switch interface, the switch can issue informational messages, discard frames from that device, or even discard frames from all devices by effectively shutting down the interface. Exactly which action the switch port takes depends on the option you configure in the **switchport port-security violation** command. Table 7-1 lists actions that the switch will take based on whether you configure the option protect, restrict, or shutdown (default).

Table 7-1   Actions When Port Security Violation Occurs

Option on the `switchport port-security violation` Command	`protect`	`restrict`	`shutdown`
Discards offending traffic	Yes	Yes	Yes
Sends log and SNMP messages	No	Yes	Yes
Disables the interface, discarding all traffic	No	No	Yes

Example 7-1 shows a port security configuration where each access interface is allowed a maximum of three MAC addresses. If a fourth MAC address is detected, only the offending device's traffic will be discarded. If the violation option is not explicitly configured, the traffic for devices that are allowed on the port would also be discarded because the port would be shut down by default.

Example 7-1   Port Security Configuration Example

```
S1(config)# interface range fa 0/5 - fa 0/24
S1(config-if-range)# switchport mode access
S1(config-if-range)# switchport port-security
S1(config-if-range)# switchport port-security maximum 3
S1(config-if-range)# switchport port-security violation restrict
S1(config-if-range)# switchport port-security mac-address sticky
```

To verify port security configuration, use the more general **show port-security** command or the more specific **show port-security interface** *type number* command. Example 7-2 demonstrates the use of both commands. In the examples, notice that only one device is currently attached to an access port on S1.

Example 7-2   Port Security Verification Command Output Examples

```
S1# show port-security
Secure Port  MaxSecureAddr  CurrentAddr  SecurityViolation  Security Action
             (Count)        (Count)      (Count)
---------------------------------------------------------------------------
     Fa0/5        3             1              0             Restrict
     Fa0/6        3             0              0             Restrict
     Fa0/7        3             0              0             Restrict
     Fa0/8        3             0              0             Restrict
```

```
         Fa0/9          3              0              0         Restrict
        Fa0/10          3              0              0         Restrict
        Fa0/11          3              0              0         Restrict
        Fa0/12          3              0              0         Restrict
        Fa0/13          3              0              0         Restrict
        Fa0/14          3              0              0         Restrict
        Fa0/15          3              0              0         Restrict
        Fa0/16          3              0              0         Restrict
        Fa0/17          3              0              0         Restrict
        Fa0/18          3              0              0         Restrict
        Fa0/19          3              0              0         Restrict
        Fa0/20          3              0              0         Restrict
        Fa0/21          3              0              0         Restrict
        Fa0/22          3              0              0         Restrict
        Fa0/23          3              0              0         Restrict
        Fa0/24          3              0              0         Restrict
---------------------------------------------------------------------------
Total Addresses in System (excluding one mac per port)      : 0
Max Addresses limit in System (excluding one mac per port) : 8320
S1#show port-security interface fastethernet 0/5
Port Security                : Enabled
Port Status                  : Secure-down
Violation Mode               : Restrict
Aging Time                   : 0 mins
Aging Type                   : Absolute
SecureStatic Address Aging   : Disabled
Maximum MAC Addresses        : 3
Total MAC Addresses          : 1
Configured MAC Addresses     : 0
Sticky MAC Addresses         : 1
Last Source Address:Vlan     : 0014.22dd.37a3:1
Security Violation Count     : 0
```

Restoring a Port After a Violation

When port security is activated on an interface, the default action when there is a violation is to shut down the port. A security violation can occur in one of two ways:

- The maximum number of secure MAC addresses has been added to the address table for that interface, and a station whose MAC address is not in the address table attempts to access the interface.

- An address learned or configured on one secure interface is seen on another secure interface in the same VLAN.

When a violation occurs, a syslog message is sent to the console stating that the interface is now in the **err-disable** state. The console messages include the port number and the MAC address that caused the violation, as shown in Example 7-3.

Example 7-3   Port Security Violation Verification and Restoration

```
S1#
Sep 20 06:44:54.966: %PM-4-ERR_DISABLE: psecure-violation error detected on Fa0/18,
  putting Fa0/18 in err-disable state
Sep 20 06:44:54.966: %PORT_SECURITY-2-PSECURE_VIOLATION: Security violation
  occurred, caused by MAC address 000c.292b.4c75 on port FastEthernet0/18.
Sep 20 06:44:55.973: %LINEPROTO-5-PPDOWN: Line protocol on Interface
FastEthernet0/18, changed state to down
Sep 20 06:44:56.971: %LINK-3-UPDOWN: Interface FastEthernet0/18, changed state to
  down
!The two following commands can be used to verify the port status.
S1# show interface fa0/18 status
Port     Name  Status        Vlan  Duplex  Speed   Type
Fa0/18         err-disabled  5     auto    auto    10/100BaseTX
S1# show port-security interface fastethernet 0/18
Port Security                : Enabled
Port Status                  : Secure-shutdown
Violation Mode               : Shutdown
Aging Time                   : 0 mins
Aging Type                   : Absolute
SecureStatic Address Aging   : Disabled
Maximum MAC Addresses        : 1
Total MAC Addresses          : 0
Configured MAC Addresses     : 0
Sticky MAC Addresses         : 0
Last Source Address:Vlan     : 000c.292b.4c75:1
Security Violation Count     : 1
!To restore a port, manually shut it down and then reactivate it.
S1(config)# interface FastEthernet 0/18
S1(config-if)# shutdown
Sep 20 06:57:28.532: %LINK-5-CHANGED: Interface FastEthernet0/18, changed state to
  administratively down
S1(config-if)# no shutdown
Sep 20 06:57:48.186: %LINK-3-UPDOWN: Interface FastEthernet0/18, changed state to
  up
Sep 20 06:57:49.193: %LINEPROTO-5-UPDOWN: Line protocol on Interface
FastEthernet0/18, changed state to up
```

You can use the **show interface** *type number* **status** or **show port-security interface** *type number* command to verify the current state of the port. To restore the port, you must first manually shut down the interface and then reactivate it, as shown in Example 7-3.

Changing the Native and Management VLANs

A native VLAN is defined in the IEEE 802.1Q specification to maintain backward compatibility with untagged traffic common to legacy LAN scenarios. A native VLAN serves as a common identifier on opposite ends of a trunk link. VLAN 1 is the native VLAN by default.

A management VLAN is any VLAN configured to access the management capabilities of a switch. VLAN 1 is the management VLAN by default. The management VLAN is assigned an IP address and subnet mask, allowing the switch to be managed through HTTP, Telnet, SSH, or SNMP.

It is a best practice to configure the native VLAN as an unused VLAN distinct from VLAN 1 and other VLANs. In fact, it is not unusual to dedicate a fixed VLAN to serve the role of the native VLAN for all trunk ports in the switched domain. Likewise, the management VLAN should also be configured as something other than VLAN 1. The management and native VLANs can be configured as the same VLAN, as shown in Example 7-4.

Example 7-4   Configuring the Native and Management VLAN

```
S1(config)# vlan 86
S1(config-vlan)# name Management&Native
S1(config-vlan)# interface vlan 86
*Jul 13 14:14:04.840: %LINEPROTO-5-UPDOWN: Line protocol on Interface Vlan86,
  changed state to down
S1(config-if)# ip address 10.10.86.10 255.255.255.0
S1(config-if)# no shutdown
S1(config-if)# ip default-gateway 10.10.86.254
S1(config)# interface range fa0/1 - 2
S1(config-if-range)# switchport mode trunk
S1(config-if-range)# switchport trunk native vlan 86
S1(config-if-range)#
*Jul 13 14:15:55.499: %LINEPROTO-5-UPDOWN: Line protocol on Interface Vlan86,
  changed state to up
S1(config-if-range)#
```

First, a VLAN is created that will be used for the management and native VLAN. Next, by activating interface VLAN 86, the switch can now be remotely managed. Finally, the trunk ports are statically configured and VLAN 86 is set as the native VLAN for all untagged traffic. After it is configured, the interface VLAN 86 will come "up."

Shutting Down and Securing Unused Interfaces

Router interfaces, as you know, must be activated with the **no shutdown** command before they become operational. The exact opposite is true for the Cisco Catalyst switches. To provide out-of-the-box functionality, Cisco chose a default configuration that included interfaces that would work without any configuration, including automatically negotiating speed and duplex. In addition, all interfaces are assigned to the default VLAN 1.

This default configuration exposes switches to some security threats. The security best practices for unused interfaces are as follows:

- Administratively disable the interface using the **shutdown** interface subcommand.

- Prevent VLAN trunking by making the port a nontrunking interface using the **switchport mode access** interface subcommand.

- Assign the port to an unused VLAN using the **switchport access vlan** *number* interface subcommand.

- Set the native VLAN to not be VLAN 1, but to instead be an unused VLAN, using the **switchport trunk native vlan** *vlan-id* interface subcommand.

Even though you shut down unused ports on the switches, if a device is connected to one of those ports and the interface is enabled, trunking could occur. In addition, all ports by default are in VLAN 1. A good practice is to put all unused ports in a "black hole" VLAN. Example 7-5 demonstrates this best practice, assuming that ports 20–24 are unused.

Example 7-5   Assigning Unused Ports to a Black Hole VLAN

```
S1(config)# vlan 999
S1(config-vlan)# name BlackHole
S1(config-vlan)# interface range fa0/20 - 24
S1(config-if-range)# shutdown
S1(config-if-range)# switchport mode access
S1(config-if-range)# switchport access vlan 999
S1(config-if-range)#
```

Study Resources

For today's exam topics, refer to the following resources for more study.

Resource	Location	Topic
Primary Resources		
Routing & Switching Essentials	2	Switch Port Security
	3	Design Best Practices for VLANs

Resource	Location	Topic
Switched Networks	2	Switch Port Security
	3	Design Best Practices for VLANs
ICND1 Official Cert Guide	8	Port Security
		Securing Unused Switch Interfaces
ICND1 Foundation Learning Guide	17	Port Security Configuration on Switches
		Securing Unused Ports
Supplemental Resources		
CCENT Practice and Study Guide	13	Configuring Port Security
	14	VLAN Security and Design
Flash Cards	8	Questions 20–35
Network Simulator	8	Switch Security II–IV
		Switch Security
		Port Security
CCNA R&S Portable Command Guide	11	Switch Port Security
		Verifying Switch Port Security
		Sticky MAC Addresses
		Configuration Example

Troubleshoot IP Addressing Issues

CCENT 100-101 ICND1 Exam Topics

- Troubleshoot and correct common problems associated with IP addressing and host configurations.

Key Topics

The last five exam topics listed in the 100-101 ICND1 Exam Topics (CCENT) are related to troubleshooting. So we will spend the next five days reviewing troubleshooting tools and skills. Today, we look at how IP addressing can cause issues in your network.

Troubleshooting Methodology

In some troubleshooting situations, the issue can be an easy, quick fix. However, other times, there can be multiple underlying issues that caused the trouble ticket to be submitted. In both cases, it is always a good idea to follow a methodical process for tracking down and resolving the problem. The following troubleshooting method is a good example of one you might use on the job.

Step 1. Gather together the relevant network documentation, including topology, addressing scheme, and any other information that might be pertinent to the problem (such as network baselines). Verify the network documentation and use tests to isolate problems.

Step 2. Generate possible solutions to the problem. Sometimes, the solution is obvious. Other times, you will need to determine the best solution from a list of possible solutions.

Step 3. Implement the best solution. Do not implement multiple solutions at the same time as this can have unforeseen consequences.

Step 4. Test to verify that the problem is resolved. If not, you might want to reverse Step 3 unless the solution resolved some of the problem. Return to Step 2.

Step 5. After the problem is resolved, fully document the solution.

Default Gateway

A misconfigured default gateway is one of the more common problems in either a static or a dynamically assigned IP addressing scheme. For a device to communicate across multiple networks, it must be configured with an IP address, a subnet mask, and a default gateway.

The default gateway is used when the host wants to send a packet to a device on another network. The default gateway address is generally the router interface address attached to the local network to which the host is connected. A wrong default gateway can occur in the following ways:

- The end device is statically configured with the wrong default gateway address. To resolve this issue, consult the topology and addressing documentation to verify what the device's default gateway should be—normally a router attached to the same LAN.

- The DHCP server is configured with the wrong default gateway. Some DHCP server configurations might require the administrator to manually configure the default gateway address—such as the Easy IP IOS feature. If this is configured incorrectly, all devices will not have access beyond the LAN.

Duplicate IP Addresses

Under some circumstances, duplicate IP address conflicts can occur between a statically configured network device and a PC obtaining automatic IP addressing information from the DHCP server. To resolve such an IP addressing conflict, you can do one of two things:

- Convert the network device with the static IP address to a DHCP client.

- On the DHCP server, exclude the static IP address of the end device from the DHCP pool of addresses.

The first solution is a quick fix that can be done in the field. However, the device more than likely needs a static configuration. The second solution might be the better long-term choice. However, it requires that you have administrative privileges to configure the DHCP server.

You might also encounter IP addressing conflicts when manually configuring IP on an end device in a network that only uses static IP addresses. In this case, you must determine which IP addresses are available on the particular IP subnet and configure accordingly. This case illustrates why it is so important for a network administrator to maintain detailed documentation, including IP address assignments and topologies, for end devices.

DHCP Issues

DHCP problems can arise for a multitude of reasons, such as software defects in operating systems, NIC drivers, or DHCP relay agents, but the most common are configuration issues.

Resolve IPv4 Address Conflicts

An IPv4 address lease can expire on a client still connected to a network. If the client does not renew the lease, the DHCP server can reassign that IPv4 address to another client. When the client reboots, it requests an IPv4 address. If the DHCP server does not respond quickly, the client uses the last IPv4 address. The situation then arises where two clients are using the same IPv4 address, creating a conflict.

The **show ip dhcp conflict** command displays all address conflicts recorded by the DHCP server. The server uses the **ping** command to detect conflicts. The client uses Address Resolution Protocol (ARP) to detect clients. If an address conflict is detected, the address is removed from the pool and not assigned until an administrator resolves the conflict.

Test Connectivity Using a Static IP Address

When troubleshooting any DHCP issue, verify network connectivity by configuring static IPv4 address information on a client workstation. If the workstation is unable to reach network resources with a statically configured IPv4 address, the root cause of the problem is not the DHCP server. At this point, network connectivity troubleshooting is required.

Verify Switch Port Configuration

If the DHCP client is unable to obtain an IPv4 address from the DHCP server on startup, attempt to obtain an IPv4 address from the DHCP server by manually forcing the client to send a DHCP request. If there is a switch between the client and the DHCP server and the client is unable to obtain the DHCP configuration, switch port configuration issues might be the cause. These causes can include issues from trunking and channeling to STP and RSTP. PortFast configuration and edge port configurations resolve the most common DHCPv4 client issues that occur with an initial installation of a Cisco switch.

Test DHCPv4 Operation on the Same Subnet or VLAN

It is important to distinguish whether DHCP is functioning correctly when the client is on the same subnet or VLAN as the DHCP server. If DHCP is working correctly when the client is on the same subnet or VLAN, the problem might be the DHCP relay agent. If the problem persists even with testing DHCP on the same subnet or VLAN as the DHCP server, the problem might be with the DHCP server.

Inter-VLAN Routing and IP Addressing Issues

For inter-VLAN routing to operate, a router must be connected to all VLANs. Each sub-interface must be assigned an IP address that corresponds to the subnet to which it is connected. This permits devices on the VLAN to communicate with the router interface and enables the routing of traffic to other VLANs connected to the router.

The following are some common IP addressing errors:

- The router is configured with an incorrect IP address for the VLAN's subinterface.

- An end device is configured with an incorrect IP address for the VLAN to which it is attached.

- An end device is configured with the wrong subnet mask for the network to which it belongs.

A common error is to incorrectly configure an IP address for a subinterface. Example 6-1 displays the output of the **show running-config** command. The highlighted area shows that subinterface G0/0.10 on Router R1 has an IP address of 172.17.20.1. The VLAN for this sub-interface should support VLAN 10 traffic. The IP address has been configured incorrectly.

Example 6-1   IP Address and VLAN Mismatch Issue

```
R1# show run
Building configuration...
<output omitted>
!
interface GigabitEthernet0/0.10
 encapsulation dot1Q 10
 ip address 172.17.20.1 255.255.255.0
!
interface GigabitEthernet0/0.30
 encapsulation dot1Q 30
 ip address 172.17.30.1 255.255.255.0
!
<output omitted>
R1#
```

Sometimes it is the end-user device, such as a personal computer, that is improperly configured. Example 6-2 shows the displayed IP configuration for a Windows PC. The IP address is 172.17.20.21. But in this scenario, the PC should be in VLAN 10, with an address of 172.17.10.21.

Example 6-2   PC IP Address Configuration Issue

```
C:\> ipconfig

Windows IP Configuration


Ethernet adapter Local Area Connection:

   Connection-specific DNS Suffix  . :
   IPv4 Address. . . . . . . . . . . : 172.17.20.21
   Subnet Mask . . . . . . . . . . . : 255.255.255.0
   Default Gateway . . . . . . . . . : 172.17.10.1
```

> **NOTE:** Although these examples used a convention of configuring subinterface IDs to match the VLAN number, doing so is not a requirement. When troubleshooting addressing issues, ensure that the subinterface is configured with the correct address for that VLAN.

Study Resources

For today's exam topics, refer to the following resources for more study.

Resource	Location	Topic
Primary Resources		
Introduction to Networks	2	Addressing Devices
Routing & Switching Essentials	5	IP Addressing Issues
	10	Troubleshoot DHCPv4
		Troubleshoot DHCPv6
ICND1 Official Cert Guide	15	Enabling IPv4 Support on Cisco Routers
	18	Verifying Host IPv4 Settings
		Testing Connectivity with ping, traceroute, and telnet
	27	All
ICND1 Foundation Learning Guide	7	Addressing Services
	11	Function of the Default Gateway
		Using Common Host Tools to Determine the Path Between Two Hosts Across a Network
	12	Verifying the Interface Configuration
Supplemental Resources		
CCENT Practice and Study Guide	2	Basic Device Configuration
	21	Troubleshoot DHCPv4
Network Simulator	18	IP Addressing and Routing
		IP Routing I
	20	VLSM Overlap I–X
CCNA R&S Portable Command Guide	25	Viewing the Routing Table
		Clearing the Routing Table
		Determining the Gateway of Last Resort
		Determining the Last Routing Update
		OSI Layer 3 Testing

Troubleshoot VLAN Issues

CCENT 100-101 ICND1 Exam Topics

- Troubleshoot and resolve VLAN problems.

Key Topics

A switch's forwarding process depends in part on VLANs. Before a switch can forward frames in a particular VLAN, the switch must know about a VLAN and the VLAN must be active. Today, we review some of the ways that VLAN misconfigurations can cause problems and which tools are available for locating the source of the issue.

VLAN Troubleshooting

If there are connectivity issues between VLANs and you have already resolved any potential IP addressing issues, you could use the flowchart in Figure 5-1 to methodically track down any issues related to VLAN configuration errors.

Figure 5-1   VLAN Troubleshooting Flowchart

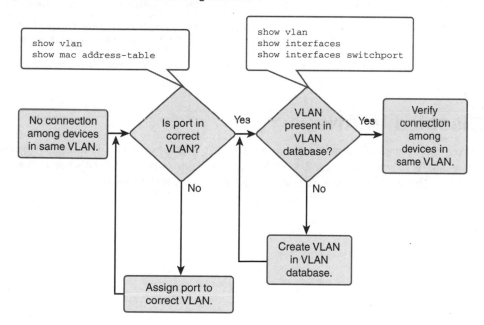

The flowchart in Figure 5-1 can be used in the following manner:

Step 1.   Use the **show vlan** command to check whether the port belongs to the expected VLAN. If the port is assigned to the wrong VLAN, use the **switchport access vlan** command to correct the VLAN membership. Use the **show mac address-table** command to check which addresses were learned on a particular port of the switch and to which VLAN that port is assigned.

Step 2.   If the VLAN to which the port is assigned is deleted, the port becomes inactive. Use the **show vlan** or **show interfaces switchport** command to discover issues with deleted VLANs. If the port is inactive, it is not functional until the missing VLAN is created using the **vlan** *vlan_id* command.

Table 5-1 summarizes these commands, which can be particularly helpful in the process of troubleshooting VLAN issues.

Table 5-1   VLAN Troubleshooting Commands

EXEC Command	Description
`show vlan` `show vlan brief`	Lists each VLAN and all interfaces assigned to that VLAN (but does not include operational trunks)
`show vlan id num`	Lists both access and trunk ports in the VLAN
`show interfaces switchport` `show interfaces type number switchport`	Identifies the interface's access VLAN and voice VLAN, plus the configured and operational mode (access or trunk) as well as the state of the port, up or down
`show mac address-table`	Lists MAC table entries, including the associated VLAN
`show interface status`	Summarizes status listing for all interfaces (connected, not-connect, err-disabled), the VLAN, duplex, speed, and type of port

Disabled VLANs

VLANs can be manually disabled. You can verify that VLANs are active with the **show vlan** command. As shown in Example 5-1, VLANs can be in one of two states: either *active* or *act/lshut*. The second of these states means that the VLAN is shut down.

Example 5-1   Enabling and Disabling VLANs on a Switch

```
S1# show vlan brief
VLAN Name                             Status    Ports
---- ------------------------------   --------- ------------------------------
1    default                          active    Fa0/1, Fa0/2, Fa0/3, Fa0/4
                                                Fa0/5, Fa0/6, Fa0/7, Fa0/8
                                                Fa0/9, Fa0/10, Fa0/11, Fa0/12
                                                Fa0/14, Fa0/15, Fa0/16, Fa0/17
                                                Fa0/18, Fa0/19, Fa0/20, Fa0/21
                                                Fa0/22, Fa0/23, Fa0/24, Gi0/1
10   VLAN0010                         act/lshut Fa0/13
20   VLAN0020                         active
30   VLAN0030                         act/lshut
40   VLAN0040                         active
S1# configure terminal
Enter configuration commands, one per line. End with CNTL/Z.
S1(config)# no shutdown vlan 10
S1(config)# vlan 30
S1(config-vlan)# no shutdown
S1(config-vlan)#
```

The highlighted commands in Example 5-1 show the two configuration methods you can use to enable a shutdown VLAN.

Study Resources

For today's exam topics, refer to the following resources for more study.

Resource	Location	Topic
Primary Resources		
Routing & Switching Essentials	3	Troubleshoot VLANs and Trunks
ICND1 Official Cert Guide	10	Analyzing VLANs and Trunks
ICND1 Foundation Learning Guide	6	Implementing VLANs and Trunks
Supplemental Resources		
CCENT Practice and Study Guide	14	Troubleshoot VLANs and Trunks
Flash Cards	9	Questions 19–24
Network Simulator	10	Topology Analysis

Troubleshoot Trunking Issues

CCENT 100-101 ICND1 Exam Topics

- Troubleshoot and resolve trunking problems on Cisco switches.

Key Topics

Trunking issues can be related to VLANs, but they can also be the result of trunking configuration errors. Today, we review methods for troubleshooting trunking.

Trunking Troubleshooting Overview

To summarize issues with VLANs and trunking, the four potential issues are as follows:

Step 1. Identify all access interfaces and their assigned access VLANs and reassign into the correct VLANs as needed. (Day 5)

Step 2. Determine whether the VLANs exist and are active on each switch. If not, configure and activate the VLANs to resolve problems as needed. (Day 5)

Step 3. Check the allowed VLAN lists on the switches on both ends of the trunk, and ensure that the lists of allowed VLANs are the same.

Step 4. Ensure that for any links that should use trunking, one switch does not think it is trunking, while the other switch does not think it is trunking because of an unfortunate choice of configuration settings.

We reviewed Step 1 and Step 2 on Day 5, "Troubleshoot VLAN Issues." Let's review Step 3 and Step 4 today.

Check Both Ends of a Trunk

For the CCENT exam, you should be ready to notice a couple of oddities that happen with some unfortunate configuration choices on trunks.

It is possible to configure a different allowed VLAN list on the opposite ends of a VLAN trunk. As shown in Figure 4-1, when the VLAN lists do not match, the trunk cannot pass traffic for that VLAN.

Figure 4-1   Mismatched VLAN-Allowed Lists on a Trunk

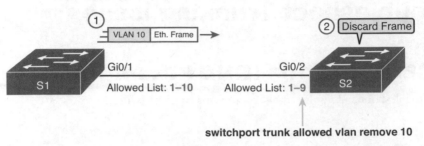

You can only isolate this problem by comparing the allowed lists on both ends of the trunk. Example 4-1 displays the output of the **show interfaces trunk** command on S2.

To compare the allowed VLANs on each switch, you need to look at the second of three lists of VLANs listed by the **show interfaces trunk** command, as highlighted in the output in Example 4-1.

Example 4-1   Verify the Allowed VLANs on S2

```
S2# show interfaces trunk
Port        Mode         Encapsulation  Status        Native vlan
Gi0/2       desirable    802.1q         trunking      1


Port        Vlans allowed on trunk
Gi0/2       1-4094


Port        Vlans allowed and active in management domain
Gi0/2       1-9


Port        Vlans in spanning tree forwarding state and not pruned
Gi0/2       1-9
```

To add VLAN 10 to S2's trunk, enter the following commands:

```
S2(config)# interface g0/2
S2(config-if)# switchport trunk allowed vlan add 10
```

The keyword **add** provides the ability to add one or more VLANs to the trunk without having to specify again all the existing VLANs that are already allowed.

Check Trunking Operational States

Trunks can also be misconfigured. In some cases, both switches conclude that their interfaces do not trunk. In other cases, one switch believes that its interface is correctly trunking, while the other switch does not.

The most common incorrect configuration—which results in both switches not trunking—is a configuration that uses the **switchport mode dynamic auto** command on both switches on the link. The keyword **auto** does not mean that trunking happens automatically. Instead, both switches passively wait on the other device on the link to begin negotiations.

With this particular incorrect configuration, the **show interfaces switchport** command on both switches confirms both the administrative state (auto) as well as the fact that both switches operate as "static access" ports. Example 4-2 highlights those parts of the output for S2.

Example 4-2   Verify the Trunking State for a Specific Interface

```
SW2# show interfaces gigabit0/2 switchport
Name: Gi0/2
Switchport: Enabled
Administrative Mode: dynamic auto
Operational Mode: static access
Administrative Trunking Encapsulation: dot1q
Operational Trunking Encapsulation: native
! lines omitted for brevity
```

Always check the trunk's operational state on both sides of the trunk. The best commands to check trunking-related facts are **show interfaces trunk** and **show interfaces switchport**.

Study Resources

For today's exam topics, refer to the following resources for more study.

Resource	Location	Topic
Primary Resources		
Routing & Switching Essentials	3	Troubleshoot VLANs and Trunks
ICND1 Official Cert Guide	10	Analyzing VLANs and Trunks
ICND1 Foundation Learning Guide	6	Implementing VLANs and Trunks
Supplemental Resources		
CCENT Practice and Study Guide	14	Troubleshoot VLANs and Trunks
Flash Cards	9	Questions 19–24
Network Simulator	10	Topology Analysis

Troubleshoot ACL Issues

CCENT 100-101 ICND1 Exam Topics

- Troubleshoot and resolve ACL issues.

Key Topics

ACLs can be particularly difficult to troubleshoot if you do not use a methodical approach to locating and resolving the issue or issues. On Day 10, "Basic ACL Configuration," we reviewed ACL configuration and verification. Today we look at some possible ACL trouble-shooting scenarios.

Troubleshooting ACLs

When you troubleshoot an ACL, check it against the rules you use for how to design ACLs correctly. Most errors occur because these basic rules are ignored. In fact, the most common errors are entering ACL statements in the wrong order and not applying adequate criteria to your rules. Let's look at a series of common problems and their solutions using the topology shown in Figure 3-1.

Figure 3-1   **Topology for Troubleshooting ACLs**

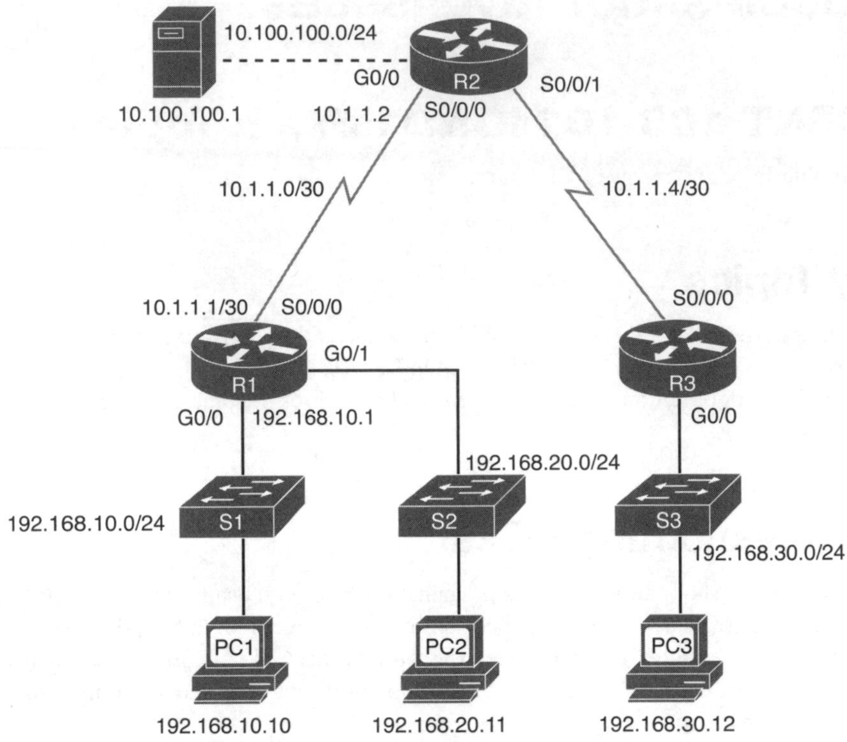

Problem 1: Host Has No Connectivity

Host 192.168.10.10 has no connectivity with 192.168.30.12. The access list shown in Example 3-1 is applied inbound to R3's s0/0/0 interface.

Example 3-1   Problem 1: Host Has No Connectivity

```
R3# show access-lists 100
Extended IP access list 100
    10 deny tcp 192.168.10.0 0.0.0.255 any
    20 permit tcp host 192.168.10.10 any
    30 permit ip any any
```

Because ACLs are processed sequentially until a match is made, traffic from host 192.168.10.10 is denied by the first statement. Statement 20, which permits host 192.168.10.10, never gets processed. The solution is to change the position of statement 20 so that it comes before statement 10. You can do this with the commands shown in Example 3-2.

Example 3-2   Solution 1: Correcting the "Host Has No Connectivity" Problem

```
R3(config)# ip access-list extended 100
R3(config-ext-nacl)# no 20 permit tcp host 192.168.10.10 any
R3(config-ext-nacl)# 5 permit tcp host 192.168.10.10 any
R3(config-ext-nacl)# end
R3# show access-lists 100
Extended IP access list 100
    5 permit tcp host 192.168.10.10 any
    10 deny tcp 192.168.10.0 0.0.0.255 any
    30 permit ip any any
```

First, notice that we entered named ACL configuration mode in order to edit the sequence numbers for the extended numbered ACL. Second, we removed statement 20. Finally, we reapplied statement 20 with a new sequence number lower than 10–5 in the example. Notice from the **show access-lists** output that the statement order is now correct. Host 192.168.10.10 will be permitted, and all other traffic from the 192.168.10.0/24 subnet will be denied.

Problem 2: Denied Protocols

The 192.168.10.0/24 network cannot use TFTP to connect to the 192.168.30.0/24 network. The access list shown in Example 3-3 is applied inbound to R1's G0/0 interface.

Example 3-3   Problem 2: Denied Protocols

```
R1# show access-lists 120
Extended IP access list 120
    10 deny tcp 192.168.10.0 0.0.0.255 any eq telnet
    20 deny tcp 192.168.10.0 0.0.0.255 host 10.100.100.1 eq smtp
    30 permit tcp any any
```

The 192.168.10.0/24 network cannot use TFTP to connect to the 192.168.30.0/24 network because TFTP uses the transport protocol UDP. Statement 30 in access list 120 allows all other TCP traffic. Because TFTP uses UDP, it is implicitly denied. One possible solution is to replace the **permit tcp any any** statement with **permit ip any any**, as shown in Example 3-4.

Example 3-4   Solution 2: Correcting the "Denied Protocols" Problem

```
R1(config)# ip access-list extended 120
R1(config-ext-nacl)# no 30 permit tcp any any
R1(config-ext-nacl)# permit ip any any
R1(config-ext-nacl)# end
R1# show access-lists 120
```

```
Extended IP access list 120
    10 deny tcp 192.168.10.0 0.0.0.255 any eq telnet
    20 deny tcp 192.168.10.0 0.0.0.255 host 10.100.100.1 eq smtp
    30 permit ip any any
```

Notice that we did not have to include a sequence number for the new **permit ip any any** statement because this statement comes at the end of the list. IOS will automatically increment it by 10.

Problem 3: Telnet Is Allowed #1

The 192.168.10.0/24 network can use Telnet to connect to 192.168.30.0/24, but this connection should not be allowed. The access list is shown in Example 3-5.

Example 3-5   Problem 3: Telnet Is Allowed #1

```
R1# show access-lists 130
Extended IP access list 130
    10 deny tcp any eq telnet any
    20 deny tcp 192.168.10.0 0.0.0.255 host 10.100.100.1 eq smtp
    30 permit ip any any
```

The 192.168.10.0/24 network can use Telnet to connect to the 192.168.30.0/24 network because Telnet in statement 10 of access list 130 is listed in the wrong position. The source port would not be Telnet's port 23, but some randomly chosen port numbered above 1024. The destination port number (or application) must be set to Telnet, as shown in the solution to this problem in Example 3-6.

Example 3-6   Solution 3: Correcting the "Telnet Is Allowed #1" Problem

```
R1(config)# ip access-list extended 130
R1(config-ext-nacl)# no 10 deny tcp any eq telnet any
R1(config-ext-nacl)# 10 deny tcp any any eq telnet
R1(config-ext-nacl)# end
R1# show access-lists 130
Extended IP access list 130
    10 deny tcp any any eq telnet
    20 deny tcp 192.168.10.0 0.0.0.255 host 10.100.100.1 eq smtp
    30 permit ip any any
```

Problem 4: Telnet Is Allowed #2

Host 192.168.10.10 can use Telnet to connect to 192.168.30.12, but this connection should not be allowed. The access list is shown in Example 3-7.

Example 3-7   Problem 4: Telnet Is Allowed #2

```
R1# show access-lists 140
Extended IP access list 140
    10 deny tcp host 192.168.10.1 any eq telnet
    20 deny tcp 192.168.10.0 0.0.0.255 host 10.100.100.1 eq smtp
    30 permit ip any any
```

Host 192.168.10.10 can use Telnet to connect to 192.168.30.12 because no rules deny host 192.168.10.10 or its network as the source. Statement 10 denies the router interface from which traffic would be departing. However, as Telnet packets depart the router, they have the source address of 192.168.10.10, not the address of the router interface. Example 3-8 shows the solution to this problem.

Example 3-8   Solution 4: Correcting the "Telnet Is Allowed #2" Problem

```
R1(config)# ip access-list extended 140
R1(config-ext-nacl)# no 10 deny tcp host 192.168.10.1 any eq telnet
R1(config-ext-nacl)# 10 deny tcp host 192.168.10.10 any eq telnet
R1(config-ext-nacl)# end
R1# show access-lists 140
Extended IP access list 140
    10 deny tcp host 192.168.10.10 any eq telnet
    20 deny tcp 192.168.10.0 0.0.0.255 host 10.100.100.1 eq smtp
    30 permit ip any any
```

Problem 5: Telnet Is Allowed #3

Host 192.168.30.12 can use Telnet to connect to 192.168.10.10, but this connection should not be allowed. The access list shown in Example 3-9 is applied inbound to R3's s0/0/0 interface.

Example 3-9   Problem 5: Telnet Is Allowed #3

```
R3# show access-lists 150
Extended IP access list 150
    10 deny tcp host 192.168.30.12 any eq telnet
    20 permit ip any any
```

Host 192.168.30.12 can use Telnet to connect to 192.168.10.10 because of the direction in which access list 150 is applied to the S0/0/0 interface. Statement 10 denies the source address of 192.168.30.12, but that address would be the source only if the traffic were outbound on S0/0/0, not inbound. Example 3-10 shows the solution to this problem.

Example 3-10   Solution 5: Correcting the "Telnet Is Allowed #3" Problem

```
R3(config)# interface serial 0/0/0
R3(config-if)# no ip access-group 150 in
R3(config-if)# ip access-group 150 out
```

Notice that this solution does not block Telnet traffic from 192.168.30.12 to the G0/0 interface on R3. A better solution might be to apply the ACL to the G0/0 interface for inbound traffic.

Study Resources

For today's exam topics, refer to the following resources for more study.

Resource	Location	Topic
Primary Resources		
Routing Protocols	9	Troubleshoot ACLs
Routing & Switching Essentials	9	Troubleshoot ACLs
ICND1 Official Cert Guide	22	Standard Numbered IPv4 ACLs
		Practice Applying Standard IP ACLs
	23	Extended Numbered IP Access Control Lists
		Named ACLs and ACL Editing
ICND1 Foundation Learning Guide	18	Troubleshooting ACLs
Supplemental Resources		
CCENT Practice and Study Guide	20	Troubleshoot ACLs
CCENT ICND1 Flash Cards	6	Managing Traffic Using Access Lists
CCNA R&S Portable Command Guide	33	Managing Traffic Using Access Control Lists (ACL)

Troubleshoot Layer 1 Issues

CCENT 100-101 ICND1 Exam Topics

- Troubleshoot and resolve Layer 1 problems.

Key Topics

We finish the troubleshooting section with Layer 1. The physical layer is often the reason a network issue exists—power outages, disconnected cables, power cycled devices, hardware failures, and so on. So let's look at some of the troubleshooting tools available to you, in addition to actually walking over to the wiring closet or network device and "physically" checking Layer 1.

Media Issues

Besides failing hardware, other common physical layer issue occurs with media. The following are a few examples:

- New equipment is installed that introduces new electromagnetic interference (EMI) sources into the environment.

- Cable runs too close to powerful motors, like an elevator.

- Poor cable management puts a strain on some RJ-45 connectors, causing one or more wires to break.

- New applications change traffic patterns.

- When new equipment is connected to a switch, the connection operates in a half-duplex mode or a duplex mismatch occurs, which could lead to an excessive number of collisions.

Figure 2-1 shows an excellent troubleshooting flowchart that you can use to aid in troubleshooting switch media issues.

Let's look at the output from the **show interface** and **show interface status** commands.

Figure 2-1   Troubleshooting Switch Media Issues

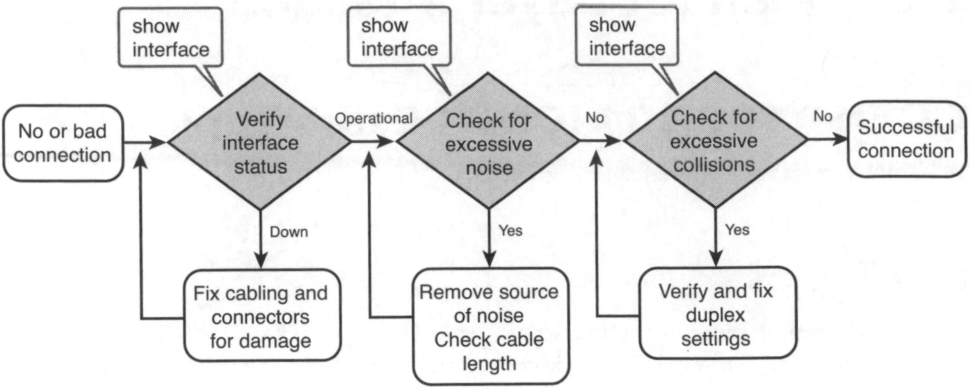

Interface Status and the Switch Configuration

Because today we are focusing on switch troubleshooting, let's look at the **show** commands that are helpful in troubleshooting your basic configuration.

Interface Status Codes

In general, interfaces are either "up" or "down." However, when an interface is down and you don't know why, the code in the **show interfaces** command provides more information to help you determine the reason. Table 2-1 lists the code combinations and some possible causes for the status indicated.

Table 2-1   LAN Switch Interface Status Codes

Line Status	Protocol Status	Interface Status	Typical Root Cause
Administratively Down	Down	disabled	The interface is configured with the **shutdown** command.
Down	Down	notconnect	No cable; bad cable; wrong cable pinouts; the speeds are mismatched on the two connected devices; the device on the other end of the cable is powered off or the other interface is shut down.
Up	Down	notconnect	An interface up/down state is not expected on LAN switch interfaces. This indicates a Layer 2 problem on Layer 3 devices.
Down	Down (err-disabled)	err-disabled	Port security has disabled the interface. The network administrator must manually reenable the interface.
Up	Up	connect	The interface is working.

Duplex and Speed Mismatches

One of the more common problems is issues with speed and/or duplex mismatches. On switches and routers, the **speed** {10 | 100 | 1000} interface subcommand and the **duplex** {half | full} interface subcommand set these values. Note that configuring both speed and duplex on a switch interface disables the IEEE-standard autonegotiation process on that interface.

The **show interface status** and **show interface** commands list both the speed and duplex settings on an interface, as shown in Example 2-1.

Example 2-1   Commands to Verify Speed and Duplex Settings

```
S1# show interface status

Port        Name              Status       Vlan      Duplex  Speed Type
Fa0/1                         connected    trunk       full    100 10/100BaseTX
Fa0/2                         connected    1           half    100 10/100BaseTX
Fa0/3                         connected    1         a-full  a-100 10/100BaseTX
Fa0/4                         disabled     1           auto   auto 10/100BaseTX
Fa0/5                         disabled     1           auto   auto 10/100BaseTX
Fa0/6                         notconnect   1           auto   auto 10/100BaseTX
!Remaining output omitted
S1# show interface fa0/3
FastEthernet0/1 is up, line protocol is up (connected)
  Hardware is Fast Ethernet, address is 001b.5302.4e81 (bia 001b.5302.4e81)
  MTU 1500 bytes, BW 100000 Kbit, DLY 100 usec,
     reliability 255/255, txload 1/255, rxload 1/255
  Encapsulation ARPA, loopback not set
  Keepalive set (10 sec)
  Full-duplex, 100Mb/s, media type is 10/100BaseTX
  input flow-control is off, output flow-control is unsupported
  ARP type: ARPA, ARP Timeout 04:00:00
  Last input never, output 00:00:00, output hang never
  Last clearing of "show interface" counters never
  Input queue: 0/75/0/0 (size/max/drops/flushes); Total output drops: 0
  Queueing strategy: fifo
  Output queue: 0/40 (size/max)
  5 minute input rate 1000 bits/sec, 1 packets/sec
  5 minute output rate 0 bits/sec, 0 packets/sec
     2745 packets input, 330885 bytes, 0 no buffer
     Received 1386 broadcasts (0 multicast)
     0 runts, 0 giants, 0 throttles
     0 input errors, 0 CRC, 0 frame, 0 overrun, 0 ignored
     0 watchdog, 425 multicast, 0 pause input
     0 input packets with dribble condition detected
```

```
56989 packets output, 4125809 bytes, 0 underruns
0 output errors, 0 collisions, 1 interface resets
0 babbles, 0 late collision, 0 deferred
0 lost carrier, 0 no carrier, 0 PAUSE output
0 output buffer failures, 0 output buffers swapped out
```

Notice that both commands will show the duplex and speed settings of the interface. However, the **show interface status** command is preferred for troubleshooting duplex or speed mismatches because it shows exactly how the switch determined the duplex and speed of the interface. In the duplex column, **a-full** means that the switch autonegotiated full duplex. The setting **full** or **half** means that the switch was configured at that duplex setting. Autonegotiation has been disabled. In the speed column, **a-100** means that the switch autonegotiated 100Mbps as the speed. The setting **10** or **100** means that the switch was configured at that speed setting.

Finding a duplex mismatch can be much more difficult than finding a speed mismatch because, if the duplex settings do not match on the ends of an Ethernet segment, the switch interface will still be in a connect (up/up) state. In this case, the interface works, but the network might work poorly, with hosts experiencing poor performance and intermittent communication problems. To identify duplex mismatch problems, check the duplex setting on each end of the link and watch for incrementing collision and late collision counters.

Common Layer 1 Problems On "Up" Interfaces

When a switch interface is "up," it does not necessarily mean that the interface is operating in an optimal state. For this reason, IOS will track certain counters to help identify problems that can occur even though the interface is in a connect state. These counters are highlighted in the output in Example 2-1. Table 2-2 summarizes three general types of Layer 1 interface problems that can occur while an interface is in the up, connected state.

Table 2-2   Common LAN Layer 1 Problem Indicators

Type of Problem	Counter Values Indicating This Problem	Common Root Causes
Excessive noise	Many input errors, few collisions.	Wrong cable category (Cat 5, 5E, 6); damaged cables; EMI
Collisions	More than roughly 0.1% of all frames are collisions.	Duplex mismatch (seen on the half-duplex side); jabber; DoS attack
Late collisions	Increasing late collisions.	Collision domain or single cable too long; duplex mismatch

CDP as a Troubleshooting Tool

CDP discovers basic information about directly connected Cisco routers and switches by sending CDP messages. Example 2-2 shows the output from a switch that is directly connected to a Cisco router.

Example 2-2   Output from the show cdp Commands

```
S1# show cdp ?
  entry      Information for specific neighbor entry
  interface  CDP interface status and configuration
  neighbors  CDP neighbor entries
  traffic    CDP statistics
  |          Output modifiers
  <cr>


S1# show cdp neighbors
Capability Codes: R - Router, T - Trans Bridge, B - Source Route Bridge
                  S - Switch, H - Host, I - IGMP, r - Repeater, P - Phone


Device ID         Local Intrfce      Holdtme   Capability    Platform    Port ID
R1                Fas 0/3            124           R S I     1841        Fas 0/0
S1# show cdp neighbors detail
-------------------------
Device ID: R1
Entry address(es):
  IP address: 192.168.1.1
Platform: Cisco 1841,  Capabilities: Router Switch IGMP
Interface: FastEthernet0/3,  Port ID (outgoing port): FastEthernet0/0
Holdtime : 175 sec


Version :
Cisco IOS Software, 1841 Software (C1841-ADVIPSERVICESK9-M), Version 12.4(10b),
RELEASE SO
FTWARE (fc3)
Technical Support: http://www.cisco.com/techsupport
Copyright (c) 1986-2007 by Cisco Systems, Inc.
Compiled Fri 19-Jan-07 15:15 by prod_rel_team


advertisement version: 2
VTP Management Domain: ''
Duplex: full
Management address(es):


S1# show cdp
```

```
Global CDP information:
        Sending CDP packets every 60 seconds
        Sending a holdtime value of 180 seconds
        Sending CDPv2 advertisements is  enabled

S1# show cdp interface
FastEthernet0/1 is up, line protocol is up
  Encapsulation ARPA
  Sending CDP packets every 60 seconds
  Holdtime is 180 seconds
FastEthernet0/2 is down, line protocol is down
  Encapsulation ARPA
  Sending CDP packets every 60 seconds
  Holdtime is 180 seconds
!
!Output is same for interface Fa0/3 through Gi0/1
!
GigabitEthernet0/2 is down, line protocol is down
  Encapsulation ARPA
  Sending CDP packets every 60 seconds
  Holdtime is 180 seconds
S1#
```

The **show cdp neighbors detail** output displays CDP messages that contain the following useful information:

- **Device ID:** Typically the hostname

- **Entry address(es):** Network and data-link addresses

- **Platform:** The model and OS level running in the device

- **Capabilities:** Information on what type of device it is (for example, a router or a switch)

- **Interface:** The interface on the router or switch issuing the **show cdp** command with which the neighbor was discovered

- **Port ID:** Text that identifies the port used by the neighboring device to send CDP messages to the local device

Also notice in the **show cdp interface** command that every interface on the switch is sending CDP messages every 60 seconds. CDP is enabled by default and thus creates a security issue because CDP messages can be intercepted and network information discovered. CDP can easily be disabled both globally for the entire device (**no cdp run**) or individually by interface (**no cdp enable**).

Study Resources

For today's exam topics, refer to the following resources for more study.

Resource	Location	Topic
Primary Resources		
Network Basics	9	Physical Layer Protocols
	11	Basic Network Performance
Introduction to Networks	4	Physical Layer Protocols
	11	Basic Network Performance
ICND1 Official Cert Guide	10	Analyzing Switch Interface Status
ICND1 Foundation Learning Guide	5	Troubleshooting Common Switch Media Issues
Supplemental Resources		
CCENT Practice and Study Guide	4	Physical Layer Protocols
CCENT ICND1 Flash Cards	2	Introducing Local-Area Networks
	3	Understanding Ethernet and Switch Operations
CCNA R&S Portable Command Guide	4	Cables and Connections
	25	Basic Troubleshooting

CCENT Skills Review and Practice

Key Topics

Tomorrow you take the CCNA exam. Therefore, today you should take the time to do some relaxed skimming of all the previous days' topics, focusing on areas where you are still weak. If you have access to a timed practice test like the ones available in the *Cisco CCENT/CCNA ICND1 100-101 Official Cert Guide*, use these to help isolate areas in which you might need a little further study.

As part of this book, I have included a CCENT Skills Practice that includes much of the CCENT configuration skills in one topology. This scenario should help you quickly review many of the commands covered by the CCENT exam.

Introduction

This culminating activity includes many of the skills you have acquired during your CCENT studies. Using the provided documentation, you will configure VLANs, trunking, port security, and SSH remote access on a switch. Then, you will implement inter-VLAN routing as well as NAT and DHCP services on a router. Finally, you will configure OSPF and default routing to provide full connectivity throughout the network.

You are responsible for configuring HQ, the Branch routers B1 and B2, and the HQ-Sw switch. Assume that routers and switches under your administration have no configuration.

Topology Diagram

Figure 1-1 shows the topology for this CCENT Skills Review.

Figure 1-1   CCENT Skills Review Topology

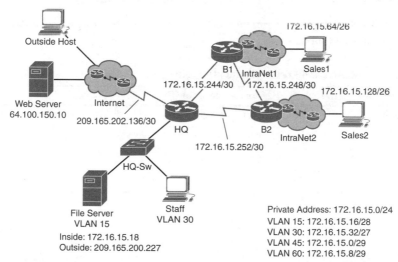

Addressing Table

Table 1-1 shows the addressing scheme for the network shown in Figure 1-1.

Table 1-1   CCENT Skills Review Addressing Scheme

Device	Interface	IP Address	Subnet Mask	Default Gateway
HQ	G0/0.15	172.16.15.17	255.255.255.240	—
	G0/0.30	172.16.15.33	255.255.255.224	—
	G0/0.45	172.16.15.1	255.255.255.248	—
	G0/0.60	172.16.15.9	255.255.255.248	—
	S0/0/0	172.16.15.245	255.255.255.252	—
	S0/0/1	172.16.15.254	255.255.255.252	—
	S0/1/0	209.165.202.138	255.255.255.252	—
B1	G0/0	172.16.15.65	255.255.255.192	—
	S0/0/0	172.16.15.249	255.255.255.252	—
	S0/0/1	172.16.15.246	255.255.255.252	—
B2	G0/0	172.16.15.129	255.255.255.192	—
	S0/0/0	172.16.15.253	255.255.255.252	—
	S0/0/1	172.16.15.250	255.255.255.252	—
HQ-Sw	VLAN 60	172.16.15.10	255.255.255.248	172.16.15.9
Staff	NIC	DHCP Assigned	DHCP Assigned	DHCP Assigned

VLANs and Port Assignments Table

Table 1-2 shows the VLAN configuration information for the B1 switches, including names, port assignments, and subnets.

Table 1-2   VLANs and Port Assignments Table

VLAN Number – Name	Port Assignment	Subnet
15 – Servers	F0/11 – F0/20	172.16.15.16/28
30 – PCs	F0/1 – F0/10	172.16.15.32/27
45 – Native	G1/1	172.16.15.0/29
60 – Management	VLAN 60	172.16.15.8/29

ISP Configuration

If you choose to configure this network on real equipment or a network simulator, use the script in Example 1-1 to configure ISP. You can also configure HQ with loopback interfaces to simulate the ISP and Web Server.

Example 1-1   ISP Configuration

```
hostname ISP
!
interface GigabitEthernet0/0
 description Link to Web Server and Outside Host
 ip address 64.100.150.1 255.255.255.0
 no shutdown
!
interface Serial0/0/0
 description Link to HQ
 ip address 209.165.202.137 255.255.255.252
 no shutdown
!
ip route 209.165.200.0 255.255.255.0 Serial0/0/0
!
end
```

Implementation

Implement the following requirements using the provided documentation.

IPv4 Addressing Configuration Requirements

At some point, you will obviously need to address all the devices. You can do that now or as you implement the requirements for each device. The requirements assume that addressing is done.

HQ-Sw Configuration Requirements

- Configure remote management access including IP addressing and SSH:
    - Domain is cisco.com.
    - User Admin with password letmein.
    - Crypto key length of 1024.
    - SSH version 2, limited to two authentication attempts and a 60-second timeout.
    - Clear-text passwords should be encrypted.

- Configure, name, and assign VLANs. Ports should be manually configured as access ports.

- Configure trunking.

- Implement port security:

  - On active ports, allow two MAC addresses that are automatically added to the configuration file when detected. The port should not be disabled, but a syslog message should be captured if a violation occurs.

  - Disable all other unused ports.

HQ Configuration Requirements

- Configure inter-VLAN routing.

- Configure DHCP services for VLAN 30. Use LAN as the case-sensitive name for the pool.

- Implement NAT:

  - All IP addresses belonging to the 172.16.15.0/24 address space are allowed.

  - Refer to your documentation and configure static NAT for the File Server.

  - Configure dynamic NAT with PAT using a pool name of your choice and these two public addresses: 209.165.200.225 and 209.165.200.226.

- Implement routing:

  - Configure OSPF, including a router ID.

  - Configure appropriate network statements.

  - Disable interfaces that should not send OSPF messages.

  - Configure a default route to the Internet.

B1 and B2 Configuration Requirements

- Implement routing:

  - Configure OSPF including a router ID.

  - Configure appropriate network statements.

  - Disable interfaces that should not send OSPF messages.

  - Configure a default route to the Internet.

❑ Verify routing:

    ❑ B1 and B2 should now be OSPF neighbors with each other and with HQ.

    ❑ B1 and B2 should be able to ping the Web Server.

Staff

❑ Verify that Staff has received full addressing information from HQ.

Verification

All devices should now be able to ping all other devices. If not, troubleshoot your configurations to isolate and solve problems. A few tests include

❑ Verify remote access to HQ-Sw by using SSH from a PC.

❑ Verify that VLANs are assigned to appropriate ports and that port security is in force.

❑ Verify OSPF neighbors and a complete routing table.

❑ Verify NAT translations and statistics:

    ❑ Outside Host should be able to access File Server at the public address.

    ❑ Inside PCs should be able to access Web Server.

❑ Document any problems you encountered and the solutions in Table 1-3.

Table 1-3   Troubleshooting Documentation

Problem	Solution

Your Notes

Answer Scripts

The following is one possible solution to implement the CCENT Skills Review and Practice requirements:

```
!HQ-Sw!!!!!!!!!!!!!!!!!!!!!!!!!!!!!!!!!
hostname HQ-Sw
!
ip domain-name cisco.com
crypto key generate rsa
1024
!
user Admin pass letmein
service password-encryption
ip ssh version 2
ip ssh authentication 2
ip ssh time-out 60
line vty 0 15
login local
transport input ssh
!
vlan 15
name Servers
vlan 30
name PCs
vlan 45
name Native
vlan 60
name Management
!
interface range FastEthernet0/1 - 10
 switchport access vlan 30
 switchport mode access
 switchport port-security
 switchport port-security maximum 2
 switchport port-security mac-address sticky
 switchport port-security violation restrict
!
interface range FastEthernet0/11  - 20
 switchport access vlan 15
 switchport mode access
 switchport port-security
 switchport port-security maximum 2
 switchport port-security mac-address sticky
 switchport port-security violation restrict
!
```

```
interface range FastEthernet0/21 - 24 , g1/2
 switchport mode access
 shutdown
!
interface GigabitEthernet1/1
 switchport trunk native vlan 45
 switchport mode trunk
!
interface Vlan60
 ip address 172.16.15.10 255.255.255.248
!
ip default-gateway 172.16.15.9
!
end
!HQ!!!!!!!!!!!!!!!!!!!!!!!!!!!!!!!!!!!!
hostname HQ
ip dhcp pool LAN
 network 172.16.15.32 255.255.255.224
 default-router 172.16.15.33
!
interface GigabitEthernet0/0
 no shutdown
!
interface GigabitEthernet0/0.15
 encapsulation dot1Q 15
 ip address 172.16.15.17 255.255.255.240
 ip nat inside
!
interface GigabitEthernet0/0.30
 encapsulation dot1Q 30
 ip address 172.16.15.33 255.255.255.224
 ip nat inside
!
interface GigabitEthernet0/0.45
 encapsulation dot1Q 45 native
 ip address 172.16.15.1 255.255.255.248
!
interface GigabitEthernet0/0.60
 encapsulation dot1Q 60
 ip address 172.16.15.9 255.255.255.248
!
interface Serial0/0/0
 ip address 172.16.15.245 255.255.255.252
 ip nat inside
!
```

```
interface Serial0/0/1
 ip address 172.16.15.254 255.255.255.252
 ip nat inside
!
interface Serial0/1/0
 ip address 209.165.202.138 255.255.255.252
 ip nat outside
!
router ospf 1
 router-id 1.1.1.1
 passive-interface GigabitEthernet0/0
 passive-interface Serial0/1/0
 network 172.16.15.0 0.0.0.255 area 0
!
ip nat pool TEST 209.165.200.225 209.165.200.226 netmask 255.255.255.252
ip nat inside source list 1 pool TEST overload
ip nat inside source static 172.16.15.18 209.165.200.227
ip route 0.0.0.0 0.0.0.0 Serial0/1/0
!
access-list 1 permit 172.16.15.0 0.0.0.255
!
end
!B1!!!!!!!!!!!!!!!!!!!!!!!!!!!!!!!!!!!!
hostname B1
!
interface GigabitEthernet0/0
 ip address 172.16.15.65 255.255.255.192
!
interface Serial0/0/0
 ip address 172.16.15.249 255.255.255.252
!
interface Serial0/0/1
 ip address 172.16.15.246 255.255.255.252
!
router ospf 1
 router-id 2.2.2.2
 passive-interface GigabitEthernet0/0
 network 172.16.15.0 0.0.0.255 area 0
!
ip route 0.0.0.0 0.0.0.0 Serial0/0/1
!
end
!B2!!!!!!!!!!!!!!!!!!!!!!!!!!!!!!!!!!!!
hostname B2
!
```

```
interface GigabitEthernet0/0
 ip address 172.16.15.129 255.255.255.192
!
interface Serial0/0/0
 ip address 172.16.15.253 255.255.255.252
!
interface Serial0/0/1
 ip address 172.16.15.250 255.255.255.252
!
router ospf 1
 router-id 3.3.3.3
 passive-interface GigabitEthernet0/0
 network 172.16.15.0 0.0.0.255 area 0
!
ip route 0.0.0.0 0.0.0.0 Serial0/0/0
!
end
```

CCENT Skills Challenge

For an extra challenge, try the following modifications to the CCENT Skills Practice:

- Make up some different host requirements and change the addressing scheme.
- Add a black hole VLAN and assign it to unused switch ports.
- Implement IPv6 addressing and OSPFv3.
- Configure the network with all static routes and no routing protocol.
- Add an ACL to give Sales1 access to FTP and HTTP on File Server. Deny Sales2 access to FTP on File Server, but permit HTTP. Make sure to take the static NAT into consideration.
- Add a Layer 3 switch and configure SVI instead of router on a stick.
- Add switches to B1 and B2 with similar VLAN configurations as used on HQ-Sw.
- Add switches to HQ and implement redundant links and trunking.
- Implement some of your own security policies by configuring more access lists.
- If you have a friend you are studying with, take turns introducing errors to the network. Then practice using **show** and **debug** commands to verify and troubleshoot the network.

Today is your opportunity to prove that you have what it takes to manage a small, enterprise branch network. Just 90 minutes and 50–60 questions stand between you and your CCENT certification. Use the following information to focus on the process details for the day of your CCENT exam.

What You Need for the Exam

Write the exam location, date, exam time, exam center phone number, and the proctor's name on the lines that follow:

Location: _____

Date: _____

Exam Time (arrive early): _____

Exam Center Phone Number: _____

Proctor's Name: _____

Remember the following items on exam day:

- You must have two forms of ID that include a photo and signature such as a driver's license, passport, or military identification. In addition, the test center admission process requires the capture of a digital photo and digital signature.

- The test proctor will take you through the agreement and set up your testing station after you have signed the agreement.

- The test proctor will give you a sheet for scratch paper or a dry erase pad. Do not take these out of the room.

- The testing center will store any personal items while you take the exam. It is best to bring only what you will need.

- You will be monitored during the entire exam.

What You Should Receive After Completion

When you complete the exam, you will see an immediate electronic response as to whether you passed or failed. The proctor will give you a certified score report with the following important information:

- Your score report including the minimum passing score and your score on the exam. The report will also include a breakout displaying your percentage for each general exam topic.

- Identification information that you will need to track your certification. *Do not lose your certified examination score report.*

Summary

Your state of mind is a key factor in your success on the CCENT exam. If you know the details of the exam topics and the details of the exam process, you can begin the exam with confidence and focus. Arrive early to the exam. Bring earplugs on the off-chance that a testing neighbor has a bad cough or any loud nervous habits. Do not let an extremely difficult or specific question impede your progress. You cannot return to questions on the exam that you have already answered, so answer each question confidently and move on.

Post-Exam Information

The accomplishment of signing up for and actually taking the CCENT exam is no small feat. Many network engineers have avoided certification exams for years. The following sections discuss your options after exam day.

Receiving Your Certificate

If you passed the exam, you will receive your official CCENT certificate in about six weeks (eight weeks internationally) after exam day. Your certificate will be mailed to the address you provided when you registered for the exam.

You will need your examination score report to access the certification tracking system and set up a login to check your certification status. If you do not receive your certificate, you open a case in the certificate online support located at the following web address:

https://ciscocert.secure.force.com/english/MainPage

When you receive your certificate, you might want to frame it and put it on a wall. A certificate hanging on a wall is much harder to lose than a certificate in a filing cabinet or random folder. You never know when an employer or academic institution could request a copy.

Your CCENT certification is valid for three years. To keep your certificate valid, you must either pass the CCENT exam again or advance to the CCNA certification before the end of the three-year period.

Determining Career Options

After passing the CCENT exam, be sure to add your CCENT certification to your resume. Matthew Moran provides the following advice for adding certifications to a resume in his book *Building Your I.T. Career: A Complete Toolkit for a Dynamic Career in Any Economy*, 2nd Edition (Pearson IT Certification, 2013. ISBN: 0789749432):

> I don't believe you should place your certifications after your name. It is presumptuous to pretend that your latest certification is the equivalent to someone who has spent 4–7 years pursuing a Ph.D. or some other advanced degree. Instead, place your certifications or degrees in a section titled *Education and Certifications*. A master's degree might be the exception to this rule.

Moran also discusses good strategies to break into the IT industry after you have earned your CCENT:

> The most important factor is that you are moving toward a career goal. You might not get the title or job you want right out of school. If you can master those skills at your current position, while simultaneously building your network of contacts that lead to your dream position, you should be satisfied. You must build your career piece by piece. It won't happen all at once.

Moran also outlines in his book that certifications such as the CCENT and CCNA are part of an overall professional skill set that you must continually enhance to further your IT career.

Your CCENT certificate proves that you are disciplined enough to commit to a rigorous course of study and follow through with your professional goals. It is unlikely that you will be hired simply because you have a CCENT, but it will place you ahead of other candidates. Even though you have listed the CCENT on your resume, it is important to highlight your networking skills that pertain to the CCENT in your job and skills descriptions on your resume.

Examining Certification Options

Although passing the CCENT exam is not an easy task, it is the starting point for more advanced Cisco certifications such as the CCNA Routing and Switching (200-120), CCNA Security (640-554), CCNA Voice (640-461), CCNA Wireless (640-722), or even CCNP-level exams. When you log in to the online certification tracking tool (use the exam report to do this), be sure to view the certification progress link. This link provides specific information about certifications that you can achieve with your CCNA as the base.

If You Failed the Exam

If you fail your first attempt at the CCENT, you must wait at least 5 calendar days after the day of the exam to retest. Stay motivated and sign up to take the exam again within a 30-day period of your first attempt. The score report outlines your weaknesses. Find a study group and use The Cisco Learning Network online community to help you with those difficult topics.

If you are familiar with the general concepts, focus on taking practice exams and memorizing the small details that make the exam so difficult. If you are a Cisco Networking Academy alumnus, you have access to the curriculum, and Packet Tracer provides an excellent network simulator. Consider your first attempt as a formal practice exam and excellent preparation to pass the second attempt.

Summary

Whether you display your certificate and update your resume or prepare to conquer the exam on your second attempt, remember to marvel at the innovation and creativity behind each concept you learn. The ability of our society to continually improve communication will keep you learning, discovering, and employed for a lifetime.

Index

Symbols

10BASE-T, 34-35

10GigE (Gigabit Ethernet), 34

100BASE-TX, 34-35

802.3 standards, 34

1000BASE-T, 34-35

2960 Catalyst switch configuration, 201-203

A

access control lists. *See* ACLs

access layer switches, 2

access-list command, 228

accessing Cisco IOS

  CLI EXEC sessions, 46

  CLI navigation and editing shortcuts, 47-48

  command history, 48

  connecting to Cisco devices, 45-46

  help, 46

  IOS examination commands, 48

  subconfiguration modes, 49

ACLs (access control lists)

  defining, 221

  design guidelines, 225-226

  extended numbered ACLs, configuring, 230-231

  identifying, 225

  interface processing, 221-222

  matching logic, 222-223

  named ACLs, configuring, 231-233

  standard numbered ACLs, configuring, 227-230

  troubleshooting, 281

    denied protocols, 283-284

    host connectivity issues, 282-283

    Telnet, 284-286

  types of, 224

  verifying, 234-235

AD (administrative distance), 126-127

Address Resolution Protocol (ARP), 20

addresses. *See* IPv4 addressing; IPv6 addressing

addressing table for CCENT skills review, 296

administrative distance (AD), 126-127

any keyword, 229

anycast addresses, 106

Application layer (OSI), 18

application layer (TCP/IP), 19-21

applications

  batch applications, 12

  common network applications, 13

  growth of, 13

    increased network usage, 14

    quality of service (QoS), 14

    Video over IP, 15

    Voice over IP (VoIP), 14-15

  interactive applications, 12

  real-time applications, 12

  user interactions, 12

area keyword, 176

ARP (Address Resolution Protocol), 20

ARPANET, 18

assigned multicast addresses, 104

assigning VLANs to interfaces, 73-75

asymmetric switching, 44

attacks, mitigating, 250

authentication, 251-253

W-X-Y-Z